MW01484514

WRITE LONG & BEAUTIFUL LETTERS

BEFORE GOLD
California under Spain and Mexico
VOLUME 9

ROSE MARIE BEEBE & ROBERT M. SENKEWICZ
Series Editors

WRITE LONG & BEAUTIFUL LETTERS

The Vallejos' Californio Correspondence 1846–1888

TRANSLATED AND EDITED BY
ROSE MARIE BEEBE AND ROBERT M. SENKEWICZ

UNIVERSITY OF OKLAHOMA PRESS ✳ NORMAN

Library of Congress Control Number: 2024059299
ISBN: 0-8061-9556-8 (hardcover)

Write Long and Beautiful Letters: The Vallejos' Californio Correspondence, 1846–1888 is Volume 9 in the series Before Gold: California under Spain and Mexico.

The paper in this book meets the guidelines for permanence and durability of the Committee on Production Guidelines for Book Longevity of the Council on Library Resources, Inc. ∞

The manufacturer's authorized representative in the EU for product safety is Mare Nostrum Group B.V., Mauritskade 21D, 1091 GC Amsterdam, The Netherlands, email: gpsr@mare-nostrum.co.uk.

1 2 3 4 5 6 7 8 9 10

To
FRANCISCA BENICIA CARRILLO DE VALLEJO

A Californio woman ahead of her time
who lived her life with dignity, grace, creativity, and courage

Contents

Illustrations

Maps

Preface

As we began translating Mariano Guadalupe Vallejo's history of Alta California, which he titled "Recuerdos," we quickly became aware that much of what he was saying was deliberately designed to counter the negative and prevalent perceptions of pre-U.S. California in the minds of the Americans who began moving into the country in great numbers during the gold rush. These negative perceptions were centered upon the Mexican inhabitants of California, many of whom could trace their ancestry to the often mestizo populations of what had been northern New Spain and was now Mexico.

These American attitudes stemmed from evaluations that American travelers to California had made even before the actual gold rush began. For example, in Richard Henry Dana's 1840 memoir *Two Years before the Mast*, a widely read book about California, Dana remarked, "The Californians are an idle, thriftless people, and can make nothing for themselves." He continued, "The men are thriftless, proud, and extravagant." Lansford Hastings, who wrote the guidebook that most overland travelers consulted during the 1840s, stated, "Ignorance and its concomitant, superstition, together with suspicion and superciliousness, constitute the chief ingredients of the Mexican character. . . . They are scarcely a visible grade, in the scale of intelligence, above the barbarous tribes by whom they are surrounded."[1]

By the time Vallejo began to compose his history, in 1874, the negative perceptions of the *Californios*,[2] as this group of Mexican inhabitants of California called themselves, began to be contrasted with a very positive perception of "Spaniards" who

---

1. The quotes are taken from Langum, "Californios and the Image of Indolence," 183, 185.
2. Regional name for a non-Indigenous inhabitant of California. All *gente de razón* (literally "people with the capacity to reason," any non-Indigenous person) reared—or later, born and reared—in California were Californios. The term was used in Baja California from 1700 on and came into popular use in Alta California by the 1820s, with the growth of the first generation of California-born Mexicans.

had first colonized the region. Many of these so-called Spaniards were missionaries, and their European background, along with their control of many Indigenous inhabitants of California at the missions, was beginning to create a narrative that would eventually mature into the "Spanish Revival" movement.

Such views permeated another widely read book about California, Alfred Robinson's 1846 *Life in California*. Robinson described one missionary, San Luis Rey's Antonio Peyri, who had been born in Spain, as "a man of great mental energy and capacity, high in favor with the government for these qualities, and being dearly loved by the people for the extreme benevolence of his disposition."[3] Vallejo was deeply aware of both the denigration of Mexicans and the exaltation of Spaniards as he composed his history. His manuscript reflected an effort to counter both of these tendencies, which he regarded as inaccurate and harmful.

As we continued our path through Vallejo's "Recuerdos," we began to realize that his manuscript provided an excellent example of the fact that historical writing involves a fundamental relationship between present and past. Questions that any historian asks of the past are inescapably formed in part by the present in which the historian is writing. The words of British historian E. H. Carr proved especially applicable to Vallejo's effort:

> The reciprocal process of interaction between the historian and his facts, what I have called the dialogue between present and past, is a dialogue not between abstract and isolated individuals, but between the society of today and the society of yesterday. . . . The past is intelligible to us only in the light of the present; and we can fully understand the present only in the light of the past. To enable man to understand the society of the past and to increase his mastery over the society of the present is the dual function of history."[4]

Accordingly, even though events described in Vallejo's manuscript ended in 1851, we realized that, if we were to fully understand what he was saying about the past, we needed to better understand the present he was experiencing in the 1850s, 1860s, and 1870s. As we did so, we came to realize that some of the key themes of his history, especially his insistence that the Californios were deeply interested in their cultural and intellectual advancement in pre-U.S. California, were themes Vallejo and his wife Francisca Benicia Carrillo de Vallejo had intentionally incorporated as a major focus in their own lives, and especially in the lives of their children.

In *Mariano Guadalupe Vallejo*, the companion volume to our published version of the "Recuerdos," we devoted the final two chapters—"Community, Culture, and Education in Mexican California" and "Family Letters"—to these issues.[5] But, as we were composing these chapters, we realized that we should delve more deeply into this complex set of issues. Though we were pleased that these chapters were

---

3. Robinson, *Life in California*, 19.
4. Carr, *What Is History*, 69.
5. Beebe and Senkewicz, *Mariano Guadalupe Vallejo*, 197–294.

good introductions to these subjects, we were left with the desire to research even deeper into the lives of Mariano Guadalupe, Francisca Benicia, their ten children (out of sixteen total) who survived into adulthood, and six children whom Mariano Guadalupe fathered by women who were not his wife.

In this book, which is the result of our further research, we present the story of this family—their struggles and conflicts against the Americans and also within their own family circles. The Vallejo family struggled to contest the triumphalist American narrative and they also struggled with each other over the best way to do that, and over the best manner in which they could survive and prosper in a land that had suddenly become different from the land of their birth.

Acknowledgments

In 2011 when we began working on transcribing and translating Vallejo's "Recuerdos," his five-volume history of Alta California from 1769 to 1849, we conducted research at numerous repositories throughout California and combed through reel upon reel of microfilm. This truly was a "primary source treasure hunt," and we were able to collect an amazing amount of material for our *Recuerdos* and *Mariano Guadalupe Vallejo: Life in Spanish, Mexican, and American California*. But we were also pleasantly surprised to find other documents, such as personal letters, in the boxes and files and on microfilm. Archive rats that we are, we decided to copy these letters just in case they might be useful at some point in the future. Little did we know back then that the letters we found would eventually evolve into *"Write Long and Beautiful Letters": The Vallejos' Californio Correspondence, 1846–1888*.

As we became more deeply involved in exploring the nineteenth-century world and the challenges Mariano Guadalupe and Francisca Benicia described in their correspondence, we again turned to the many people who had assisted us previously. We discovered that the greatest number of Vallejo family letters were in collections at The Bancroft Library. As we had experienced on multiple occasions in the past, the Bancroft staff was unfailingly helpful. Bancroft Director Elaine Tennant, Interim Director Charles Faulhaber, Associate Director Peter Hanff, Curator of The Bancroft Collection Teresa Salazar, and Curator of Latin Americana José Adrián Barragán-Alvarez were consistently accommodating in allowing us access to the Vallejo-related collections and often suggested other manuscript collections we had not yet considered. Collections Manager Lorna Kirwan was, as she had been in the past, extremely helpful in obtaining images. And Diana Vergil, as always, provided us with constant encouragement along with office support.

The California State Parks repository at the Sonoma Barracks contained letters and other manuscript sources not available elsewhere. Carol Dodge, Ronnie Cline, Tyler Markley, Ward Eldredge, Deborah Lee, and April Farnham were extremely obliging, during both our in-person visits and our subsequent requests by email and phone. Their enthusiasm for our project was contagious!

In conceptualizing how we might structure and present a volume of these letters and graphics, we greatly profited from conversations and email exchanges with Janet Fireman, Judy Fireman, Iris Engstrand, Martha McGettigan, and Molly McGettigan Arthur. Brian McGinty was very generous in sharing information about his Vallejo-Haraszthy ancestors.

Other scholars offered crucial advice on our written efforts. Chuck Rankin, whose own wonderful book on the Civil War correspondence between Frederic and Elizabeth Lockley was an important inspiration for us, offered penetrating and incisive comments on an earlier manuscript draft of what would eventually become *"Write Long and Beautiful Letters."*

We were very fortunate to locate images of people and places mentioned by Mariano Guadalupe and Francisca Benicia in their correspondence to each other, which added an incredible visual dimension and energy to letters that were already very descriptive. We are especially grateful for the outstanding support from staff members at many institutions as well as private collectors we contacted electronically who provided prompt responses to our requests. These dedicated people are Nancy Meddings and Susie Kopecky at Allan Hancock College; Selena Capraro at the Amon Carter Museum of American Art; Jane K. Newell at the Anaheim Public Library; Marilyn Van Winkle at the Autry Museum of the American West; Erin García and Debra Kaufman at the California Historical Society; Marie Silva at the California Judicial Center Library; Stephanie Geller at the California State Library; David Newman; Terre Heydari at the De Golyer Library, Southern Methodist University; Michelle M. Frauenberger at the Franklin D. Roosevelt Presidential Library and Museum; Holly Hoods at the Healdsburg Museum; Michael Lara at the San José Public Library, California Room; Mónica Orozco, Fr. Jack Clark Robinson, Andrew Walsh, Laura Bang, and Lee Noemí Leal-Ramírez at the Santa Bárbara Mission Archive-Library; Nadia Nasr and Taylor Garvey at the Santa Clara University Archives and Special Collections; Lauren Menzies at the Society of California Pioneers; Sonoma County Library staff; Patricia Cullinan at the Sonoma Valley Historical Society; staff of the University of Southern California and California Historical Society; and Deya Terrafranca at the Ventura County Museum.

At the University of Oklahoma Press we are grateful to our acquisitions editor, Joe Schiller, for his steadfast support of this project and of the Before Gold series as a whole. Steven Baker is the consummate editor and we feel privileged to have been able to work with him on our publications. We so appreciate his critical eye and expertise. We were privileged to be able to work once again with John Thomas, from whom we always learn something new. He is definitely the copy editor extraordinaire. We have worked with Ariane Smith on different projects throughout the years, and we were thrilled that she was able to make time in her busy schedule to work her book design magic on this latest publication. The maps in this book were created by Tom Jonas. His creative eye and attention to detail are why we have chosen him to create maps for our books in the Before Gold series. He never disappoints.

Closer to home, we could not ask for a more supportive team than my sister Chrisanne Beebe and her husband, Steven Taddei. We especially appreciate the many times they took care of our dog, Cody, when we were out of town conducting research or giving presentations. Last but not least, our canine supervisor Cody helped us maintain a good balance between work and play, which always kept us smiling.

Notes on Correspondence and Documentation

*I*n our typographic translations of the handwritten correspondence, underscoring, parentheses, quotation marks, and similar indicators are presented as seen in the original letters. We make an exception where translation to conventions of modern English calls for italics, such as for the names of ships. Additionally, square brackets indicate our own editorial insertions unless otherwise noted. Where Spanish is not the original language in the correspondence, we indicate this in footnotes.

In the documentation, we accessed all U.S. Census data through Ancestry.com. Sacramental demographic information came from the Early California Population Project, Huntington Library, unless otherwise noted.

Because letters to and from Francisca Benicia Carrillo de Vallejo and Mariano Guadalupe Vallejo are numerous, we employ the abbreviations F.B.C.V. and M.G.V. for their names as letter writers and recipients in our documentation. Additionally, we use the following abbreviations for the two heavily cited archival sources:

DLG-V   De la Guerra Collection–Vallejo Papers, Santa Bárbara Mission Archive-Library, Santa Bárbara, California

TBL   The Bancroft Library, University of California, Berkeley

WRITE
LONG
&
BEAUTIFUL
LETTERS

Introduction

S OUTHERN ALTA CALIFORNIA, 1775. December 17, 1775, was a day of great rejoicing for the more than two hundred members of the expedition that was bringing soldiers, settlers, and their families from northern New Spain to Alta California. A week and a half earlier, Commander Juan Bautista de Anza had divided his party into three distinct groups to facilitate their crossing the desert between the Colorado River and the Salton Sea. Each group would leave one day after the previous group, so that the scarce water to be found along the trail could be more easily rationed by smaller groups. Today was the fourth day after the first group had crossed the desert and set up camp, but the last group had yet to appear. When the last group finally arrived toward the end of the day, the entire expedition was united once again, and the campsite erupted into a spontaneous celebration. One member of the expedition, María Feliciana Arballo, a widow from Culiacán traveling with two small children, proved to be quite exuberant in her delight. The expedition's chaplain, Father Pedro Font, described her behavior in his diary:

> At nightfall, what with the joy of all the people having arrived, some rather unruly party-ing broke out over there. A woman, a widow who was traveling with the expedition, quite brazenly sang some *glosas* that were not so nice. Her singing was acknowledged by the applause and shouting from the rabble. Her companion, that is the man with whom she was traveling, became angered at this and punished her. Our commander overheard this and it caused him to come out of his tent and scold the man for punishing her. I said to him, "Let it be, sir, he is doing the right thing," and he answered, "No, Father, I must not allow these excesses in my presence." He was strict about this excess and not about the excess of the party!—which went on until quite late.[1]

---

1. Bolton, *Anza's California Expeditions* 1:304–13; *glosas* are songs, and what she sang apparently contained irreverent lyrics. "Her companion" was probably Agustín Valenzuela, a soldier from Los Alamos in Sonora, with whose wife and child Arballo and her children had apparently partnered during the journey. See Font, *With Anza to California*, 154, 338, 343.

Father Font was so upset that he returned to the subject during his remarks at Mass the next morning. He recounted,

> I said Mass, during which I spoke four words concerning the party last night, condemning the act, since instead of giving thanks to God for their having reached here alive and not having died during all those hardships, as the animals did, it seemed we were thanking the Devil with that kind of festivity, and so forth. I imagine that this did not sit very well with our commander, who all during the morning did not speak to me.

This action by a forceful woman foreshadowed and symbolized what would become one of the most significant rifts during the Spanish era in California, the tension between the missionaries on one side and the military and settlers on the other. They consistently argued over a variety of issues, often over who might possess the most desirable land in California and who might be able to conscript the most Indigenous people to work that land. With secularization of the missions in the 1830s, the military and settlers prevailed.

SONOMA, 1846. ON JUNE 14, 1846, A DISORGANIZED GROUP OF APPROXImately thirty or forty American settlers, apparently motivated by unsubstantiated rumors that the Mexican authorities wanted to expel them from Alta California, took control of the Sonoma Plaza and of Mariano Guadalupe Vallejo's Casa Grande. After some discussion among themselves and with Vallejo, they decided to move Vallejo, his brother Salvador, his brother-in-law Jacob P. Leese, and his secretary Víctor Prudón to John C. Frémont's camp near Sutter's Fort. The men were soon imprisoned at the fort, where they remained for almost two months. Other Californios in Sonoma were also held under arrest there as the rebelling band eventually declared California an independent republic.

For the rest of the month of June, Sonoma remained under the control of this group, who adopted a flag with a drawing of a bear as their standard. During that time, Frémont remained near Sutter's Fort and some Californios in the vicinity began to collect arms with the ultimate aim of driving the Bear Flaggers out of Sonoma. During this period of confusion, three Californios who were heading to Sonoma to try to get some of the prisoners in Sonoma released were killed by forces associated with the Bear Flaggers.[2]

Francisca Benicia Carrillo, the wife of Mariano Guadalupe Vallejo, remained in Sonoma after her husband was sent to Sutter's Fort. She was a granddaughter of María Feliciana Arballo, and she quickly exhibited her grandmother's initiative and vigor. Her brother Ramón was one of the Californios collecting arms in the countryside, and toward the end of June she was able to secretly send him a dozen pistols, ten pounds of gunpowder, four flintlock shotguns, and six sabers.

---

2. Warren, *Men of the California Bear Flag Revolt*, 63–67.

At the beginning of July, Frémont left Sutter's Fort and established himself as head of the movement in Sonoma. He had been told what Francisca Benicia had done, and he and one of his officers, Archibald Gillespie, went to the Casa Grande to confront her. Frémont said to her, "Señora, do you not realize that you are deserving of a very serious punishment for having supplied arms to the enemies of the government of California?" Undaunted by his presence, she brazenly replied,

> I have not given arms to the enemies, but rather to the friends of the government of California. Those people under your command have no God and no laws. They have placed on the flagpole a rag that has a bear painted on it, and that is the same as saying they are thieves. If you want there to be peace on the frontier, order that the rag be taken down and raise the American flag. Under the protection of that flag, we will be able to live tranquilly and perhaps even united, for many of my sisters are married to Americans and you know that family ties are powerful.[3]

Gillespie then asked her if she had any weapons left at home. According to her husband's account, she said that "she only had four pistols, which she had locked up in the chest of drawers in her room. She was keeping them to defend her honor and the lives of her daughters in case some of the 'Bears' tried to barge into their bedrooms, and she would not turn those pistols over to him or to the Californios."

This action by another forceful woman foreshadowed and symbolized what would become one of the most significant rifts during the American era in California. This rift would not be between missionaries and soldiers/settlers but between people who had been born in California and those who had come from afar and who now controlled it.

When the United States declared war on Mexico in 1846, the fighting in California was brief. Despite one defeat at the hands of Californio forces at San Pasqual in December of that year, the American military quickly established control over most of the territory. Writing in 1851, Antonio María Osio, a Mexican official and landowner, dramatically described how the situation looked five years earlier:

> The flag of the North Americans waved in all the populated areas of Alta California, but the Mexican tricolor still flew in a few places as it wandered about its own country, passing through the deserted fields, unable to find shelter from the bad weather. It seemed as if the flag were revealing its despair. Its brilliant colors had been stained by the strong rays of the sun, it had been torn by bullets and thorny branches, and worst of all, it had been orphaned with no hope of being helped. Nevertheless, the flag proudly waved in the wind, sensing the courageous heartbeats of the brave men who supported it. If they could not obtain an honorable surrender, they vowed to fight to the bitter end and die defending the flag. Let it be known for all time that even though they were unable to do more for their native land and for the country of their birth, these men should serve as an example for other places invaded by forces from the United States.[4]

---

3. Vallejo, *Recuerdos*, 2:1271–73.
4. Osio, *History of Alta California*, 241.

Early in 1847, the Californio forces surrendered to John C. Frémont at Cahuenga. These forces were under the command of Andrés Pico, who was, like Francisca Benicia Carrillo de Vallejo, a grandchild of María Feliciana Arballo. In surrendering his forces to the Americans, Arballo's descendent was participating in the creation of a new era, with its own tensions. As Osio said, "To their dismay, these Mexicans would be viewed as foreigners in their own country."[5]

THIS BOOK DEALS WITH HOW ONE CALIFORNIO FAMILY, THE VALLEJOS, experienced the end of the Mexican era and the first decades of American rule in California. They were soldiers and settlers who became quite prominent and successful after the secularization of the missions, but the American conquest brought them into a new and challenging environment.

This family, as we have seen, traced its ancestry to María Feliciana Arballo. When she arrived with the Anza expedition at Mission San Gabriel in early 1776, she and her two children remained there. In the spring of that year she married soldier Juan Francisco López, a native of Baja California who was currently serving at Mission San Gabriel. The family lived in several southern Alta California locations, as López served at Mission San Juan Capistrano and the San Diego presidio. The youngest of their eight children, María Ignacia de la Candelaria López, was born in San Diego in 1793. In 1809, María Ignacia married Baja California native and San Diego soldier Joaquín Víctor Carrillo at Mission San Diego. Their fourth child, a girl born in 1815 whom they named Francisca Benicia, would in 1832 become Mariano Guadalupe Vallejo's wife.[6]

On her father's side, Francisca Benicia's family had deep Baja California roots. Her father's great-grandfather, Juan Carrillo, had served as a soldier in Baja California in the first half of the eighteenth century. Those Baja California connections worked to Joaquín Víctor Carrillo's advantage in the early nineteenth century, for the military commander of the San Diego presidio, Francisco María Ruiz, was a distant relative of his.[7] Ruiz served as godfather for several of Joaquín and María Ignacia's children, including Francisca Benicia. He eventually allowed Joaquín and his family the use of his house, which was situated near the presidio grounds.[8]

Francisca grew up with three sisters who were five, three, and one year older than her. As they were growing up, they found that San Diego had turned into

5. Andrés Pico's mother, María Eustaquia Gutiérrez, was one of the two young daughters by her deceased husband whom María Feliciana Arballo brought with her on the Anza expedition. See Northrop, *Spanish-Mexican Families*, 2:213–14; Osio, *History of Alta California*, 243.

6. Northrop, *Spanish-Mexican Families*, 1:200–202, 2:46–47, 150.

7. Ruiz's mother was a daughter of Joaquín's great-grandfather, Juan Carrillo. See Crosby, *Antigua California*, 262, 415, 420.

8. Martínez, *Guía Familiar*, 28–30; Crosby, *Antigua California*, 262, 415, 420; McGinty, "Carrillos of San Diego," 4–7; San Diego Baptism 4235, August 24, 1815.

Francisca Benicia Carrillo de
Vallejo, ca. 1830. *Courtesy of the
Sonoma County Library. Photograph
Collection: cstr_pho 007331.*

something of a political and social center. José de Echeandía, appointed governor
of the territory by the Mexican central government in 1825, found that he preferred
the warmer climate of San Diego to the more foggy and chilly environment of
Monterey, the formal capital of Alta California. Accordingly, he spent a good
amount of time in San Diego and conducted much of his official business there.[9]

Francisca's life began to change in 1830. During a November 1829 mutiny by some
soldiers in Monterey over their lack of pay, some officers there were held prisoner.
When they were released, most of them were allowed to remain in Monterey, but
two who had apparently irritated the mutineers more than their fellow officers
were sent to San Diego. One of these officers was Mariano Guadalupe Vallejo.

Like Francisca's family, Vallejo's ancestry reached back to northern New Spain.
His father Ignacio's family was locally prominent in Las Cañadas, a town outside
of Guadalajara. After studying briefly for the priesthood, Ignacio Vallejo joined
the military and was eventually recruited by Fernando de Rivera y Moncada in
1773 to go to Alta California. Ignacio served at several locations, including San

---

9. Bancroft, *History of California*, 3:31–55.

Mariano Guadalupe
Vallejo, 1830. *Courtesy
of The Bancroft Library,
University of California,
Berkeley.* POR: *Vallejo,
Mariano Guadalupe: 18.*

Diego during the Kumeyaay revolt of 1775. In 1776 he served at San Luis Obispo
after the local Chumash had set a fire that destroyed part of the mission complex
and his carpentry skills made him very useful in the rebuilding task. In 1791, Ignacio married María Antonia Lugo, the fourteen-year-old daughter of one of his
military companions. Mariano Guadalupe, born in Monterey in 1807, was their
eighth child.[10]

Mariano Guadalupe followed his father and older brother José de Jesús into the
military. He enlisted at the end of 1823 and by 1827 had reached the rank of *alférez*.[11]
In the same year, he was appointed to the *Diputación*.[12] He served as treasurer and
paymaster of the Monterey presidio and, for a time, was even acting commander
of the presidio. In 1829, Mariano Guadalupe led an expedition into the interior
in an attempt to defeat a group of Indigenous people who had left Missions San
José and Santa Clara and refused to return. The group was led by Cucunuchi, an

10. More detail on Mariano Guadalupe Vallejo and Francisca Benicia Carrillo de Vallejo's activities and lives before
    1846 may be found in Beebe and Senkewicz, *Mariano Guadalupe Vallejo*, 3–110.
11. Ensign; the lowest-ranked military officer, approximately equal to today's rank of second lieutenant.
12. The *Diputación* is an elected assembly of a province, territory, or department (a government unit corresponding
    to a state or territory). Under the centralist Mexican government after 1836, Alta California, formerly a territory,
    became a department.

Indigenous resident of Mission San José whose Christian name was Estanislao. Vallejo's expedition was unsuccessful, much to the displeasure of his commander, Ignacio Martínez. Cucunuchi/Estanislao, however, soon returned to the mission, where he was forgiven by resident priest Narciso Durán. It was shortly after he returned from this expedition that Vallejo was imprisoned by the group of mutinous soldiers mentioned above. He was released on the condition that he leave Monterey and go to San Diego.

Vallejo knew virtually no one in San Diego, but he did have some potential contacts there. One of the members of newly appointed Governor Echeandía's staff was Alférez Romualdo Pacheco. When Echeandía decided to make his headquarters in San Diego, Pacheco met and courted Ramona Carrillo, daughter of Joaquín Carrillo and María Ignacia López. They were married in August 1826 and moved to Monterey the following year.[13] Since Vallejo and Pacheco were serving together at the Monterey presidio, Vallejo became acquainted with Ramona. So when he arrived in San Diego, which for him was an unfamiliar region, it was only natural that he sought to make contact with Ramona's parents. He became acquainted with Ramona's younger sister, Francisca Benicia, and they became close fairly quickly.

But the Carrillo household was hardly tranquil. Eight months earlier, the oldest Carrillo daughter, Josefa, had eloped with American trader Henry Delano Fitch. They had sailed south and the family had not received any word from them since they left. Joaquín and María's only other married daughter was Ramona, who had been living in Monterey and then in Santa Bárbara with her husband Pacheco. So when Vallejo met and became attracted to another Carrillo daughter, Francisca Benicia, her parents were probably of two minds. Since Vallejo was from northern California, a marriage between him and Francisca would separate yet another daughter from close contact with the family. On the other hand, the marriage of this daughter to a young and dashing military officer might help restore the family honor that had been stained by the elopement of Josefa and Fitch.

Vallejo spent only a few weeks in San Diego before returning north, but that proved to be enough time to begin to convince Francisca and himself that marriage might be a good possibility. In March, when Vallejo was in Santa Bárbara serving on a court-martial of some of the mutineers, he undoubtedly told Ramona Carrillo, who was there with her husband, about his interest in Francisca. Her parents eventually came around and approved the match. Still, as a soldier, Vallejo was required to obtain official approval to marry. In October he wrote a formal request from Monterey to the authorities in Mexico City for permission to wed Francisca.[14]

Echeandía was replaced by Manuel Victoria in 1830. The new governor attempted to reverse the secularization policies his predecessor had initiated. Victoria's

---

13. Bancroft, *History of California*, 4:764; San Diego Marriage 1609a, August 4, 1826.
14. The request was dated October 15, 1830, C-B 30, doc. 137, TBL; Vallejo, *Recuerdos*, 1:453.

reversals of Echeandía's policies proved highly unpopular among many soldiers and settlers, who were intending to gain possession of the extensive mission lands secularization would remove from the control of the missionaries. Victoria was driven from Alta California in 1831 after a battle in which Romualdo Pacheco was killed. Echeandía, still in Alta California, summoned the Diputación to meet in Los Angeles. Vallejo, who was a member of that body, went south. As he was traveling from Los Angeles to San Diego to visit Francisca in March, he received a letter granting formal approval of the marriage, which took place two days later in San Diego. In his "Recuerdos," Vallejo gave a dramatic, but inaccurate, account of the event. He stated that Echeandía ended his toast to the couple with this message to the new bridegroom: "My young friend, times of unrest are not the best for getting married. The news I have received today makes it imperative that we move rapidly to the north, and you should accompany the expedition."[15] And so Vallejo recounted that he had to leave San Diego at six o'clock the following morning. However, he actually was summoned by Echeandía to a meeting in San Diego, where he remained for the next few months.

During that time Alta California experienced considerable political instability, occasioned by disputes between Echeandía and Monterey commander Agustín Zamorano over the political leadership. The instability was ended by Mexico's appointment of José Figueroa as governor. At the beginning of 1833, Vallejo returned to northern California as commander of the San Francisco presidio. Francisca remained in San Diego until the birth of their first child, Andrónico, on March 14, and then she and the new baby traveled to San Francisco. However, the child did not survive his first year and died on January 21, 1834.[16]

Francisca would spend the rest of her life in northern California. She remained at San Francisco during 1834 and gave birth there to another boy, whom they also named Andrónico. In June 1835 she and the infant moved to the new Pueblo de Sonoma, which her husband had established after he oversaw the secularization of Mission San Francisco Solano. Vallejo and his family lived in the former priest quarters at the mission until the construction of their new house on the plaza was completed. The new two-story residence on the plaza, with an accompanying tower and extensive servants' quarters, was completed by the end of 1836 and became known as the Casa Grande. As a leading military officer, Vallejo also received several land grants from the properties of the secularized missions in the North Bay region, San Rafael and San Francisco Solano, as well as from hitherto uncolonized Indigenous lands. His major ranchos were Petaluma, Suscol, and Suisun.

Vallejo also formed an alliance with Suisun chief Sem-Yeto, known throughout northern California by his Christian name, Solano. Vallejo's troops helped Solano

---

15. Vallejo, *Recuerdos*, 1:456.

16. Vallejo, *Recuerdos*, 1:456; Los Angeles Plaza Church Baptism 367, April 11, 1833; San Francisco Death 5334, January 21, 1834.

(*left*) Josefa Carrillo, late nineteenth century.
Courtesy of the Healdsburg Museum, Healdsburg, California. 567–49.
(*right*) Henry Delano Fitch. *Courtesy of The Bancroft Library,*
University of California, Berkeley. POR: *Fitch, Henry Delano:* 1.

in his struggles against his tribe's traditional enemies, the Satiyomis. In turn, Solano helped Vallejo acquire Indigenous laborers from other groups to work on his expanding rancho holdings, with estates comprising many thousands of acres at ranchos Petaluma, Suisun, and Suscol. In 1875, Francisca's brother Julio remembered, "General Vallejo in his Petaluma estate often employed one hundred and fifty pairs of oxen plowing his very extensive fields. Each Indian was in charge of a pair of oxen and for his troubles the Indian only obtained a scanty amount of clothing and food he required for the support of his family."[17]

When Vallejo was sent to Sutter's Fort by the Bear Flaggers, Francisca had already given birth to ten of their children. Two of them—Andrónico (b. 1833) and Plutarco (b. 1839)—died in infancy. The remaining eight children were living with Francisca at the Casa Grande: Andrónico (b. 1834), Epifania (b. 1835), Adela (b. 1837), Natalia (b. 1838), Platón (b. 1841), Guadalupe (b. 1843), Jovita (b. 1844), and Uladislao (b. 1845).

Francisca did not, however, have to face the challenge of raising so many children all on her own, for she had assistance from a large number of Indigenous servants. When Manuel Torres visited the Casa Grande in 1844, he remembered, "The patio of his [Vallejo's] Casa Grande was filled with servants, both male and female, but

17. Carrillo, "Statement," C-E 67, 5, TBL.

Presumable appearance of the Mission of SAN FRANCISCO SOLANO (SONOMA) about the Year 1832. in its primitive state, or rather with Pater Quijas' contemplated renovations.

The roof of the old church, taken off by order of Padre Quijas, for the purpose of a complete renovation of its facade, of probably the design given above. Before the completion of that change, while yet unroofed, the Secularization took place, and with it and the political turmoil of that period, the unprotected walls fell in, and the church became a ruin long before the rest of the Mission buildings.

The above elevation is drawn from a ground-plan kindly furnished by Gen: M.S. Vallejo at Lachryma Montis October 1878.

(*above*) Mission San Francisco Solano, ca. 1832, by Mariano Guadalupe Vallejo.
Drawn for Edward Vischer in 1878. *Courtesy of The Bancroft Library,
University of California, Berkeley.* BANC PIC 19XX.039:44b-ALB.
(*below*) Sonoma Plaza, Casa Grande, 1839. *Courtesy of
California State Parks, Sonoma Barracks.* No. 243-x-5006.

RES. OF SALVADOR VALLEJO   EL TOREON   LA CASA GRANDE   BARRACKS   MISSION CHU
JACOB P. LEESE
· SONOMA · 1839 ·

Drawn under Direct

the majority of the servants were women." He continued, "I was not used to seeing such a thing so I asked the general's wife what type of work so many Indians did there."[18] This is how he recounted her response:

> Each of my children has their own servant, who has no other job than to look after the child in their care. I have two servants who attend to my personal needs. Because we have so many visitors here, four or five are in charge of grinding corn and making tortillas, since three women working at that task is no longer enough to prepare food for everyone. Six or seven women are assigned to work in the kitchen. Five or six women are constantly busy washing the children's clothing, as well as the clothing of everyone who works at the house. And, finally, close to a dozen women are in charge of sewing and spinning.

Francisca also told Torres how she said the Indigenous servants were treated:

> You probably know that in general Indian women are not very inclined to learning how to do many things, therefore the woman who is taught how to cook does not want to hear any talk about washing clothes. And a good washerwoman becomes quite irritated if one wants her to do some sewing or spinning. All the women servants whom we have at home are very loyal to us. They are not in the habit of asking us for money, nor do they have a fixed wage. We give them everything they need. If they get sick, we take care of them as if they were members of our family. If they end up having children, we act as godparents and we take it upon ourselves to educate their children. If they want to travel a great distance to visit a family member, we provide them with animals to ride and an escort. In a word, we treat our servants more like friends than like servants. You can ask any of the servants whom you see here, and you will be assured that what I have told you is exactly how things are.

Francisca was also maintaining close contact with her birth family. After her father died around 1836, her mother, accompanied by the children who were still at home, journeyed north and settled in Santa Rosa, about twenty miles north of Sonoma. She was formally granted a rancho there, Cabeza de Santa Rosa, in 1841, and her son Joaquín, a younger brother of Francisca, was granted a nearby rancho, Llano de Santa Rosa, in 1844.

During the 1830s and 1840s, Vallejo was at times military commander of northern Alta California and at other times military commander of Alta California as a whole. But his consistent focus was generally on the North Bay, and he did not actively participate in the north-south sectional struggles that plagued Alta California in the 1830s. His lack of engagement irritated the northern Alta California leadership, especially Juan Bautista Alvarado and José Castro, who had been his childhood friends in Monterey. Vallejo also proved friendly to North American immigrants who came overland into Alta California in increasing numbers in the 1840s. He calculated that friendship with these groups, who were settling in the northern Sacramento Valley area, would give him greater leverage with the Alta California Mexican authorities.

---

18. Torres, "Peripecias de la vida Californiana, 1843–1850," C-D 15, 52–53, TBL.

In early 1846, Thomas O. Larkin, the American consul in Monterey, reported to the federal government in Washington, D.C., that Vallejo "has been formal, stiff, pompous, and exacting towards his countrymen and foreigners of the lower or middle classes." However, he continued, Vallejo also "has given much work and employment to the laboring American Emigrants, always speaking in their favour."[19] But Vallejo would shortly find that always speaking in their favor did not guarantee him favorable treatment from the newly arrived Americans. And his experience, along with that of Francisca and their children over the next four decades, as revealed in their extensive correspondence, would be anything but uniformly favorable. They would be, as Antonio María Osio had presciently predicted in 1851, "foreigners in their own country."

In this book, we employ 183 letters exchanged between Mariano Guadalupe and Francisca Benicia between 1846 and 1888 as a way of recovering the experience of people who had been born in California and were living in a state now controlled by the American conquerors. Mariano Guadalupe was a prolific letter writer and strongly encouraged his family members, friends, and others to maintain frequent contact with him through letters. We are fortunate that, in addition to the letters this couple wrote to one another, many other letters written by Mariano Guadalupe, Francisca Benicia, and their family members and friends have been saved in various repositories. So, in addition to the correspondence between Mariano Guadalupe and Francisca Benicia, we include 139 letters and excerpts of letters this couple wrote to or received from their children and other acquaintances. We are acutely aware that the letters in this book are nineteenth-century letters, not contemporary documents, and we attempt to read them as such. We have desired to listen to these family conversations in the manner in which Walt Whitman listened to Civil War soldiers and discovered that such conversations provided "glimpses of many things untold in any official reports."[20] These letters share much with "common lives" studied by Christopher Hager; notably, these correspondents were interested in "maintaining family and community across space and time" as well as "meeting the challenges that tested those bonds." At times in their correspondence, Mariano Guadalupe and Francisca Benicia struggled, both successfully and unsuccessfully, in "achieving, finally, the kinds of intimacy that written letters sometimes can forge better than anything else."[21] And, as even extremely close correspondents often do, they both could withhold some items and exaggerate others as they were writing to each other.[22] Both Mariano Guadalupe and Francisca Benicia found that they had to make and often remake their own self-identities as they migrated into a new world. As we occasionally lamented the incompleteness

19. Larkin, "Notes on the Personal Character of the Principal Men," in Larkin, *Larkin Papers*, 4:331.
20. Cited in Bonner, *Soldier's Pen*, 6.
21. Hager, *I Remain Yours*, 12–13.
22. Gerber, "Acts of Deceiving and Withholding," 322.

of some of the correspondence, we always tried to remember the sage words of Miroslava Chávez-García, that "the letter writing process . . . is imperfect . . . as are all source materials, including oral histories, census records, and government reports, which also suffer from manipulations, silences, and distortions."[23]

The Vallejo letters cover a wide variety of issues that this family confronted as they attempted to adjust to life in U.S. California. Financial issues were often paramount, for landowning families like the Vallejos had to defend their property claims before an expensive, unfamiliar, and often hostile legal system. Vallejo's need to travel frequently to San Francisco to testify before courts and legal panels meant that he and Francisca were often separated. Vallejo often told her how discouraged he was by these judicial proceedings and by the physical distance between himself and his family. He often expressed a sense of isolation and disappointment over not receiving more letters from them, for he regarded letters from Francisca and the children as his only way of maintaining an emotional closeness to them. And Francisca, greatly burdened by the responsibilities of maintaining their house and raising their children by herself, constantly urged him in her own letters not to be consumed by public affairs and to spend more time at home. For both of them, their disappointments with their social situations would often boil over into anger with each other, each one resenting what they felt was their spouse's lack of understanding of their personal difficulties.

These issues played out in a variety of situations, often involving their children. Both of them wanted their children, the girls as well as the boys, to be schooled and educated, so that they could prosper in the new social order in which they and their compatriots found themselves. Although they wanted their children to adjust to this new order, they were at times frustrated by the nontraditional directions in which this process of adjustment sometimes took their children. They often reacted to their children's changes in different ways. Mariano tended to become dismayed over the progressive decline of the patriarchal authority he had routinely exercised in his family during the Mexican era. Francisca, on the other hand, was more accepting of these changes and, at times, became somewhat envious of the greater freedom available to her daughters but not to herself.

Toward the end of their long lives, they could both look back. They continued to resent how the American conquerors had behaved toward them and their fellow Mexican Americans, taking their property and treating them as second-class residents of the land in which they had been born. But they also could view with some satisfaction the way they had raised their family and dealt with the financial and social obstacles the American conquest of California had placed before them.

This type of correspondence among members of various Mexican American families has been used in many recent books that dramatically widen and deepen

---

23. Chávez-García, *Migrant Longing*, 28.

our understanding of the diverse peoples who constituted nineteenth-century California. By and large, however, most of this material has come from southern California and been used in works in which that region is the primary focus.[24] This makes sense, since the Latino presence in nineteenth-century California persisted more deeply and longer in the southland, which was comparatively less affected by the massive Anglo immigration associated with the gold rush. We hope that this book, which deals with one family from the north, can help fill out the picture.

At various times Francisca Benicia and Mariano Guadalupe refer to letters between them that are not in this book. We understand that our collection is not complete. Doubtless many of their letters were not preserved or are in various other archival collections. Also, there often are gaps. In addition, some of the letters are very short and deal with topics not mentioned elsewhere in the correspondence and about which we have discovered very little. And we have not been able to identify all of the individuals mentioned. In our various introductory sections we include selections from letters Mariano Guadalupe and Francisca Benicia wrote to some of their children, as well as letters their children wrote to them. These letters throw light upon many issues that appear in the husband-wife correspondence. But, again, they do not explain everything. Yet, even with those gaps, we have decided to include these letters, since we want to offer as full a picture as possible of the relationship between these two important people, and of the family dynamics, business, and social relationships in which they were involved.

We have indicated earlier in this introduction some of the major themes that appear in the correspondence. The letters themselves do not offer one coherent and consistent narrative related to any of these themes. But we think that is actually for the better, since the letters reflect the ambiguities, contradictions, and nuances of the everyday life of this remarkable couple. We believe that the words of Mariano Guadalupe, Francisca Benicia, and their children constitute a unique and important vantage point that enables a deeper understanding of the Mexican American experience in California as a whole.

---

24. Among these important works are Monroy, *Thrown among Strangers*; Chávez-García, *Negotiating Conquest*; Camarillo, *Chicanos in a Changing Society*; Casas, *Married to a Daughter of the Land*; Pérez, *Colonial Intimacies*; Chávez-García and Castillo-Muñoz, "Gender and Intimacy"; Brown-Coronel, "Intimacy and Family"; and Pérez, "Dalton-Zamoranos."

CHAPTER I

From Bear Flag Prisoner to the Early American Years 1846–1858

As we narrate in the introduction, on June 14, 1846, a group of North Americans entered the Sonoma Plaza, barged into the Casa Grande, and eventually declared Alta California independent of Mexico. When the Bear Flaggers, as they became known, first approached the Casa Grande, Francisca's immediate advice to her husband was that he "escape through the back door." Vallejo replied that "under no circumstances could I decide to abandon my young family during such a critical time." The rebels eventually took Vallejo to Sutter's Fort along with his younger brother Salvador, his secretary Víctor Prudón, and his sister Rosalía's husband, Jacob P. Leese. Francisca was left at the Casa Grande with her eight children, ranging in age from twelve to less than one year.[1]

Before his departure, Vallejo managed to send one of his men, José (Pepe) de la Rosa, to Sausalito to ask for help from John Montgomery, captain of an American vessel anchored there. Vallejo had met Montgomery some months earlier in Monterey. Although the American captain replied that he could not get involved in affairs involving the Californios, he did send one officer, John Missroon, to check on the condition of the Vallejo family in Sonoma. Francisca prevailed upon Missroon to issue a safe-conduct pass to her brother Julio so that he could go to Sutter's Fort and check up on the condition of her husband. But Julio was arrested by the Bears and was kept with Vallejo at the fort.[2]

---

1. Vallejo, *Recuerdos*, 2:1249.
2. Vallejo, *Recuerdos*, 2:1262; José (Pepe) de la Rosa, who came to California with the Híjar-Padrés party in 1834, became an important friend and companion of Vallejo and Francisca. Hutchinson, "Official List," 409.

(left) Commodore J. B. Montgomery, U.S.N., ca. 1869.
Civil War photographs, 1861–1865, Library of Congress, Prints Division.
LC-8813–2078 B. *(right)* John S. Missroon, ca. 1861.
Courtesy of the Naval History and Heritage Command.
Washington, D.C. W9–4540.

Julio's arrest prompted Francisca to send arms to her brother Ramón and his compatriots in the countryside who were preparing to attack the Bear Flag stronghold. With the assistance of American settler and Bear Flagger John Grigsby, she also managed to hide another of her brothers, Joaquín, at the Casa Grande, out of view of Frémont and his men who were looking for him.

Francisca was not the only woman in Sonoma who attempted to resist the Bear Flaggers in the best manner she could. Her sister-in-law Rosalía later recounted what she had done:

> During the whole time that Frémont and his ring of thieves were in Sonoma, robberies were very common. The women did not dare go out for a walk unless they were escorted by their husband or their brothers. One of my servants was a young Indian girl who was about seventeen years old. I swear that John C. Frémont ordered me to send that girl to the officers' barracks many times. However, by resorting to tricks, I was able to save that poor girl from falling into the hands of that lawless band of thugs who had imprisoned my husband.[3]

With her husband gone, Francisca tried to take care of her eight children while keeping track of affairs at the nearby ranchos of Petaluma and Suscol.[4] By the end of the first week of July, the Bears had been dissolved and

---

3. Beebe and Senkewicz, *Testimonios*, 29.
4. Vallejo, *Recuerdos*, 2:1272–74.

John C. Frémont. *Courtesy of the California History Room, California State Library, Sacramento, California. Neg. 2832.*

Sonoma was under the control of the U.S. Army. Vallejo and Francisca hoped the army would release the prisoners, but that did not happen immediately, so she continued to use her letters to update her husband about affairs in Sonoma. Many of the people whom Vallejo and Francisca mentioned in their letters were Indigenous servants of the Vallejo family or former soldiers who had settled in the Sonoma area.

Sacramento
July 4, 1846[5]

My dear Francisca,

   A month ago today I left home. But since I am hopeful that I will be able to return, I can cope with it, even though one of the officials who was at our home some days ago wrote to me saying that he would return very soon. Understand that you are in charge of everything at the ranchos and you should do whatever you think is appropriate. It would be a good idea not to continue with the house at Petaluma, because it is necessary for me to be there. It might be a good idea to work on the kitchen in Sonoma, as you were planning on doing. The papers dealing with the rancho are in a small box in my desk. Take them out and put them in a place where they will be safe.

---

5. DLG-V 45, letter 1.

Jacob P. Leese and Rosalía Vallejo de Leese.
Courtesy of the California Historical Society.
FN-25806.

If Salazar returns after you receive this letter, have him bring me some money, if you can sell some hides. Or else ask Señor Vaca for some money in my name.[6]

I heard that Andrónico acquired some horses and that the whole family is well.

Salazar, Julio, Prudón, and Don Luis are well and send their regards to their families.[7]

I am so anxious to return home. Have Señor Eleuterio stay at the house and tell him to go from time to time to Suscol to check on the property.[8] Give my regards to Don Pepe.

M. G. Vallejo

1846[9]
Guadalupe Vallejo,

Your children and I are fine. Don't worry too much about the family because the señores are taking good care of us. We are sad because we don't know when you will

---

6. Manuel Vaca owned a rancho in the region. Bancroft, *History of California*, 5:753–54.

7. Salazar is probably Fulgencio Salazar, a former soldier who said a few years earlier that he was going to move to Sonoma after his retirement. Fulgencio Salazar al Comandante General del Departamento, May 11, 1840, C-B 9, doc. 137, TBL. "Don Luis" is his brother-in-law, Jacob P. Leese.

8. "Señor Eleuterio" is probably Eleuterio Villavicencio, a retired soldier. See José Abrego, "Revista y presupuesto de gefes, oficios, y soldados retirados," October 9, 1844, C-A 20, 392–93, TBL.

9. C-B 441, box 6, folder 5, TBL. Julio Carrillo was imprisoned on June 20, so we believe this letter was probably written before the July 12 letter that follows.

return. My Mamá sends you many greetings. She says for you to take good care of Julio. Not much can be done at the ranchos because the Indians are running away. Alvarado is harvesting at Petaluma and Señor Eleuterio is slaughtering cattle at Suscol.[10] Your papers are being well taken care of. I am sending you some money, a little bit of pinole, and bread. When you write to me, write more legibly because I can't read your handwriting.

Francisca Carrillo de Vallejo

Sacramento
July 12, 1846[11]

Francisca,

We are still fine. Since Salazar is heading back there to get some clothing, I am sending you this letter so that you can give everyone my greetings. Salazar will probably return right away, and I hope he will bring me news about the family. Tell Rosalía that Leese received the few things he requested. I also received what you sent me, especially the corn tortillas.

We still don't have any news as to whether we will be set free soon, and this has us worried.

We send many blessings to all of you,

M. G. Vallejo

P.S. Julio is also fine, and he sends greetings to the family.

July 12, 1846[12]

I am sending Agapito and Tomás with a basket for you that contains some loaves of bread. Inside every loaf placed in the third and fourth layers you will find small gold coins, which might be of use to you for buying what you need. For two nights the servants have not slept in my room, because the danger has passed. On the 10th a captain sent by Montgomery came from Sausalito with an open letter.[13] He strongly urged me to read it. He put the American flag on the flagpole where the Bear was before. Since then there are no longer any robberies that I know of, but your sister Rosalía says it is always that way. During these days there have been

---

10. Miguel Alvarado was the mayordomo at Rancho Petaluma. Miguel Alvarado to M.G.V., January 9, 1845 and February 25, 1845, C-B 12, docs. 131, 138, TBL.

11. C-B 441, box 1, folder 2, TBL.

12. C-B 441, box 6, folder 5, TBL.

13. The officer was Lt. Joseph Warren Revere. Bancroft, *History of California*, 5:242.

many celebrations. Each and every one of us was cheering with delight and waving our handkerchiefs, but the "Bears" were very sad. I have heard the wife of good Captain Sears say that her husband was saying that "the American flag had come too soon, and that is why all their work was for nothing."[14] Your sister Rosalía and I no longer fear for your life or that of your brother Salvador and Don Luis.

Sacramento
July 22, 1846[15]

My dear Francisca,

By means of a vaquero who came from Napa on some errands for Salvador and Julio, I know that the whole family is fine. And I also know from the same messenger that Salazar should be arriving very soon. I am anxiously awaiting his arrival to hear news from home. We are all fine.

Even though Salazar may have already left to come here, I want you to send me two quires of paper, that is to say, ten folders, with one of the Indians from Suscol who knows the way (Petronio knows it well), because there is no paper here.[16] If we wait much longer, we won't have anything to write on. Also, send me the small ivory chess set that is in one of the desk drawers, as well as some salt laxatives.

Have someone tell Alvarado to write to me and report on the work going on and the harvests. And tell him not to kill more than 100 fat steers at Petaluma for their tallow, and tell Señor Eleuterio no more than 150 at Suscol. Have them take the hides from Suscol to Sonoma.

Every day we wait for the mail to arrive from Monterey. Maybe when it arrives, we will be free to return to our homes. Tell the mayordomos to keep a close watch. We know that the señora is at home and that all the girls are fine. We send them our greetings.

Julio is fine and sends his greetings to everyone, as do I. Take care of the children and give them an affectionate hug in my name, and don't forget about Rosalía and her children.

Your affectionate M. G. Vallejo wishes you happiness.

P.S. José has written to me and also to Andrónico, and he is sending you the attached letter with some drawings.[17]

---

14. "Captain Sears" is Franklin Sears. See Warner, *Men of the California Bear Flag Revolt*, 297–300.

15. C-B 441, box 1, folder 1, TBL.

16. A quire is four sheets of paper folded to form eight leaves. Petronio is the Spanish name given to a sixteen-year-old Suisun youth whose Indigenous name was recorded as Ayesa when he was baptized at Mission San Francisco de Asís in 1815. He moved to Mission San Francisco Solano soon after it was opened and in 1830 was married there to a Suisun woman from Tolenas whose Indigenous name was recorded as Chalachesma and who was given the Spanish name Emerenciana. San Francisco de Asís Baptism 4475, 5099; San Francisco Solano Marriage 192a.

17. As discussed later in this chapter, José was an illegitimate son of Vallejo.

Original Bear Flag. *Courtesy of the California History Room,
California State Library, Sacramento, California. Neg.1182.*

Sacramento
July 23, 1846[18]

My dear Francisca,

I finally received your letter and Andrónico's, which gave me such great pleasure because now I can be assured that you are living safely.

If a courier arrives with a letter that will be given to you from the commander, send it to me by means of a vaquero whom you trust. We are hopeful that we will leave here and head back to Sonoma within ten days. I am just waiting for the courier who delivered the letter to the Commodore to return.

My mother sent a letter to find out the whereabouts of Salvador and myself. I already answered and consoled her. I send my regards to you, my Señora. Kiss all the children.

Your,
M. G. Vallejo

---

18. DLG-V 45, letter 2.

Sutter's Fort—New Helvetia, ca. 1849, by Joseph Warren Revere, U.S.N.
Courtesy of The Bancroft Library, University of California, Berkeley. xF865.R4.

July 1846[19]

Guadalupe,

Señor Laugriano went into the granary and stole some things, and he was caus-ing a commotion with the Indians.[20] I told the captain about this and Laugriano was arrested. I am very afraid of him.

A man arrived here and showed me two letters. He said they were about setting you free. He also told me that it was necessary for you to bring some men with you because there were some bad people on the road who wanted to kill you and the others. Ask some good men to come with you.

I'm fine and so is everyone here at home.

Francisca Carrillo de Vallejo

I'm sending paper to you.

ON AUGUST I, VALLEJO WROTE HIS ELDEST SON, ANDRÓNICO, AND TOLD him, "I want you to take care of the house and follow Mamá's advice. You must

---

19. C-B 441, box 6, folder 5, TBL.

20. Perhaps this is Laureano Guzmán, one of the soldiers who arrived with Governor Micheltorena in 1842. Bancroft, *History of California*, 4:289.

Thomas O. Larkin.
Courtesy of The Bancroft
Library, University of California,
*Berkeley.*BANC PIC 1963.002:04585-A.

write every day because it is necessary for all educated people to do so. I understand that Captain Frémont returned some horses to you. Your Papá embraces you."[21]

On the next day, however, he and Francisca's brother Julio were released from Sutter's Fort after they signed a document in which they promised "not to take up arms against the United States of North America" and "not to furnish supplies, carry communications or in any way assist any person or persons who may be opposed to the United States of North America."[22] After his release, Vallejo first spent some time at the Casa Grande recuperating from his ordeal. He also had to calculate the livestock and property losses he had suffered during his imprisonment. As he told Thomas O. Larkin, "I have lost more than a thousand live horses, cattle, 600 tame horses, and many other things of value which were taken from my house here and at Petaluma."[23]

Nevertheless, Vallejo quickly became involved in a variety of projects, through which he attempted to create a bond between himself and the newly arrived Americans. This was not a surprise to those Americans who knew him. Merchant Faxon D. Atherton, who had met Vallejo during a three-year stint in Alta California in the late 1830s, wrote Larkin from Valparaíso, Chile, in December 1846, "If he has not been too excited in the [Bear Flag] matter, I think he knows too well which side his bread is buttered to kick very hard against the fates, especially if he is left with the semblance of a little authority, which it might be good policy to do."[24]

21. M.G.V. to Andrónico, August 1, 1846, DLG-V 46, letter 1.
22. C-B 441, box 11, folder 9, TBL.
23. M.G.V. to Thomas O. Larkin, September 15, 1846, Larkin, *Papers*, 5:237.
24. Faxon D. Atherton to Thomas O. Larkin, December 3, 1846, Larkin, *Papers*, 5:290–91.

In September, rumors spread through the Central Valley that a large war party of Walla Walla Indians was moving south toward Sacramento. Naval commander John Montgomery asked Vallejo to organize a party to keep track of the intruders, and Vallejo gladly accepted. Although the rumor turned out to be greatly exaggerated, Vallejo continued to seek to cement his ties with the Americans. In April 1847 he accepted an appointment as an Indian subagent for the North Bay from the new American military commander, Robert Stockton. In October of that same year, Vallejo participated in a reception for Stockton at Yerba Buena. The Monterey *Californian* reported that "General Mariano Guadalupe Vallejo, with several others who have held office under the late government, took their appropriate places in the line" to greet Stockton.[25]

He also spent some time with Robert Semple and Thomas O. Larkin as they attempted to establish a town on the Carquínez Strait that they hoped would become the major port for the San Francisco Bay area. The venture failed because the discovery of gold in 1848 ensured the preeminence of Yerba Buena, renamed San Francisco, at the tip of the peninsula on the western side of the bay. Nevertheless, Vallejo maintained his reputation as a leading figure. In January 1849, Larkin characterized his wealth as "immense."[26]

In the meantime, family life continued at the Casa Grande. In January 1847, four-year old Guadalupe died. And in November of that same year Francisca gave birth to a son, whom they named Plutarco, after the son who had passed away at the age of two in 1841. Unfortunately, this Plutarco suffered the same fate as his older brother and died several months after his birth. In January 1849, Francisca gave birth to a girl, whom they named Benicia.

In 1849, Vallejo was elected as a delegate from Sonoma to the Constitutional Convention in Monterey, which lasted from September through the middle of October. On the way to Monterey he stopped at San Francisco and used his trip to the convention as a way to make some contacts with various Americans. Being in the capital of Spanish and Mexican California where he had been born also allowed him to renew contact with some of his family members. In addition, he expressed to Francisca the hope that his oldest daughter, Epifania, was learning some American social customs that she might be able to teach him. He also was aware that she was beginning to become romantically involved with John Frisbie, an American who had arrived in California as a member of the New York Volunteers during the Mexican War. John Frisbie had spent most of the war in San Francisco but was stationed in Sonoma during August 1848. It was there that he met and became attracted to Epifania.

---

25. *Californian*, October 24, 1846.
26. Thomas O. Larkin to Faxon D. Atherton, January 19, 1849, Larkin, *Papers*, 8:103.

(*left*) Robert Field Stockton, ca. 1860s. *Courtesy of The Bancroft Library,*
University of California, Berkeley. POR: *Stockton, Robert Field: 3.*
(*right*) Major Samuel J. Hensley, 1850. *Courtesy of the*
California Room, San José Public Library,
Clyde Arbuckle Photograph Collection. csj_*ARB-B0101.*

Yerba Buena
August 30, 1849[27]

Francisca,

The bearer of this letter is Mr. Henly, who is going to take a look at the wood
that has been cut.[28] If he likes it, he will build four sawmills, giving me half [of the
wood]. So have José or Antonio take him to the old logging area in Petaluma that I
bought from Alvarado, so he can see it. Tell them to take him along the best road.

Give my greetings to the family,

Your Guadalupe

27. C-B 441, box 1, folder 2, TBL.
28. "Mr. Henly" is Samuel Hensley, a former Bear Flagger who had worked for Sutter in the 1840s. Bancroft, *History of California*, 3:781.

Yerba Buena
September 1, 1849[29]

Francisca,

This afternoon I will be leaving on the steamer for Monterey, after waiting here for five days, with a high temperature and a strong and unrelenting cough that takes away any desire I have to go outside.

I am heading to Monterey totally against my will. I feel quite sick, but if I return quickly perhaps I can get my business affairs in order in a definitive and efficient way.

Take care of yourself and take care of the family, especially the older children. Each day I see a thousand examples of immorality, and this causes me great sorrow.

Hug Uladislao and Benicia a thousand times, and give my greetings to the rest of the family.

Don't get sick, take care of yourself, don't go outside too much, but doing some moderate exercise would be good for you.

As always, I am your

Guadalupe

VALLEJO WAS ONE OF THE EIGHT CALIFORNIOS WHO ATTENDED THE Constitutional Convention. They unanimously opposed a proposal that would have denied Indigenous people the right to vote. Since many Californios were of mestizo descent and many had darker complexions than the North Americans, they feared that if the proposal were adopted it would be used to deny the franchise to many Californios. In an awkward compromise, the convention gave the legislature the power to enfranchise certain Indigenous persons by a two-thirds vote. When the design of the state seal was under discussion, and the proposed design included a grizzly bear, Vallejo wryly proposed "that the bear be taken out of the design for the Seal of California or, if it do remain, that it be represented as made fast by a lasso in the hands of a Vaquero." This proposal was not adopted.[30]

---

29. C-B 441, box 1, folder 2, TBL.

30. Hargis, "Native Californians in the Constitutional Convention," 7; Browne, *Report of the Debates in the Convention*, 323.

Monterey
September 28, 1849[31]

Francisca,

We are finishing the work that we all came here to do, and I think I will be leaving here by October 7.

Take care of everything.

My mother and all my brothers and sisters send you affectionate greetings.

From now on the Pueblo de San José will be the capital.

Tell Fanita that I hope by the time I arrive in Sonoma she will already know how to waltz so she can teach it to me.[32]

Your husband,
Guadalupe

WHEN VALLEJO RETURNED TO SONOMA AT THE CONCLUSION OF THE CON-vention in mid-October, he quickly became involved in electoral politics as a candidate for the state senate in the election scheduled for November. After some uncertainty in the counting process, he was declared the victor and assumed his legislative seat in San José at the end of December. He arrived too late to participate in the voting for California's U.S. senators, but he urged Pablo de la Guerra, also a newly elected state senator, to vote for John C. Frémont, who had sought Vallejo's support. When Vallejo did arrive, he quickly seized the opportunity to try to establish good relationships with the Americans he was meeting, such as San Francisco lawyer Elbert Jones.[33]

San José
December 30, 1849[34]

Señora Doña Benicia F. Carrillo de Vallejo,

Señor Jones, the bearer of this letter, is a personal friend of mine and he is going to Sonoma to pick up some law books. I have offered him any of the books from my library that he might need. Therefore, it will be necessary for him to take a look at my books and select the ones he wants to bring back, leaving a list of the ones he has taken. I hope that Señor Jones will be warmly welcomed at home.

---

31. C-B 441, box 1, folder 2, TBL.

32. "Fanita" was their nickname for their oldest daughter, Epifania.

33. Elbert Jones, a San Francisco lawyer originally from Kentucky. See Soule, *Annals*, 174, 196; Bancroft, *History of California*, 4:694.

34. C-B 441, box 1, folder 3, TBL.

Pablo de la Guerra, Salvador Vallejo, and Andrés Pico.
Courtesy of The Bancroft Library, University of California, Berkeley.
POR: *Guerra, Pablo de la: 1.*

Ever since I left home, I have been very battered by the rains along the way. It took me sixteen days to get here. I hope that once the weather settles I can go out and visit the family. I will give them your good wishes, as always.

Make sure that the children read, write, and practice the piano regularly.[35]

Hug all the older children and give Jovita, Uladislao, and Benicia a kiss.

I hope to see all of you soon.

Yours,
M. G. Vallejo

P.S. Tell Andrónico that Señor Jones is my friend and that he might need a horse to go to the pier.

In these next two letters, written during the legislative session, Vallejo mentioned several of his children and urged Francisca to care for them during his absence at the legislature. Included among the children he named were two boys, José and Enrique, whom he fathered with women who were not his wife Francisca. Children whose parents were not married were not unusual in California during this time. Although precise records are difficult to obtain, scattered evidence indicates that such births increased during the Mexican era. One reason was that the power and prestige of the Catholic Church had declined since the Spanish era. During the 1830s and 1840s, at Mission San Gabriel and the Los Angeles Plaza church, about 14 percent of children born to Spanish-surnamed couples were birthed by mothers who were not married to the child's father. Few records indicate what degree of coercion or consent was involved in these pregnancies, and that is certainly true in the case of Vallejo's illegitimate children. But we do know that he fathered at least twenty-two children and that Francisca was not the mother of at least six of them.[36]

We have not been able to find any baptismal record for José. Family tradition and genealogical speculation are varied, although there seems to be a consistent Indigenous connection. He is sometimes referred to as a "foster" son whom Vallejo adopted as a reward for warning him of an impending Indigenous attack. Other references indicate that his mother was an Indigenous woman, and this seems to be more plausible.[37] Since he is referred to in Vallejo's January 9, 1850 letter in the

---

35. Vallejo had purchased a piano from an American trader in 1844. Two years later he hired Andrew Hoeppner to teach his children how to play. In 1847 a visiting American naval officer reported that Vallejo's children could play the instrument "remarkably well." Beebe and Senkewicz, *Mariano Guadalupe Vallejo*, 205–6; Wise, *Los Gringos*, 109; Andrónico to María Antonia Lugo, August 16, 1850, C-B 441, box 6, folder 3, TBL.

36. Chávez-García, *Negotiating Conquest*, 159–61.

37. Emparán, *Vallejos*, 90–95; Northrop, *Spanish-Mexican Families*, 2:310.

Faxon Dean Atherton.
From Gullard and Lund,
Under the Oaks, 17.

same sentence as Andrónico, who was born in 1834, it is reasonable to suspect that he was born at some point in the early to mid-1830s, perhaps before Vallejo and Francisca were married. Where he lived and who took care of him in the late 1830s and early 1840s is not clear. But there is documentation that in 1843 Vallejo sent José to Valparaíso, Chile, on a boat commanded by John Wilson, who was married to Francisca's sister, Ramona Carrillo.[38] In Valparaíso, Wilson entrusted José's care to Faxon D. Atherton, who enrolled José in a school run by a group of French clergy. Vallejo sent Atherton money to pay for José's studies at the school, but after a few years the boy expressed a desire to return to California. Atherton was able to find transportation for him in 1847, and he returned to California at the end of that year.[39] José worked at the Petaluma rancho and while there had some kind of serious disagreement with his father, which resulted in their estrangement. He remained in contact with Francisca, whom he called "Madre," and lived for a time with Ramona and John Wilson at their rancho in San Luis Obispo.[40]

Enrique was born in March 1839, well after Vallejo and Francisca's marriage. His mother, Juana María Pacheco, was the older sister of Ignacio Pacheco, one of

38. Ramona's first husband, Romualdo Pacheco, had been killed in a battle in 1831. She married John Wilson, a Scottish ship master, in 1835. Santa Bárbara Presidio Marriage 211.

39. The basic story is told in Atherton, *California Diary*, 102; Pomerleau, "French Missionaries;" John Wilson to M.G.V., May 18, 1843, C-B 11, doc. 374; José Vallejo to M.G.V., July 6, 1843, C-B 11, doc. 423; M.G.V. to Father Patrick Short, November 11, 1846, C-B 12, doc. 248; M.G.V. to Faxon D. Atherton, November 20, 1846, C-B 12, doc. 251; José Vallejo to M.G.V., December 1, 1846, C-B 12, doc, 252; José Vallejo to M.G.V., December 11, 1846, C-B 12, doc. 254; Thomas O. Larkin to M.G.V., June 3, 1847, C-B 12, doc. 295; José Vallejo to M.G.V. June 19, 1847, C-B 12, doc. 300, all in TBL.

40. Emparán, *Vallejos*, 94–95; José Vallejo to F.B.C.V., December 24, 1853, C-B 13, doc. 321, TBL.

Vallejo's Sonoma soldiers. Ignacio's wife, Josefa Higuera, died in January 1838, and his older sister Juana María left her home in Santa Clara and went to Sonoma to comfort her brother.[41] During her stay in Sonoma, she conceived a child who was born in Santa Clara in early 1839 and given the name José Enrique. In the baptismal register, Father Rafael Moreno recorded that the father was "Guadalupe Vallejo." Where Enrique spent his earliest years is not clear. In 1841, Juana María, who was forty-six years old, married a forty-five-year-old cousin, José Dolores Pacheco, and they may have cared for him in his infancy.[42] In any event, by 1850 he was living with the Vallejo family at Sonoma, and he appears to have established close relationships with at least some of the other Vallejo children. For instance, in a letter to his father in 1860, a few months after he had arrived in New York to study, Platón said, "Tell Henry [Enrique] I would be glad to have him write me a little letter and that I would like to see him very much." Enrique did write to Platón and told him, "After spending so many years together and never having had a disagreement, because we are so much alike, it made me feel even more sad that you are so far away from me. If I could see you, even for a moment, my sad heart and mind would feel some comfort. If only I could be with you to reminisce about our time together, when we would go on walks together, when we would go to partes [parties] and picnics, always together having fun."[43]

Given these relationships, it is highly unlikely that Francisca was unaware of the boy's origin. It is not clear, though, whether she was aware of three other *hijos naturales*, as they were termed in the sacramental registers, children whom Vallejo had fathered earlier. In 1827 two such children, José Ramón and María Antonia, were born in Monterey, in March and April, respectively. Their mothers were two sisters, Ana María Avila and Rosalía Joaquina Avila. The sisters' father, Guadalupe Avila, was a Monterey soldier who had died in June 1825. Father Ramón Abella, the priest who baptized José Ramón, noted in the register that Vallejo had admitted to being the boy's father.[44] A month later, when Father Abella baptized María Antonia, he noted in the register that the presidio commander had told him that Vallejo was the child's father.[45] The children were most likely raised in the Monterey region by their mothers.

In the mid-1840s, María Antonia married William Reed, an English sailor who arrived in California in the mid-1830s. Reed acquired some Mission San Miguel land in 1846, and María Antonia and her brother José Ramón settled there with him. In December 1848 they were visited by a group of Americans who were passing

---

41. Mission Santa Clara Baptism 9932; Mission San José Death 5781.
42. Mission Santa Clara Marriage 2751.
43. Platón to M.G.V., July 20, 1860, C-B 441, box 6, folder 2, TBL (written in English); Enrique to Platón, April 4, 1861, C-B 441 FILM, reel 3, 16–19, TBL.
44. Mission San Carlos Baptism 3480.
45. Mission San Carlos Baptism 3482.

Mission San Miguel, 1875, by Carleton E. Watkins.
*Courtesy of the California Historical Society and the University of
Southern California Digital Library.* CHS-m14757, USC 1–1-1–14093.

through. These men noticed that Reed had recently obtained money from the sale
of some sheep destined for the miners in the newly discovered gold fields. The
Americans murdered all of them for the money.[46]

Vallejo fathered another child, a girl named Pía Juana, in Monterey in 1831.
Her mother was María Gaudiosa Zúñiga, the seventeen-year-old daughter of
Buenaventura Zúñiga, a soldier who had died in December 1829. In the baptismal
register, Father Abella stated that it was reported that Vallejo was the father. María
Gaudiosa died in August 1832, and her daughter Pía passed away a month later.[47]

San José
January 9, 1850[48]

Francisca,

The gentleman who will be delivering this letter to you is Mr. Robert Hopkins,

46. Ohles, *Lands of Mission San Miguel*, 52–55.
47. Mission San Carlos Baptism 3731; Mission San Carlos Death 2820, 2824.
48. C-B 441, box 1, folder 3, TBL.

William Montgomery Boggs, ca.
1870s. *Courtesy of Sonoma County
Library Photograph Collection. cstr_
pho 043244.jp2.*

the person who has asked to rent a room to set up an office.[49] I told him that I would rent him the room between the billiard room and William Boggs's room.[50] If that room isn't occupied, have Andrónico turn it over to him. I imagine that the carpenter Andrés is no longer staying there. If he is, have him move to the tower.

Since leaving Sonoma I haven't had one good day. I experienced many difficulties along the way and here as well. As soon as the weather settles, I think I'll head home to see the whole family. I am not happy being away from home. When I can't see all of you, I feel that I have nothing. This enormous emptiness causes me to suffer greatly both physically and emotionally.

Take good care of the whole family and make sure they study every day. Encourage José and Andrónico to study because they are young, and they need to do this. So do the girls, who are also young and need good examples and good advice. Hug and kiss the younger children, especially Uladislao. Tell him to be happy. When you receive this letter, give all the children some money so they can buy sweets. Also, give some money to the little Indian children. Give Don Pepe my greetings and have him fix up the place where he is living.

I am, as always, your

Guadalupe

---

49. Robert Hopkins was a lawyer in Sonoma. Munro-Fraser, *History of Sonoma County*, 142. He was elected district judge. Vallejo supported him in 1850. *Journal of the Senate of the State of California at Their First Session*, 170, 263.

50. William Boggs was the son of Lilburn Boggs, former governor of Missouri, who had spent the winter of 1846 at the Vallejo rancho in Petaluma and had been *alcalde* (local magistrate) of the Northern District from 1847–49. Bancroft, *History of California*, 2:722–23; Hyde, *Empires, Nations, and Families*, 352–53; Palmer, *History of Napa and Lake Counties*, 384 (Napa County section).

California's first state house, San José, 1849.
*Courtesy of the California Historical Society and the University
of Southern California Digital Library.* CHS-929, USC-1-1-1-14352.

San José
January 28, 1850[51]

Francisca,

I am writing this letter to you with the sole purpose of sending you and the whole family my greetings. I think about you with fondness. Give all the children good advice. Tell them that their Papá hasn't forgotten about them for an instant. He blesses them every day and prays to the Supreme Being to enlighten them so they will live up to their parents' expectations. Their parents pray for their present and future well-being and take pride in having such good children. Give kisses to all the little ones. Tell Uladislao to take care of my room and my weapons, tell Jovita to sweep my room, and tell Platón to keep speaking English. Give Benicia one, two, three, four, five thousand kisses. Tell Enrique to take care of the laying hens.

---

51. C-B 441, box 1, folder 3, TBL.

Tomorrow I'll be very busy trying to see if I can move the capital to Sonoma or to Suscol near the mouth of the Suscol estuary, where I have offered to donate some land.[52] It hasn't stopped raining since I arrived and I'm rather stiff from the cold. Make sure the drains are open so that water doesn't back up and stain the walls of the house.

I have received two letters, but I don't know who they are from because there is no signature. I imagine that one is from Andrónico and the other is from José.

I hope you and the girls will write to me. Send all the letters in the same envelope by way of Benicia. Give Don Pepe my greetings and tell him that very soon I'll go and see if his room is ready.

I am your
Guadalupe

* * *

VALLEJO REMAINED IN SAN JOSÉ WORKING IN THE LEGISLATURE UNTIL its adjournment on April 22. As part of its business, the legislature formally divided the state into counties. Since the counties were named after the larger population centers or significant natural landmarks within them, most of them had Spanish names. Vallejo authored an important report for the legislature on the historical background of the county names. In this report he sought to emphasize the Mexican heritage of the new American state of California.[53]

The winter proved especially rainy, and he complained that his accommodations were very cramped and inconvenient. As a result, he became somewhat lonely. He often complained that few members of his family were writing to him and keeping him apprised of events at home. Yet at the same time he would give Francisca instructions on how to treat the strangers he would occasionally send to the Casa Grande. But she, finding herself once again with increased responsibilities while he was so far away, was in no mood to listen to his complaints or his orders. She was also quite concerned about one of her children. In November 1849 she told her sister Josefa that Benicia, who was less than a year old, was very sick with a form of dysentery that required constant medication and sometimes daily visits from a doctor.[54]

---

52. This effort to locate the permanent state capital on some of his rancho lands in the North Bay was ultimately unsuccessful.

53. "Report of Mr. Vallejo on the Derivation and Definition of Names of the Several Counties of California," *Journal of the Senate of the State of California at Their First Session*, Appendix, 522–37.

54. F.B.C.V. to Josefa, November 24, 1849. C-B 441 FILM, reel 4, 146–47, TBL.

San José
February 4, 1850[55]

Francisca,

You already know how to write quite well, yet you still don't send me anything written in your own hand. Why? Don't you think that I'm always anxious to hear from you and to know what everybody is doing? Don't you trust me? Is it possible that you are ashamed of me? Do you believe that even a minute goes by when I don't think about my family? Why don't all the boys write to me? And Fanita, has she forgotten her Papá? Isn't Adelita talented enough to write a few stanzas and send them to her Papá? And has Natalia forgotten that her Papá always keeps her close in his heart? And why doesn't Andrónico, who is the oldest child at home, think about his Papá more often? His Papá always, always has such high hopes for him. So has everybody forgotten about me? Have they forgotten that the main reason they learned how to write was so they could write to me with confidence, which is something of utmost importance to me? Isn't that what the head of a family deserves? All of this causes me a great deal of worry, for I deserve their utmost trust.

I am attaching two letters that I received. I suppose that one of them is from José and the other is from Andrónico. Tell them, in my name, that when they write to me it is necessary for them to sign their letters.

Kiss and hug all the little ones and accept the sincere affection that is sent to you by your

Guadalupe

To Don M. Guadalupe Vallejo in San José
Sonoma
February 8, 1850[56]

Guadalupe,

You tell me that I don't write to you in my own hand! You are correct. The letter I wrote to you was in Don Pepe's hand because I was very busy. That is why I asked him to do it. You tell me that you think about your family a lot. If that is true, then why don't you come home? Yes, I trust you. I imagine that you are busy. I am not ashamed of you, but I do believe that your government and your capitals keep you very occupied . . .

Yes, I truly believe that you can go about your business without even thinking about your family because, if you did remember them and stopped to think about it, you would realize that your family needs you more than the government does.

55. C-B 441, box 1, folder 3, TBL.
56. C-B 441, box 6, folder 5, TBL.

(*left*) José (Pepe) de la Rosa.
Courtesy of Ventura County Research Library and Archives. JDF-*daguerre (Collections).*
(*right*) Vicenta Sepúlveda Yorba Carrillo. *Courtesy of the Anaheim Public Library. No. P8754.*

Don't you remember that you have the same obligations toward them that I do, and perhaps even more? Don't you remember that the family needs you to take care of them and advise them? Don't you remember that I get tired?

Why don't you come home and take care of your family and your interests? Don't you remember how much work you put into this? Why are you letting all of this slip away, everything that has cost you the sweat of your brow, to go and earn one more peso? I don't want a single peso, nor hundreds of thousands of them from you. Your family and I love you more than all the millions of pesos in the world.

Why are you working so much? Isn't what we have enough for you? Neither I nor your family want anything more. All of the children think about you a lot. They didn't write to you because everyone who comes here from San José says that you are on your way home. But since so many weeks went by, they lost hope and started writing to you. Andrónico wanted to go with Captain Frisbie so he could see you. Uladislao, Jovita, and Benicia are waiting for you. They go outside every so often to see if you are coming.

My sister Vicenta arrived three days ago.[57] Everyone here is fine.

I am always thinking about you,

Francisca Benicia de Vallejo

57. This was how Francisca referred to María Vicenta Sepúlveda. She first married Tomás Yorba in 1834. He died in 1845, and she married Francisca's brother José Ramón in 1847. See Northrop, *Spanish-Mexican Families*, 1:310, 364; 2:47.

San José
February 19, 1850[58]

Francisca,

You are correct in believing that you alone bear the full responsibility for caring for the family and that I have put you in that situation. I know you have no reason to think differently. I'm working on behalf of the family and their [economic] security. There is no doubt that I have very sacred obligations with regard to the family, but I also have obligations with respect to society in general. The way to settle that matter is to cooperate by just and fair means (under the present circumstances it still seems difficult) in terms of the organization of the government. Once this has been achieved, it will give me great satisfaction to have been one of the people who assisted in this.

Are you not suffering in the same way that I am? I would bet you anything that after reading this explanation you will forgive me for my absence. Do you believe that I can be happy away from your side and that of our children? I only want to be away so that I can receive letters from you and from the whole family and have the pleasure of reading them. When you realize what it means to receive <u>good</u> news from one's entire family, you will understand the pleasure I derived the other day when I received your letters and the other ones, as well.

Yesterday I also received the first letters that were written to me shortly after I left Sonoma.

Several days ago I asked you for two books. If you had sent them to me, I already would have returned home. But the books still haven't arrived, so I need to ask Don Juan Padilla to go and get them.[59] M. Hansen, the gardener, can give the books to Padilla. They are the ones with the parchment covers that contain Father Junípero Serra's work, as well as another old book with a parchment cover that has been in my safekeeping.

I sent you some onion seeds. Give everyone in the family a hug. Give Ramón's family greetings on my behalf.

Tell Ula that I'm on my way and for him to be happy. Tell Platón that we will see one another soon. Tell Jovita that her Papá will look for some pretty things for her. Give Benicia a kiss.

And what shall I say to you? Nothing . . . except that . . .

I am your
Guadalupe

---

58. C-B 441, box 1, folder 3, TBL.

59. Juan Padilla was associated with Ramón Carrillo's anti–Bear Flag activities in 1846. Bancroft, *History of California*, 4:765. Padilla gave power of attorney to Vallejo in 1849. C-B 35, doc. 114, TBL.

San José
February 28, 1850[60]

Francisca,

The books I have been waiting for, for so long, the ones that I wrote to you about in several letters, didn't arrive until today. Now I definitely can get ready to head home soon.

Don't believe that I am here because it is my choice. I am sick and tired of this place, and I am bored. The rains have been very heavy and, as a result, the mud in the streets is unbearable. Besides, I am lacking the comforts that old men like me greatly need. I am in a small room where five of us are living together, with no other comfort than being able to sleep under a roof. My eyes are bad, perhaps from stoking a very small and very bad iron fireplace and then having to go out into the cold air.

Take care of the family. Give them advice, and that way you will be fulfilling your duties as a mother and more in my absence.

Why haven't you written to me again? And the girls, why don't they write to me? How can writing just one letter tire them out? And how is it that I am always able to write a letter?

Give everyone my greetings. Give Jovita and Uladislao a kiss. Tell Platón that I am very happy with his letters. Tell Andrónico to write to me as well, telling me everything he has been doing during my absence, such as the improvements at the house, and what is happening at the ranchos.

I am your
Guadalupe

San José
April 2, 1850[61]

Francisca,

I am sending this letter to you for the sole purpose of greeting you and the whole family. Hug all of them, give Uladislao and Benicita a kiss, and give them some sweets, too. Soon I will be home and I, your husband, will give you a thousand embraces.

M. G. Vallejo

---

60. C-B 13, doc. 37, TBL.
61. C-B 441, box 1, folder 3, TBL.

AFTER THE ADJOURNMENT OF THE LEGISLATURE, VALLEJO HURRIED BACK to Sonoma. On April 25 he and Francisca were the godparents at the Catholic baptism of John Frisbie. During the Spanish and Mexican eras, a non-Catholic foreigner wishing to marry a Californiana had to be baptized first, and Frisbie's decision to become a Catholic signaled his intention eventually to seek Epifania's parents' permission to marry her. During this same time Frisbie was also establishing a close relationship with Vallejo. Together they set up a series of stores that sold provisions to newly arrived miners anxious to head for the gold fields in 1849. Frisbie, an unsuccessful candidate for lieutenant governor in the state's first election at the end of that year, provided organizational assistance to Vallejo in his successful campaign for the state senate at that same election.

A few months after Frisbie's baptism, Vallejo made him his personal lawyer. On January 1, 1851, at a gala event held by the newly established Society of California Pioneers, Frisbie, who was a main speaker, invited Vallejo to make some remarks. As the local newspaper reported, "General Vallejo was called for most vociferously, and replied in a few remarks and sentiments in his own native magnificent language, to which the audience loudly responded. He is a popular man."[62]

Even though his senate term was only for one year, Vallejo remained in contact with the legislature when it convened for its second session in San José on January 6, 1851, as he attempted to make the city of Vallejo the capital of California.

San José
January 17, 1851[63]

Dear Francisca,

All the children wrote to me, but you didn't because you are ill and that is forgivable, even though the collective family voice assures me that this illness is nothing new.

I'm certain that you probably were listening to everyone's letters being read aloud, sometimes laughing and at other times correcting my nonsense.

Take care of everyone until I can return to help you. Don Juan Cooper offered to look for a nice house in Monterey for me and will write to me later.[64] That is why I'm not going to Monterey now.

I think I will leave here next Wednesday, even though I haven't been able to finish the business regarding the capital. But in any case, I unexpectedly managed to secure $150,000, which seems to have come from heaven.

---

62. *Daily Alta California*, January 3, 1851.

63. DLG-V 45, letter 3. On this same day, Vallejo also wrote short letters to his children Adela (DLG-V 47, letter 1), Enrique (DLG-V 48, letter 1), Epifania (DLG-V 49, letter 1), and Uladislao (DLG-V 52, letter 1).

64. John Cooper, a mariner, arrived in Monterey in 1823 and married Vallejo's sister Encarnación in 1827. Bancroft, *History of California*, 2:765–66, Northrop, *Spanish-Mexican Families*, 1:351.

Captain John Rogers Cooper, 1851.
Courtesy of The Bancroft Library,
University of California, Berkeley.
BANC PIC 2000.047-CASE.

Colonel Frémont reconciled honorably with me, and we remain friends.

I can't be separated from you or the family. I feel an immense emptiness. Nothing can make life pleasant when I'm away from you. I'm always thinking about domestic responsibilities. My heart is sad, and I think I will die very soon if I remain separated from home. Perhaps that is the reason the boys and girls love me so much and I them.

Have the children kiss your hand after they read this letter.

Your husband,
M. G. Vallejo

ALTHOUGH THE EFFORT TO MAKE VALLEJO THE STATE CAPITAL WAS successful, the legislature met there for only a few days in 1852 because the lack of suitable accommodations forced it to move to Sacramento. By this time, Frisbie had become a member of the family; he and Epifania were married on April 3, 1851, at the church of San Francisco Solano. On the day of the marriage Vallejo wrote to his mother, "Señor Frisbie is a fine man. I held that opinion of him before and I still feel the same way, for he has given the proof that I am correct."[65] The couple took up residence in Benicia. By that time, Francisca had given birth to another child, Napoleón, who was born in December 1850.

---

65. M.G.V. to María Antonia Lugo, April 3, 1850, C-B 441, box 1, folder 3, TBL.

(left) Fannie Vallejo Frisbie, ca. 1865. *Courtesy of The Bancroft Library,*
University of California, Berkeley. BANC PIC 1978.195:11-PIC.
(right) John B. Frisbie. *Courtesy of the Autry Museum of*
the American West, Los Angeles. No. 2002.1.3.23.

In 1851, Congress passed the California Land Act. The presumption behind
the legislation was that many of the land grants issued by the authorities during
California's Mexican era were invalid. The law required all holders of Mexican land
grants to provide documentation proving the validity of their grants. Since Frisbie
had spent some years in Albany, New York, clerking at a law office before he came
to California, Vallejo relied on his advice on legal matters related to the Land
Act. Frisbie was also able to use his contacts in the legislature to try to soften the
financial liabilities Vallejo had accrued in his attempts to make the city of Vallejo
the state capital. Vallejo also used Frisbie and other legal contacts to try to help
other Californios, such as his sister-in-law Josefa Carrillo de Fitch, maintain their
properties. He also consulted with other landowners throughout the state, such
as Pablo de la Guerra of Santa Bárbara.[66]

Vallejo was elected to a term as mayor of Sonoma in 1852. He also spent considerable time away from home during the first half of the 1850s, especially since the Land
Commission met in San Francisco and Vallejo needed to be there. He testified in
the cases that involved the ranchos he had been granted, such as Petaluma, Suisun,

66. M.G.V. to Josefa Carrillo de Fitch, June 29, 1851, C-B 441, box 1, folder 3, TBL; M.G.V. to Pablo de la Guerra, January 18, 1856, DLG 998, letter 3, Santa Bárbara Mission Archive-Library.

and Suscol. He also testified for other Californios who had been granted ranchos in the Bay Area. Vallejo very much understood that the legal proceedings were stacked against the Californios. In 1856 he told Pablo de la Guerra, "The squatters, for their part, say whatever they like and come and take the land. Meanwhile, the <u>lawyers</u> could care less about any of it."[67]

Francisca was left to manage the household, and a variety of matters were in flux. For instance, as the children were growing up the family quarters on the second floor of the Casa Grande was becoming more and more crowded. As early as 1849 the family purchased a group of lots about half a mile northwest of the plaza. They eventually built a Gothic style "Boston" house on that land and Vallejo gave it the name Lachryma Montis, after a spring on the property. The family moved into the home in late 1853. Frisbie and Epifania's first child was born in 1852. They named him Mariano Vallejo Frisbie. However, the child, whom the proud grandparents called "Lupe," died four years later. A year before Lupe's death, Epifania bore a girl, whom they named Fanita Natalia. She was often called "Fannie."

In the midst of so much upheaval and sadness, Vallejo and Francisca were very concerned about the ability of their children to adapt to the new world the Treaty of Guadalupe Hidalgo had created. They were extremely anxious to educate all their boys and girls and set them up with at-home tutors as often as they could. Vallejo and Juan Bautista Alvarado had been personally tutored in Monterey by Governor Pablo Vicente de Solá after the pueblo schoolteacher, Sergeant Miguel Archuleta, had told the newly arrived governor that Vallejo and Alvarado "were the most advanced students at the school, because they could sing a Mass of Thanksgiving very well."[68]

Vallejo and Francisca also made sure to take advantage of any opportunities that might allow them to provide their children with more formal educational opportunities. Given his experience of following his own father into the military, it was natural for Vallejo to seek a similar path for his oldest son, Andrónico. Using the political contacts he had made at the Constitutional Convention and in the legislature, in 1851 he was able to secure an appointment for his son to West Point. At first Andrónico was pleased by this possibility. In March he excitedly wrote his grandmother, "Very soon I will be leaving for the United States. I have been accepted as a cadet in the prestigious military college called West Point."[69] But further reflection on his temperament and abilities soon cooled his ardor, and he decided not to enter the military. He did go east, but to a different destination.

At this time Vallejo was using the legal services of Robert McLane, a former U.S. congressman who had moved to California to practice law, in his efforts to have the

67. M.V.G. to Pablo de la Guerra, March 3, 1856, DLG 998, letter 4, Santa Bárbara Mission Archive-Library. In this letter, the word "lawyers" is written in English.
68. "Manuscript Made for Theodore Hittell by Gov. J.B. Alvarado," Engelhardt Papers, Santa Bárbara Mission Archive-Library.
69. Andrónico to María Antonia Lugo, March 28, 1851, C-B 441, box 6, folder 3, TBL.

city of Vallejo made the state capital. McLane was a graduate of Mount St. Mary's College in Emmitsburg, Maryland. When McLane returned to Baltimore in early 1852, he took Andrónico with him and enrolled him at Mount St. Mary's. The very next year, when Frisbie and Epifania traveled east to visit his family, they took Vallejo and Francisca's second-oldest son, Platón, with them and enrolled him in the same college.[70]

As Andrónico was beginning his studies, his father wrote him a long letter. Reflecting on his own experiences, he passionately told his child how important he regarded the educational opportunities he hoped to provide not only to his eldest son but to all of his children.

> Up until now, ignorance and stupidity have reigned in California. I hope that very soon we will have schools filled with skilled teachers who can shine a ray of light on the darkness in which we have lived until now. How fortunate young people would be if that were so! My dearest son, if only I had been given the opportunity to acquire an education such as that which has been afforded you and perhaps to your siblings! Take advantage of it, Andrónico. It is important for you to have some inkling about mythology, such as knowing that Saturn had wings. Yes, my son, time flies and its flight is very rapid. I would gladly give everything I own to be your age again and find myself in the position in which you now find yourself. You know very well that up until now there has been an absolute lack of all means of education here in California. And the little education I managed to acquire was thanks to sleepless nights and constant study and dedication. I didn't have teachers to guide me, but you do, and they are capable as well as dedicated. Therefore, you need to repay them for their efforts, and also live up to my expectations, by applying yourself to your studies. A person's fate can change. You know that Lady Luck is portrayed blindfolded, with one foot on a wheel that spins at random. One day you have everything and the next day it is all gone. But knowledge is not exposed to the vicissitudes and losses that affect one's life. Knowledge is a type of wealth that is secure and long-lasting. He who possesses knowledge is viewed as a god and is deemed to be worthy even if he is lacking in material things. For it is with knowledge that one can acquire material wealth. So many mistakes are made due to ignorance! But so many bad decisions are held in check because of education. Here is another mythological reference: pagans thought that all the troubles of the world were released from Pandora's box. But I would say that all the troubles derive from ignorance as well as Midas's chest of gold.
>
> I don't think I need to tell you, but it is my duty to remind you to be respectful and deferential to your instructors, to keep your distance from all bad company, and to make sure that all your friendships are honorable and not detrimental. For knowledge paired with virtue is the complement of human perfection. But knowledge paired with vice camouflages vice and gives it an appearance of honor. Read good books filled with moral principles. Don't buy or open any books without the permission of your instructors.[71]

---

70. The question of the state capital was dealt with in two letters McLane wrote to Vallejo on July 26 and November 6, 1851 in C-B 13, docs. 182, 208, respectively, TBL; two other McLane letters to Vallejo report on Andrónico's trip east and his enrollment at Mount St. Mary's: McLane to Vallejo on February 2 and April 1, 1852, in C-B 13, docs. 226, 230, respectively, TBL; Emparán, *Vallejos*, 315.

71. M.G.V. to Andrónico Vallejo, July 15, 1852, DLG-V 46, letter 3.

(*left*) Natalia Vallejo. *Courtesy of California State Parks,*
Sonoma Barracks. No. 243–1-369.
(*right*) Jovita Vallejo. *Courtesy of California State Parks,*
Sonoma Barracks. No. 243–1-368.

When the family moved from the Casa Grande into Lachryma Montis, an opportunity arose to further the education of their daughters. John L. Ver Mehr, an
Episcopalian clergyman, had opened a girls' school in Sonoma, named St. Mary's
Hall. Ver Mehr first operated the school out of the Leese adobe on the plaza, but
then Vallejo and Francisca rented the Casa Grande to him at a reduced rate on the
condition that their three eldest daughters who were still at home—sixteen-year-
old Adela, fifteen-year-old Natalia, and nine-year-old Jovita—could attend.[72] The
Vallejos and the Ver Mehrs became close. When Epifania's child Mariano Vallejo
Frisbie died in 1856, two months shy of his fourth birthday, Ver Mehr conducted
the burial service.[73] At the same time, nine-year-old Uladislao was sent to Benicia
to attend a boarding school for boys located there. The school's director reported
to Vallejo that the boy "needs drilling to acquire habits of study."[74]

Through all of this, Francisca remained as unconvinced as ever that her husband
needed to spend so much time in public affairs, such as when he served in the
Constitutional Convention and the state senate. The health of baby Benicia did
not improve, and she died in January 1853.[75] Four months later another child was
born. This child was a girl, and her parents named her Benicia, in memory of their

72. Ver Mehr, *Checkered Life*, 379; Peeke, "Forgotten Man," 177; "Female Education," *Alta*, October 6, 1855.
73. Ver Mehr, *Checkered Life*, 395.
74. C. M. Blake to M.G.V., October 12, 1854, Benicia Historical Museum Collection, 1985.015.0009.
75. M.G.V. to María Antonia Lugo, February 12, 1853, C-B 441, box 1, folder 3, TBL.

recently departed daughter. But the death of the girl heightened Francisca's concern for the well-being of her children. She was distraught when she learned that Vallejo had not kept a close enough eye on four-year-old Napoleón during a visit he made to his father in San Francisco. She was not happy that she had to send her children on voyages to San Francisco or Benicia so that they could have contact with their father. She bluntly indicated her displeasure in an 1854 letter when Mariano Guadalupe was in Benicia consulting with Frisbie about various legal and land matters.

Sonoma Springs
September 12, 1854[76]

Guadalupe,

I was sitting on my sewing chair waiting for you for quite a while, thinking perhaps that you wouldn't be coming, because the stagecoaches had arrived some time ago, and you weren't on any of them. Then, all of a sudden Billy came in with a letter from you in which you told me about the trouble we were going to have with Napoleón. I realized and understood very well how you must have felt during those moments when you were looking for him and couldn't find him. Oh my God! What would I have done if Napoleón had been lost! Guadalupe, take good care of Nápoles.[77] From the moment I put him on the steamer, I have not been at ease, not even for an instant. The days seem longer to me than ever before. All I do is think about that little boy because I know he is so mischievous. If he doesn't see you, he is capable of wandering about until he finds you, and you might lose him again.

The rest of the family is fine. It's true that I had planned on going to San Francisco if you thought it would be a good idea. I would leave next Tuesday, if the captain arrived, as you say in your letter. I have all the girls here at the house so they can make their dresses. Tell Fanita that the girls are sending her two bonnets so that she can have them covered in green on the outside and lined in purple on the inside, or whatever she thinks is best. But don't put any flowers on the outside or perfume on the inside, and have the captain bring them when he comes back.

I will take care of everything that you have asked me to do, Guadalupe, as soon as you leave that room where you are living.

Tell Fanita to take care of Nápoles, or take him with you wherever you go. It weighs heavily on me that I let him go with Don Pepe, with so much work that you have to do, and now Nápoles will create even more work for you.

---

76. C-B 441, box 6, folder 5, TBL.

77. Napoleón and his father had become separated on the steamer that was carrying them to San Francisco. Emparán, *Vallejos*, 379. Billy was an Indigenous servant in the household who was the second husband of Isidora Filomena, the widow of Vallejo's important Indigenous ally, the Suisun chief Sem-Yeto, better known by his Christian name Solano. See Beebe and Senkewicz, *Testimonios*, 3–15. "Nápoles" was Francisca's nickname for Napoleón.

Give Fanita all my love and give my best to the captain. Give Nápoles and Lupe many kisses. Have some coffee and toast prepared and enjoy it with the two of them in my name.

Benicia F. de Vallejo

P.S. Papá, since Saturday we have been in the house busily sewing our woolen dresses, the ones you told us to make for when we go to see you, Fannie, Nápoles, Lupe, and the captain, and to give each of you many kisses. Papá, if you see Felicidad, ask her why she tricked us, and the same goes for the captain.[78] The other day he promised us that he would write to us as soon as he arrived in San Francisco.

Your affectionate children,[79]
Adela, Natalia, Jovita, Uladislao, Benicia

AT THE END OF 1855, ANDRÓNICO AND PLATÓN LEFT MOUNT ST. MARY'S and returned to California. Andrónico began working at the Petaluma rancho while Platón, and eventually Uladislao, entered San Francisco College on Bush Street, which was run by Englishman John Chittenden. Soon after entering the school, Uladislao wrote enthusiastically to his father of the progress he hoped to make: "I began to study French and I think I will get along very quick. . . . I am going to study Latin very quick and maybe philosophy and a few other things."[80]

In November 1856 an epidemic of diphtheria broke out in Sonoma and four of Ver Mehr's daughters died from it. He decided to close St. Mary's Hall in Sonoma and move to San Francisco, where he reopened the school. Adela and Natalia had already finished their course of studies at Sonoma, but Jovita became a student at the new St. Mary's Hall on the corner of Geary and Powell.

San Francisco
June 11, 1857[81]

Francisca,
    Do as much as you can to get Platón ready so he can go to school as soon as

---

78. Felicidad is Francisca's sister, who lived at the Carrillo adobe in Santa Rosa. She married Víctor Castro in 1855 and died after a difficult childbirth the next year. McGinty, "Carrillos of San Diego," 143–44.
79. "Affectionate" is in English in the original letter.
80. *Daily Alta California*, October 27, 1857, contains an advertisement for San Francisco College with some information about Chittenden; Uladislao to M.G.V., June 16, 1858, C-B 441, box 6, folder 16, TBL (written in English).
81. C-B 441, box 1, folder 3, TBL.

(above) San Francisco College receipt, November 1858. Board and tuition costs for
Platón and Uladislao Vallejo from September 1 to December 31, 1858.
Courtesy of The Bancroft Library, University of California, Berkeley. C-B 441, box 5.
(below) St. Mary's Hall, Bush Street, San Francisco, July 14, 1859.
Courtesy of The Bancroft Library, University of California, Berkeley. C-B 441, box 11, folder 10.

possible. When I return from Monterey, I'll arrange everything with the professors. I'll have to pay $40 a month for the course of study.

It's also necessary to get Jovita ready, as best you can, so as not to lose time. Send her to Dr. Ver Mehr's school with Natalia and have Natalia wait there for me. When I return, I'll settle that matter and bring Natalia home if she doesn't wish to stay for the school term.

I am well, give the young ones a kiss,

M. G. Vallejo

P.S. In my absence, the attached letters should suffice and can be presented to the interested parties so that the girls can be admitted.

THE MALE STUDENTS AT SAN FRANCISCO COLLEGE AND THE FEMALE students at St. Mary's Hall would socialize together on various occasions, such as the July 4 fireworks celebrations overseen by Mrs. Ver Mehr. Platón wrote to his father a few days after such an occasion, "We bought a few fireworks on the Fourth." "Not wishing to have all the fun to ourselves," he, Uladislao, and another young man "went up near St. Mary's Hall and had the greatest fun you ever saw. The young ladies shared also in our exploits."[82] At home, two girls joined the Vallejo family as Francisca gave birth to Luisa in 1856 and María the following year. They were her final children.

In 1858, with several land cases still undecided, Vallejo had to go to Monterey. His mother, María Antonia Isabela Lugo, had died in 1855. In her will she left her property to two of her children—an unmarried son, Juan Antonio, and María de Jesús, who was married to French merchant Víctor Fortoul. The property consisted mainly of Rancho San Cayetano in Monterey County, which had been granted to her husband, Ignacio Vallejo, in the 1820s. Juan Antonio was the original executor of her will, but he died after falling from a horse in May 1857, and Vallejo was then named executor. He traveled to Monterey and sought to have his sister Prudenciana, whose husband, José Amesti, had died in 1855, included in the will. Fortoul, however, raised a series of objections, and the case dragged on for years.[83]

While Vallejo was in Monterey, it became clear in Sonoma that Adela wished to marry John Frisbie's older brother Levi, a medical doctor who had come to California in 1850 to recover his health. Levi was sixteen years older than Adela. Francisca and Vallejo both objected to this marriage. Adela, reflecting the attitudes about companionate, as opposed to arranged, marriage that had become fairly standard

82. Platón to M.G.V., July 8, 1857, C-B 441, box 6, folder 12, TBL (written in English).
83. Emparán, *Vallejos*, 98–103.

in the United States by the mid-nineteenth century, argued that she should not be bound by the Mexican custom of contracting matrimony only if she had the consent of her parents.[84] She apparently also insinuated that her own parents had not felt themselves bound to that custom when they decided to wed in the 1830s. Adela set the wedding date herself. Francisca and some of her children appear to have become more reconciled to Adela's plans than Vallejo himself. In June, a few days before the wedding was scheduled, Platón, a student at San Francisco College along with Uladislao, wrote his father:

> Adela will marry on Saturday. Mamá told us we might go up there to see the wedding and then come back again on Monday. I think that since they are really going to get married, it is right to make them, for Adela's sake, a nice little party, to make it look well, even if it be against one's own will. Don't you think so? I think it will be a great deal better. Adela is quite determined, and I hope it is all for the best.[85]

Nevertheless, Vallejo remained in Monterey, and the date on which the wedding was scheduled passed without a ceremony. Francisca informed Vallejo of the situation and begged him to return as soon as he could, but he remained in Monterey.

Monterey
June 30, 1858[86]

Francisca,

The mail has been delivered three times already and I have been anxiously awaiting your letters, as well as those from the whole family. I suppose either that everyone is away or that they had many commitments. But there is a well-known proverb that begins, "One who loves well, loves easily." So my complaint is not particularly with you, but you have asked me to forgive you several times. My complaint is more with Andrónico, Adela, Natalia, and Jovita. I will never forgive such negligence on their part with regard to their Papá, because all of them promised me that they would write at least one letter every week.

I know nothing about the marriage of Adela, to whom I wrote in response to your letter. If she is at home, tell her not to forget her promise and that I would like to hear her speak in her own defense. She is very unwavering in terms of her feelings, and even though those feelings are about the same thing (me), her argument lacks truth. I did not get married against the will of my wife's parents, even though they resisted at first. Before marrying, I never disrespected the family's domestic rules. I

84. See, for instance, Rothman, *Hands and Hearts*, 87–176; Lystra, *Searching the Heart*, 227–258; Sollors, *Beyond Ethnicity*, 102–30; Farmer, *On Zion's Mount*, 300.
85. Platón to M.G.V., June 16, 1858, C-B 441, box 6, folder 1, TBL (written in English).
86. C-B 441, box 1, folder 3, TBL.

Prudenciana Vallejo Amesti (*left*).
*Courtesy of California State Parks,
Sonoma Barracks. No. 243-x-3502.*

never saw my wife more than twice and I did not speak to her directly about getting married, but rather indirectly. I asked her parents for her hand in marriage by means of a letter written from 300 leagues away. I have never behaved in any other manner, and you yourself know that. In short, when you write to me, I would like for you to do so with no other purpose than to tell me what happens.

I presume that Jovita has probably returned to school. Her tuition is paid for.

You already know me. I see things differently than most people normally do. I love my family dearly, from my wife down to my youngest child. I sacrifice myself for them. We raise them, we educate them, etc. and that is the proof. If they are grateful, there is no doubt that they will not forget what we did for them, because few children can expect to receive gifts such as these from their parents.

Platón and Uladislao are in San Francisco. If Jovita and Benicita go to school, that will make four of them. Then you only have Natalia and two little girls left, which means that there is not much for us to do at home.

I will be finished here soon, and then I promise you that I will stay home for several weeks so that I can kiss the little ones and you, too.

Take care of yourself, take care of the children, and don't forget the one who loves you,

M. G. Vallejo

Monterey
July 10, 1858[87]

Francisca,

The steamer is going to be heading out of the bay and I'm writing this letter before it arrives. If it works out that way, I can take advantage of this opportunity to greet you.

I have written you many letters, ever since before Adela's wedding, because you indicated that it was what you wanted me to do. You wanted me to write letters like the very first one I sent you. Isn't that right? That's why I am writing to you, and I would like you to write to me as well. But no, you don't even bother. Take care of the younger children, for that is a duty. The older children are always <u>guilty of neglect</u> when it comes to us. Instead of trying to help you, they irritate you.

No one has written to me in a long time regarding Adela's marriage. Poor soul! I hope she doesn't regret having entered so quickly into that ill-fated arrangement! I know nothing more than what Platón has written to me. He says that <u>everyone at home is fine</u> without alluding to anything. Natalia wrote to me a few days ago and said nothing about the marriage, which leads me to believe that everything is finished.

Day after tomorrow I'll head north. I can't forget the last two nights I was at home. The first one was so bitter and the last one so sweet. Do you remember? You said so many things to me! And I, what did I say to you? I was looking at you, smiling, without revealing on my face how I felt, but it was as if there were a <u>volcano</u> inside of me. The storm passed, calm reigned again, and I think your heart told you, "He does not deserve such a scolding, he is a good man, and he loves me." Isn't that right? The last night was divine! So many things! Do you remember?

Give Napoleón, Luisa, and María a kiss. Remember me as a good friend who loves you unconditionally.

M. G. Vallejo

When Francisca concluded that Adela remained resolved to marry Levi, she took her daughter to San Francisco and purchased an expensive wedding gown for her with money she borrowed from her husband's lawyer, but she did not tell her husband about this.

---

87. C-B 441, box 1, folder 3, TBL.

(*above*) Rassette House, southwest corner of Bush and Sansome Streets, San Francisco.
Courtesy of the San Francisco History Center, San Francisco Public Library. Neg. 4265.
(*below*) Rassette House receipt, June 15, 1858, for Mrs. Vallejo and Miss Vallejo.
Courtesy of California State Parks, Sonoma Barracks. No. 243–366–313.

Lachryma Montis
July 14, 1858[88]

Guadalupe,

Adela's wedding came to nothing in the end. The doctor always had difficulties. I tried to make plans for this wedding three or four weeks ago, but there always was some sort of problem, and I think there always will be. This tires me out. Adela is more deserving of pity than anything else. Don't believe the stories you hear.

Jovita is still sick with a cough. Benicia is much better. Marillita is almost well. Andrónico, Adela, Natalia, Jovita, Napoleón, little Benicia, Luisita, Marillita, and I send you many hugs, many kisses, much affection, and many other things.

Come, come, come, come, come, come. You say that you love me and the family so much. If what you say is true, why do you leave me alone for so long now that the family needs your guidance? Remember, we are not talking about one or two children, there are many of them. You say that your duty and your obligations detain you. I don't know which obligation is more important to you, if it is taking care of your old sisters who no longer need to be taken care of, or coming home to take care of your family. I cannot take care of everything alone. I am very tired and very angry. The work in the orchards or the garden is so-so. Some fruit is beginning to ripen. They already harvested the oats. It is very hot in Sonoma.

I had written this letter two weeks ago and I didn't send it to you because I was embarrassed to have you see my bad writing. But I finally decided to write to you. You have every reason to be angry because the children don't write to you. Every day I tell them to write to you. I think that Adela's wedding will be next week or whenever the doctor feels like having it.

I am very ill and sad because you no longer love me . . . at all. What are we going to do? Patience.

Benicia F. de Vallejo

Monterey
July 18, 1858[89]

Francisca,

I finally received your letter dated the 14th of this month. It was all in your own handwriting and you didn't have to resort to having someone else write it for you.

---

88. Vallejo Family Papers, 243–366–314, California State Parks, Sonoma Barracks.
89. C-B 441, box, 1, folder 3, TBL.

Francisca Benicia Vallejo.
Courtesy of California State Parks,
Sonoma Barracks. No. 243–1-1403.

The letter is filled with all your own thoughts, which I recognize and always want to be aware of. So now you use ellipses, eh? So much can be said by using them! Isn't that so? Do you remember how much I said to you in my last letter? Did you understand it well? I still can't forget what you said to me the night before I came back here. You were seated on top of my pile of clothes, removing <u>one of your stockings</u> . . . and I was watching you. . . . So many different sensations at that moment! But I would rather not remember. But no, I do want to remember. You said so many things to me! And I, the way I was looking at you. So philosophical! Isn't that true? Such circumspection! Isn't that so?! But, how beautiful you seemed to me! Do you believe me? Yes, you have to believe me, because if you don't, I will die from sorrow.

I think you will be happy with this letter, and much more, because I'm going to see you very soon. Keep in mind that as soon as I arrive I'm going to give you a kiss that comes straight from my heart. Will you give me one in return? . . . yes . . . yes . . . yes . . . yes. . . . I'm on my way. . . . I'm on my way. . . . I'm on my way. . . . I'm on my way. . . .

Yours always,
M. G. Vallejo

P.S. A thousand kisses for everyone, everyone, everyone.

(*left*) Adela Vallejo Frisbie. *Courtesy of the California History Room,
California State Library, Sacramento, California.*
(*right*) Dr. Levi C. Frisbie. *Courtesy of California State Parks,
Sonoma Barracks. No. 243-x-3141.*

ON JULY 23, ADELA WROTE HER FATHER IN ENGLISH AND TOLD HIM THAT
Levi was becoming impatient and that if the wedding did not happen on July 26
there would be "an end to this affair." She told him that the day was fixed. She
begged him, "Do come, Papá, and all of us will be very glad to have you here on that
occasion. Dear Papá, if you love your child, you must come. It is my only wish, and I
pray you will not be angry with me."[90] Vallejo went to San Francisco, but he was in
a very foul mood. He wrote to Francisca a few hours before the wedding occurred.

San Francisco
July 26, 1858[91]
One o'clock in the afternoon

Francisca,

   I arrived here last night, and I haven't been able to obtain any news regarding
Adela's marriage. I <u>should not</u> go to the house if the doctor is there, nor should I
allow them to remain there for a moment even if she has gotten married.

---

90. Adela to M.G.V., July 20, 1858, C-B 441, box 4, folder 8, TBL.
91. C-B 441, box 1, folder 3, TBL.

I'm tired of playing the fool and suffering so many insults from that man on account of a crazy and silly girl, and perhaps other members of the family. I want to go to the house without the doctor being there. If I arrive tomorrow and if he's there, he can just leave immediately so I can avoid having to throw him out.

My regards to the children,

M. G. Vallejo

P.S. Answer me tomorrow.

VALLEJO STAYED IN SONOMA FOR ABOUT A MONTH AFTER THE WEDDING. He had always wanted his children to adjust to the new order of things in California. A large part of that was his desire that his children learn English, which they more than satisfied. As early as 1851 their oldest child Andrónico boasted to his parents that he spoke English every day.[92] And in 1858, Jovita apologized for writing a letter in English to her mother from her school in San Francisco. She said, "Dear Mamacita, you must excuse me for writing to you in English, but I had to do it to improve my English."[93] All of the children continued to do this.

An 1874 visitor reported that the two youngest daughters, Lulú and María, both spoke English very well as teenagers.[94] Vallejo realized that his children were learning English better than he ever would, and he was able to talk to them about this fact. In a letter to Jovita at the beginning of 1861 he playfully wrote a section in English, saying to her, "¿How you like my inglés? ¿You understan [sic] it? If not tell me the truth about it."[95]

In a letter Vallejo wrote to Frisbie as he, Epifania, and their child Lupe were heading to New York in 1853, he described Epifania in terms that summarized his hopes for all his acculturating children:

> Fanita is my favorite daughter and I have reason to say this. She has very special qualities, which, developed with sensitivity and skill, will bring joy and good fortune to you and your children. Therefore, I am entrusting you with not losing sight of that important goal. When I think about when you will be presenting her at a social gathering, I feel proud, for she will not belie the fact that she comes from a family that is deserving of some esteem. Even though she may display some innocence in her behavior, she is aware of her position in the new society that she will be a part of.[96]

92. Andrónico to F.B.C.V., February 27, 1851; Andrónico to M.G.V., February 27, 1851, C-B 441 FILM, reel 4, 115–16, both in TBL.
93. Jovita to F.B.C.V., April 1, 1858, C-B 441, box 4, folder 28, TBL.
94. Kate Bancroft, "Journal: My Trip to Sonoma," 71/18c, vol. 3, 7–8, TBL.
95. M.G.V. to Jovita, January 17, 1861, C-B 441 FILM, reel 4, 105, TBL.
96. M.G.V. to Frisbie, January 21, 1853, C-B 441, box 1, folder 3, TBL.

He had provided his daughter Adela with an English-language education so that she might be able to cope with the new political and social order of things in California. But she had made that adjustment in a manner he had not expected, one that went against the traditional values he assumed would remain strong in the life of his family. That troubled him. When he returned to Monterey in August, his foul mood colored the manner in which he related to the city of his birth. He now regarded the Mexican inhabitants and neighborhoods of Monterey as "a cemetery of the living dead who are in agony." He was referring not only to Monterey but also to the entire cultural and familial landscape in which he had been raised and which he continued to value even as he realized it was being swallowed up by something else.

Monterey
August 24, 1858[97]

Francisca,

I left San Francisco on the 18th at 9:00 o'clock in the morning. After a voyage of eight hours, with perfect weather and a very tranquil ocean, I arrived at this place. I felt sad until I just had to stop feeling that way, as the saying goes. At first I was happy to return to the place of my birth to see the people with whom I had grown up from childhood to puberty. After reliving those early memories I carry in my heart, it pains me to say that there is no place more humdrum than Monterey. And there aren't any people who are less cultured than these miserable inhabitants. Everything here reeks of envy, discord, disunity, rancor, gossip, and general unrest. If only I could rectify all of it! It galls me to no end that I can't find a single soul with whom to interact in my own way. This is what I desire, but I can't find anyone with any bright ideas.

Yesterday I went to the Carmel River with the sole purpose of bringing back a few demijohns of water to drink, since they don't even have water here. Imagine my surprise when I arrived at the river and saw that it was totally dry, so dry that I had to return without any water. Such an astounding thing had never been seen before. I walked for three miles down the riverbed and there was not even a sprig of watercress to be found, nor any water to fill half a demijohn. After I returned from the Carmel River the only thing I could do was join a small group of people who were heading to the Cañada Verde, which is a favorite spot of Mexican women, Rosalía's family, and Carmelita Soberanes. We went and ate some stew made of beef jerky, drank several bottles of wine, and tumbled about in the sand like children who don't know how to pass the time.[98]

97. C-B 441, box 1, folder 3, TBL.
98. Vallejo's sister Rosalía, her husband Jacob P. Leese, and their family moved to Monterey in 1849. Carmelita Soberanes was married to Frenchman Charles Cambuston and lived in San Antonio in Monterey County. Northrop, *Spanish-Mexican Families*, 2:267; 1860 U.S. Census, San Antonio Township, Monterey County, 43.

(left) Luisa "Lulú" Vallejo. *Courtesy of the Autry Museum of the American West, Los Angeles. No. 2002–1-3–6.*
(right) María Vallejo. *Courtesy of the Autry Museum of the American West, Los Angeles. No. 2002–1-3–54.*

On the way back I got so dusty that I couldn't stand being around myself. Then I thought of Lachryma Montis and wished that I could have flown there to enjoy the benefits of the water. What a difference from one place to the other! And you probably believe I wasn't thinking about you, isn't that so? Yes, yes, I did think about you as well as all the children. What would I do if I had to live here? I surely would die. The mere thought of it frightens and sickens me.

This whole place looks like a cemetery of the living dead who are in agony. These walking skeletons belong to another world, one without blood, without a soul, without a life of their own. These people are inhaling breath they have borrowed. In short, they are not living. Instead, they are wandering about by some sort of mechanical and involuntary impulse of creation.

I have finished describing the people. I will now leave this sad episode behind in order to create memories that are of you. Don't you think that would be good to do? Yes, I believe that you will cherish my dreams, my thoughts, and my way of creating those memories. Isn't that true? Yet, why do this if you aren't doing it with me? If I begin, I will not finish. Because I have such a tendency of letting my pen have free rein, I would never finish recalling happy memories, especially of our last nighttime conversations. Do you remember?

The stagecoach driver is on his way. I must hurry and finish this letter, but I do so with great sorrow in my heart. I only have time to send you my heartfelt regards and ask you to kiss all the little ones.

M. G. Vallejo

WHEN VALLEJO RETURNED TO SAN FRANCISCO IN OCTOBER, HE MADE a point of telling Francisca that he had managed to pay off most of the debts she had incurred in planning and executing their daughter's wedding.

San Francisco
October 7, 1858[99]

Francisca,

I think tomorrow I'll finish everything I have to do here, at least for now. I'll then be back in Sonoma so I can rest.

With much effort I have obtained 5,000 pesos and I have paid all, all, all of your small accounts, as well as a few of my own. But I still need to receive 2,000 pesos (of the 5,000) on November 1.

I no longer have to hide from anyone . . . with regard to debts. I'm bringing you a very small gift, but when you see it I want you to tell me it's pretty. Will you say that to me? You will, right?

Write to me tomorrow if you need something so that I can bring it to you.

Give all the children a kiss.

M. G. Vallejo

P.S. When I arrive, I want you to be happy. Will you be happy?

---

99. C-B 441, box 1, folder 3, TBL.

CHAPTER 2

Struggles over Land and Money
1858–1864

*I*n December 1858, María Amparo Ruiz, who at the time was visiting San Francisco, asked Vallejo to visit her at her home.[1] A native of Baja California, she boasted a distinguished pedigree. Her grandfather on her mother's side, José Manuel Ruiz, was a former governor of Baja California. María Amparo Ruiz was also a distant relative of Francisca Benicia Carrillo de Vallejo, since both women were descended from children of a prominent eighteenth-century Baja California couple, Juan Carrillo and Efigenia Millán.[2]

During Mexico's war with the United States, some American troops occupied La Paz, the capital of Baja California. The city and its surroundings were suffering from drought and a lack of food, so many residents, including María Amparo, welcomed the Americans, who were able to assist them with provisions. But when it became known that the Treaty of Guadalupe Hidalgo left Baja California as a part of Mexico, some residents became fearful of the retribution they might experience from other Mexicans after the American troops left. So the troops commanded by U.S. Army captain Henry S. Burton offered to take any of these residents who wished to accompany the Americans to Alta California when they evacuated Baja California. María Amparo was one of the 350 people who accepted the offer. Soon after the group arrived in Monterey, she and Captain Burton were married.[3]

Burton was first stationed in northern California. He and his wife met Vallejo in either Monterey or the North Bay area. María Amparo and Vallejo had met

1. Sánchez and Pita, *Conflicts of Interest*, 154; biographical information about Ruiz de Burton comes from this volume.
2. Carrillo and Millán's son Hilario was Francisca's great-grandfather, and their daughter Isabel was María Amparo's great-grandmother. Crosby, *Antigua California*, 254, 262, 420, 468n76.
3. Sánchez and Pita, *Conflicts of Interest*, 2–4, 10–14.

U.S. ship Dale *lying at La Paz, Lower California, ca. 1846–1848*, by William H. Meyers.
*Courtesy of the National Archives and Records Administration, Franklin D. Roosevelt
Presidential Library and Museum, Hyde Park, New York.* MO 1975.33a.17.

occasionally in northern California before Burton was transferred to San Diego
in 1852. As Mariano Guadalupe's account of their December 1858 meeting in San
Francisco indicates, they had a warm relationship and found each other to be
excellent companions. The next year María Amparo left California as Burton was
assigned back east.

San Francisco
December 22, 1858[4]

Francisca,

   After repeated visits looking for Doña Amparo, I found her at her home, as wonderful and charming as ever. I didn't kiss her (even though I was tempted to do so). I
find her to be very beautiful. You should know that after the initial pleasantries, we
conversed privately for two and one-half hours, during which time I was mesmer-
ized. I don't know who spoke more—if it was her or me. I spent the time in a most
agreeable fashion with a woman I like very much, a woman who has the qualities

4. C-B 441, box 1, folder 3, TBL.

(*left*) Henry S. Burton. Reproduced by permission of
the Huntington Library, San Marino, California.
Helen Long Collection of Moreno Documents, box 29.
(*right*) María Amparo Ruiz de Burton, ca. 1874–1886.
Courtesy of the California Judicial Center Library. PC 002.

of being a fellow compatriot. With her frank and cheerful nature she told me some juicy gossip, which I believe originated with you. I also believe that she understands me and knows how to appreciate my character and my intentions. I invited her and her husband to pay the family a visit. They promised me that they will be in Sonoma on Monday afternoon and will stay there for a day. I'll try to be in Sonoma by that day, but if I'm not there, make sure that you welcome them most warmly.

I haven't been able to finish my business dealings related to Petaluma.[5] Yesterday and today I've been very bored and tired. San Francisco can tire a person out when money can't be earned. And even more so when on every street someone is asking you for a loan, another begs for alms, and someone else wants to sell a subscription. This is in addition to the thousand other essential commitments that arise because of one's circumstances and place in society.

Give my regards to all the children.

M. G. Vallejo

P.S. This writing paper is horrible.

---

5. Vallejo's title to Rancho Petaluma was confirmed in July 1857. He sold parts of the land over the next few years. See Hoffman, *Reports*, Appendix, 35; Emparán, *Vallejos*, 106.

*Petaluma in 1857. Courtesy of the California Room,
California State Library, Sacramento, California.* FL 281056.

San Francisco
June 30, 1859[6]

Francisca,

If you think Napoleón can travel on the steamer from Petaluma so that I can buy him some clothing, have someone take him to Lakeville, where the captain or some other man can look after him.[7] I'll make sure to go to the steamer and bring him to the house.

If you are planning to come on July 4, come on Saturday. If you can't come on account of the children, but Jovita wants to, then have her come. Do whatever works best for you.

If Ula wants to come, have him come. I'll see how we can manage things.

Your cousin Amparo is here. She is headed to the United States.

M. G. Vallejo

---

6. C-B 441, box 1, folder 3, TBL.

7. Lakeville, about five miles outside of Petaluma on the Petaluma River, was the northern terminus of the steamship route between Petaluma and San Francisco. A road connected Sonoma and the steamer landing at Lakeville. Tuomey, *History of Sonoma County,* 1:477.

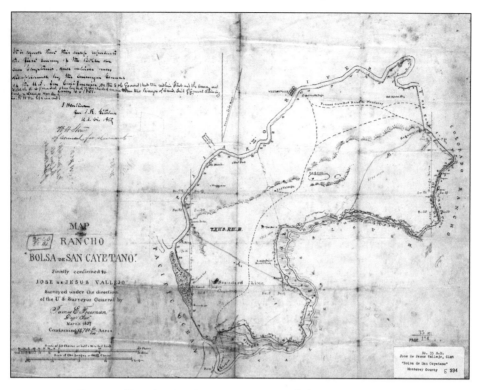

Diseño of Rancho San Cayetano. *Courtesy of The Bancroft Library,
University of California, Berkeley. Land Case Map E-994.*

THE LATE 1850S WAS A MIXED TIME FOR THE VALLEJO FAMILY.
The U.S. District Court did uphold Vallejo's claim to Rancho Petaluma in 1857,
but the legal bills he had acquired during the confirmation process were daunting. Also, the dispute with Fortoul over Rancho San Cayetano in the Monterey
region continued. Vallejo's trips there were far from pleasant, and they often put
him in a bad mood.

But Mariano Guadalupe and Francisca continued to attempt to provide as many
educational opportunities as they could for their children. Platón and Jovita were
attending schools in San Francisco, and Uladislao was attending the Family Boarding School for Boys in Benicia. Napoleón began to attend a local district school in
Sonoma. By 1858, Uladislao had joined Platón in San Francisco, and in April 1860

both of them went to New York. Platón began the study of medicine at Columbia College, and Uladislao went to the Bronx to study at St. John's College at Fordham. After his two brothers left for New York, Napoleón entered San Francisco College. When he was at home, he continued playing with the Indigenous children of the region, whom he had come to know. Some of those children were undoubtedly Vallejo's house servants. On January 1, 1861, Napoleón wrote in English to Platón, "I am having a very good fun since I came home, playing with all the little Indian 'chaps' playing marbles from morning till night, good fun 'you bet' but with all that Papá made us clean the place after we get through."[8]

When Vallejo learned that Platón and Uladislao had arrived in New York, he wrote Uladislao in June: "I am very hopeful that you will soon enter the Colegio and that you will dedicate yourself wholeheartedly to your studies so that you can live up to your parents' expectations. Obey your teachers, for that is how you will be able to learn about the sciences, which is a course of study that is quite difficult in the beginning. But with time and dedication it will become easier and even pleasant." Uladislao wrote to his father that same month, "I am getting along very well in the college." He added, "If you let me stay here for six more years, I will be all right with that."[9] With the same enthusiasm he had shown when he had entered San Francisco College a few years earlier, he predicted that by that time he would have earned three degrees, including an M.D.

Platón also reported to his father about Uladislao's excitement. He wrote, "The vacation at St. John's College commenced on Wednesday the 11th of this month. Ula was here in N. York and spent the Sunday with me. He left again on Monday and went back to the College to study. He says that he is going to study up this vacation and make up for one year. He likes the College much, and his professors. He is bent on study and is determined he shall lose no time. I am glad to see the boy in such good earnest." Part of Uladislao's enthusiasm may have resulted from the fact that he was very impressed by what Platón was doing. In a letter the next month he told his father, "The other day I went to see Platón and what do you think I saw in his room? He had a great big skeleton standing against the wall and he was finding the names of the bones. He has another box full of bones that he studies at night." But Platón was well aware of the rigorous demands of the medical studies he was beginning. In October he told his father, "Today the preliminary lectures of the college have ceased, to begin the Regular Course on the 24th, after leaving us with a sufficient knowledge of that which we did not know before." A month later he reported, "I am getting along slowly with the medicine business. I like it well and hope to like it more."[10]

8. Napoleón to Platón, January 1, 1861, C-B 441 FILM, reel 3, 10, TBL. This was still occurring two years later. See M.G.V. to Lulú, April 15, 1863, C-B 441 FILM, reel 4, 149, TBL.

9. M.G.V. to Uladislao, June 15, 1860, C-B 441 FILM, reel 3, 7; Uladislao to M.G.V., June 21, 1860, C-B 441, box 6, folder 16, both in TBL.

10. Platón to M.G.V., July 20, 1860, C-B 441, box 6, folder 12 (written in English); Uladislao to M.G.V., July 21, 1860, C-B 441, box 6, folder 16; Platón to M.G.V., October 20, 1860, C-B 441, box 6, folder 12 (written in English); Platón to M.G.V., November 30, 1860, C-B 441 FILM, reel 2, 23–24, all in TBL.

Arrival of the Pony Express at San Francisco. Courtesy of the
California Room, California State Library, Sacramento, California. No. 22299.

At home, family life was marked by disappointment and tragedy, as five-and-a-half-year-old Benicia Isabel died in January 1859. On the other hand, the vineyards, under the direction of two individuals hired by Vallejo, produced good-quality wines.[11] And the fruits Vallejo planted also won various prizes. Matters seemed to be looking up. In March 1860 the U.S. District Court in San Francisco confirmed Vallejo's claim to Rancho Suscol. Two months later Vallejo was elected mayor of Sonoma for a second time. At the end of the summer the family decided to upgrade their accommodations at Lachryma Montis. So they moved back to the Casa Grande on the plaza while the renovations were occurring.

163 Montgomery St.
San Francisco
July 17, 1860[12]

Francisca,
   Napoleón arrived fine. I'm sending you under separate cover Platón and Ula's letters. I'm also sending you by "express" a piece of ham. It's a small piece, but it's good. Do you like that?
   Have the girls write letters to Platón and Ula right away so that they can be sent

---

11. McGinty, *Strong Wine*, 317,
12. C-B 441, box 1, folder 4, TBL.

by Pony Express. It will be leaving very soon, which means that within ten days they will receive news from the family.

Give kisses to the little ones.

M. G. Vallejo

San Francisco
August 11, 1860[13]

Francisca,

Today I'm leaving for Monterey in order to return as quickly as possible.

Take care of the children and give kisses to all of them. And you, be <u>prudent</u> and <u>judicious</u>. Remember how the saying goes, "It is better to be alone than in bad company." You already know that the current people are dangerous. I can see far into the future and I'm aware of how all of this is going to end. Domestic happiness cannot be obtained if it is not accompanied by certain rules. Balance is lost and the building collapses if the rules are not followed.

Goodbye,
M. G. Vallejo

P.S. Next week an agricultural commission is supposed to go and inspect the orchards and the house. Make sure that everything is clean and show them the garden. Let's see if we win the <u>prize</u>.

San Francisco
September 2, 1860[14]

Francisca,

I haven't been able to strike any sort of deal with Larkin's children regarding the black horse. Therefore, have Jaime turn it over to Mr. Clark immediately.

Regards,
M. G. Vallejo

---

13. C-B 441, box 1, folder 4, TBL.
14. C-B 441, box 1, folder 4, TBL.

San Francisco
September 15, 1860[15]

Francisca,

I was planning on leaving today, but a thousand things have kept me from doing so, among them the death of Señor Larrain at two o'clock this afternoon.[16] Napoleón is at school and is very happy. The other day I had a long discussion with Captain Frisbie about Natalia's trip to the United States and also about some properties at Suscol. I'll be in Sonoma on Tuesday to move us to the Casa Grande until the other house is finished.

M.G.V.

TOWARD THE END OF 1860, JOHN AND EPIFANIA FRISBIE TOOK THEIR three young girls on a trip to the East Coast to visit his family. Natalia Vallejo accompanied them to help her sister care for the children because Epifania was again pregnant. They sailed first to New York City, then went to Syracuse and Albany before returning to New York City. Natalia did not care for upstate New York. Her reaction demonstrated that she was in the process of becoming a California booster. This is how she described Syracuse in a letter she wrote to her mother in English:

> Syracuse [is] a city that I don't like very much—it horrifies me—I don't know why. It isn't worth leaving California to go and live in a place like Syracuse, which is so far away from New York City. For example, it's the same as if someone were to leave here to visit California and end up staying in Santa Rosa. But at least there is something to see in Santa Rosa—beautiful countryside, trees, fields—where a person can be entertained to a certain degree, unlike here, where there is nothing. It's true, there is no place like California.[17]

A few days later, writing again in English from the Metropolitan Hotel on Broadway and Prince Street, she called New York City "this grand city."[18] But on the West Coast her father—with four of his children three thousand miles distant, with the San Cayetano matter still unresolved, and often spending much time in San Francisco engaged in seemingly endless legal matters—was lonely and anxious.

---

15. C-B 441, box 1, folder 4, TBL.

16. Antonio Larrain was a participant in a complex series of real estate transactions related to Rinconada de San Francisquito in Santa Clara County. These transactions involved, among others, Mariano Guadalupe and his brother Salvador. The land dealings eventually led to a series of litigations that went up to the California Supreme Court. *Sacramento Daily Union*, June 27 and July 26, 1864.

17. Natalia to F.B.C.V., November 25, 1860, C-B 441 FILM, reel 2, 24–25, TBL.

18. Natalia to M.G.V. and F.B.C.V., C-B 441, box 4, folder 29, TBL.

San Francisco
December 20, 1860[19]

Francisca,

I've been at the dock since 10:00 pm waiting for the steamer to arrive, expecting that you and the family would be on it. Since it hasn't arrived yet, I decided to return to my room. I'm filled with worry, wondering if there has been some horrible accident. It's 3:00 am and I still can't calm down. I left a carriage at the docks in case you should arrive. But I'm hoping that the steamer didn't leave because of the heavy rain, which has been very strong here, too. I think that Napoleón and Enrique will be coming tomorrow, the 21st. I'll write to them today so that they can be here on Friday.

I really want for you to come and for you to be happy. You know how much I'm suffering, but it's even more than you can imagine. For us to live happily, it's necessary for you to believe everything I told you before I left home. Take pity on me, don't think ill of me, remember that we have very little time left to live, that we have many children for whom we must set an example of peace and morality, and we still have young children to educate. For me it's a very daunting and exhausting task. And it seems that for you it's very important that I fulfill that duty before my days come to an end, a duty that I've always fulfilled despite financial difficulties and my unfortunate situation. Why do you want to increase my emotional suffering? Why aren't you happy? I can't be more than I am, and I shouldn't have to be. I consider myself blameless (up to a point) and not guilty of the things that some sharp tongues or malicious minds have led you to believe. I shouldn't allow anyone's reputation to suffer because of a misunderstanding. It's better to free ninety-nine guilty people than to punish one innocent person. I'm not referring to myself, I'm referring to <u>other people</u> who should be considered blameless regarding the person you mentioned.[20] I don't know how to deceive when I swear an oath, and even if I didn't swear an oath you know that I'm not afraid to tell the truth even if it were to disrupt my domestic tranquility. I beg you to think it over carefully and believe in the one who loves you and is your best friend.

M.G.V.

---

19. C-B 441, box 1, folder 4, TBL.

20. We suspect that this letter, in which Mariano Guadalupe is deliberately vague about the people to whom he is referring, relates to Francisca's developing awareness that a child whom her husband had fathered with another woman had been born fourteen months after the two of them had married. If this is the case, "the person you [Francisca] mentioned" is most likely that child, Prudenciana López. We treat this matter more fully in chapter 3, in our introduction to Mariano Guadalupe's September 29, 1869, letter to Prudenciana.

Receipt made out to Mrs. F. Vallejo from Mr. Ryan for $103.40 for the purchase of fruit trees and plants for Lachryma Montis, March 17, 1861. Types of trees: plum, apricot, nectarine, almond, cherry, pear, apple, white fig. Types of plants: gooseberry, raspberry.
Courtesy of California State Parks, Sonoma Barracks. No. 243–330–1.

THE CIVIL WAR STARTED IN THE SPRING OF 1861, AND PLATÓN SPENT A year as a volunteer surgeon for the Union forces, after which he returned to Columbia to finish his medical studies. Uladislao, on the other hand, was not enthralled with the academic life and decided to leave New York and return to California after spending less than a year at Fordham. Vallejo wrote to Platón about Uladislao's decision to leave his studies:

> This has saddened me greatly. It is also very disagreeable to me.... What bothers and alarms me the most is that if he hasn't been able to remain at such a respected school that is at a great distance, I have very few hopes for that boy. In terms of his studies, he has demonstrated a repugnance, as well as a fickle, disobedient, and stubborn nature. It's very upsetting that, after incurring so many expenses to help him obtain an education, he's incapable of listening or appreciating the efforts I've made on his behalf. This all seems to me to be a bad omen. I hope that I'm wrong. I hope that Ula's faults don't lead him over a precipice.[21]

When the Frisbie family returned to Vallejo during the summer, Francisca spent time with them as she helped her daughter care for her newest child, who had been born in New York. Vallejo tried to cheer up his wife with reports of the progress of the Lachryma Montis renovation. He also continued to make frequent trips to San Francisco.

21. M.G.V. to Platón, November 11, 1861, C-B 441 FILM, reel 3, 20–21, TBL.

Devil's head fountain, Lachryma Montis, ca. 1892.
Courtesy of Sonoma County Library Photograph Collection. cstr_pho 018717.

Lachryma Montis
August 12, 1861[22]

Francisca,

The girls have stayed longer than they thought they would. I think the reason is that the members of the Bachelor Club are hosting a dance on Thursday.[23] Also, they have been <u>very busy</u> eating the fruit that is in abundance: fresh peaches, grapes, pears, and apples. There is so much fruit that we actually have too much of it. I'm preserving fruit, painting, and beginning work on the house. I'm making you a very, very beautiful and elegant bath house. I'm also rebuilding the common rooms and the kitchen and making flour and peach aguardiente that I think will

---

22. C-B 441, box 1, folder 4, TBL.

23. Young unmarried Anglo men referred to themselves as the Bachelor Club. A ravine slightly north of Clear Lake that was first settled by four such men, for example, was called "Bachelor Valley." See Palmer, *History of Napa and Lake Counties*, 67, 197 (Lake County section).

María de la Luz Carrillo de
Vallejo. *Courtesy of California
State Parks, Sonoma Barracks.*
No. 243-x-3220.

be very tasty.[24] I paid the man who worked on the basement of the house and who also cleared out the weeds from the vineyards, watered the grove of trees, painted Napoleón's boat, and watered the orange trees, which have a lot of fruit. The areas around the house are very beautiful and tidy, and they are watered in the afternoon and in the morning. The fountain was recently painted.

I don't want to tell you anything else so that you will be surprised when you return. Take care of the little ones, give them a kiss, and go for a stroll whenever you can. Give my regards to Doña Carolina.[25] I imagine she is at the house every afternoon keeping you company. I do think about her a lot from time to time!

Wishing you good health and I'll be seeing you soon.

M. G. Vallejo

San Francisco
November 30, 1861[26]

Francisca,

I'm sending you the document that we agreed on. Apparently, Luz has the house for one hundred pesos a month, for one year, with the option for two.[27] It's necessary

---

24. *Aguardiente* is a hard liquor, often brandy.
25. Carolina Días. See biographical sketches.
26. C-B 441, box 1, folder 4, TBL.
27. Francisca's sister María de la Luz Carrillo (Luz) was married to Mariano Guadalupe's brother Salvador. They lived in Napa. McKittrick, "Salvador Vallejo," 311–12, 318.

Receipt for $54.50 of purchases made by "Mrs. Genl. Vallejo" in San Francisco,
January 27, 1860, at Jos. Genella. *Courtesy of California State Parks,*
Sonoma Barracks, No. 243–366–303.

that a notary public witness her signature. If you want, wait for me to return and
we can do it together.

I've been very busy and sick (thankfully, it's nothing serious).

I tried to leave today, but I can't until Tuesday.

Give my regards to the children.

M. G. Vallejo

❋

San Francisco
December 5, 1861[28]

Francisca,

I'm sending you a sack of vegetables on the steamer from Sonoma.

---

28. C-B 441, box 1, folder 4, TBL.

Report card for Henry Vallejo (*left*) and Napoleón Vallejo (*right*),
Santa Clara College, September through November 1860. *Courtesy of
The Bancroft Library, University of California, Berkeley. C-B 441, box 11, folder 10.*

Have someone tell Mr. Ryan to send one or two wagons to the pier on Saturday
so that the furniture I have here can be taken to Lachryma Montis.[29] I think that
I also will be going. I bought (on credit) a set of living room furniture, very similar
to what is in the small room here. Together, the two sets should be enough for
Your Majesties' living room.

I also might send some rugs for the rooms. I'm tired, bored, furious, and I feel
denigrated. The other day I sent you the document that you spoke about. The
lawyers representing El Pájaro, which belongs to my brother Uncle Jesús and to
all the Vallejos, have not been able to reach an agreement with my lawyers.[30] Since
this matter is very important to me, I've wanted to give them more time.

Regards to all the children.

M. G. Vallejo

✳ ✳ ✳

29. Mortimer Ryan was the overseer of the Lachryma Montis properties. Andrónico to M.G.V., January 27, 1858, C-B
441, box 6, folder 3, TBL; Emparán, *Vallejos*, 115, 246, 315.
30. "Uncle Jesús" is in English in the original letter.

Napoleón Vallejo, ca. 1863.
Courtesy of The Bancroft Library,
University of California, Berkeley.
BANC PIC 1978.195.08-PIC.

WITH FRISBIE'S HELP, ULADISLAO GOT A JOB AT A SAN FRANCISCO STORE.
Vallejo asked Francisca to exert as tight a control as she could over Uladislao's movements when he was in Sonoma. In the meantime, Enrique enrolled at Santa Clara
College and appeared to have had a rocky start there. Indeed, his fall 1860 report
card said that, while his application to his studies was "sufficient," his improvement was "rather slow." Matters, however, did seem to improve. He told Platón
in an April 1861 letter that he was studying English and Spanish and added, "I'm
advancing rapidly, even though not enough to be able to explain what I'm doing
at the colegio." He was excited that he had learned how to sign his name but
confessed, "I'm still not skilled enough to begin a class on commerce."[31] A month
later he wrote to Francisca, whom he addressed as "my very esteemed, worthy, and
loving mother." He asked if she might send him "five or ten cents, which I really
need in order to buy some items for myself, such as ointment, dental powder, and
a few other essential things." He invited her, "with the rest of the family," to visit
and witness the final public examinations that were to take place in June. At the
commencement exercises, Enrique was awarded a prize for the way he was able
to play the violin.[32] Enrique's younger brother Napoleón was also at Santa Clara,
in the pre-college division. His fall 1860 report card stated that his application to
study was "not very great," and his improvement was "slow."[33]

---

31. Enrique to Platón, C-B 441 FILM, reel 3, 16–19, TBL.
32. Enrique to F.B.C.V., C-B 441 FILM, reel 2, 26–27, TBL; Santa Clara College Prospectus for the Year 1860–1861, 30,
     Santa Clara University Archives and Special Collections.
33. The 1860 report cards for Enrique and Napoleón are in C-B 441, box 11, folder 10, TBL.

While she was in school in San Francisco, Jovita had begun to study music more intensely. She became quite proficient at playing the piano and guitar. In April 1858 she told her mother, "I am getting along very well in all my lessons and guitar." She sang regularly at church services at Mission San Francisco Solano in Sonoma. Her accomplishments, as well as the ability some of the other children had attained on the piano their father had purchased in the 1840s, fit very well with his desires to educate his children as broadly as possible. He believed that music was an indispensable part of that broad education. In an undated note that has survived in his papers, he wrote, "Parents should teach their children the secret of musical notes at the same time they are teaching them the alphabet, because music is a valuable resource in life. Music is an art of such sublime perfection that can be expressed and written in a universal language."[34] With this in mind, he came up with a plan that he hoped would affirm his daughter Jovita's accomplishments in music and, at the same time, give Uladislao and Enrique, who was at home after having finished at Santa Clara College, some direction. He drew up a contract by which Jovita would serve as a music teacher for Enrique and Uladislao:

April 4, 1862

In the city of Sonoma, on the fourth day of the month of April of the year 1862, Señorita Jovita Vallejo, Enrique Vallejo, and Uladislao Vallejo agreed to the following contract:
1. Mis Jovita will give guitar lessons to Enrique for the period of one year, consisting of three lessons per week.[35]
2. As compensation for the lessons. Enrique will give Mis a milk cow, reddish in color.
3. Mis Jovita agrees to provide weekly music lessons to Uladislao for the period of one year.
4. As compensation for the lessons, Uladislao will give Jovita a young colt named Barragán, and both Señores will turn over sole ownership of the colt and the cow to Mis Jovita.
As evidence that we are in agreement, we sign this contract today, before witnesses.

Jovita A. Vallejo, E. Vallejo, Uladislao E. Vallejo

Witness   Witness

M. G. Vallejo   Natalia V. Vallejo

---

34. Jovita to F.B.C.V., April 1, 1858, C-B 441, box 4, folder 28, TBL; C-B 441, box 11, folder 3, TBL.
35. Vallejo uses the English word "Miss" and spells it "Mis."

One of the first pianos to
arrive in Alta California. The
family of José Abrego donated
the piano to the California
Historical Society in the 1940s.
*Photograph courtesy of David
Newman, great-grandson of
Abrego granddaughter Dulce
Bolado Davis.*

Marshfield Landing
April 25, 1862[36]

Francisca,

I think that it's better if you have someone bring the provisions that are upstairs
and put them in the room downstairs, just as you had suggested. I also think it's
better for Tomás to bring the meat from the slaughterhouse to make sure that
there's enough meat for the workers.

Tell Ula that I say he is not to leave the house at night under any circumstances.

M. G. Vallejo

THE EXPERIENCES OF SOME OF THE OTHER CHILDREN DURING THE EARLY
and mid-1860s were mixed. José appears to have lived in several locations in the
Bay Area before settling in the East Bay region. There in 1862 he married Loreto
Peralta, daughter of Domingo Peralta and Eduviges García, who lived in the San
Pablo region of the East Bay.[37] They had two children. The oldest was a boy whom
they named Mariano Guadalupe, and the younger was a girl whom they named

---

36. C-B 441, box 1, folder 4, TBL.
37. José Vallejo to F.B.C.V., undated [early 1860s], C-B 441, box 6, folder 7, TBL.

Benicia. The birth of Benicia, however, was a tragic affair, for Loreto died during or shortly after the 1867 childbirth and Benicia passed away a few days later.[38]

Andrónico's situation with his family was complex. When he returned from school in Baltimore at the end of 1855, he worked for a time as a ranch hand for his father, but he then left that job. Confused about what role his father was expecting him to play, Andrónico eventually went to San Francisco, where he rented a room as a boarder. He confessed his doubts to his mother: "It is true that I have been poor, and still am, but this isn't important. I was in a state of poverty when Papá was here and I couldn't find the nerve to ask him for money so I could eat." She told him that his father seemed not to know how to deal with growing boys and young men:

> The only person to blame is your Papá because he hasn't known how to behave and he has ruined everything. He is going to act the same way with Platón, Ula, Enrique, and Napoleón as he has with you. If they don't find a way to make a living, I know that your Papá won't find it for them. And what is the remedy for this? There isn't one, except for patience and the willingness to conform to the will of God. One must take a firm stand and refuse to pay attention to what everyone else says and does. It doesn't matter if you are poor. Be mindful of your health and your honor. Be charitable to those who need help. This is what God wants. And your Mamá says that she would rather see you as a poor man with honor than a rich man with many faults.[39]

Andrónico also complained that his father treated his secretary, Francisco Estrada, better than he treated his own son. Francisca told him that she had no warm feelings for Estrada either and urged him to be careful around him. She said:

> Forget about Señor Estrada, the secretary, the saint, the Sota de Oros, the faithful companion, the man who doesn't speak ill of your Papá, the great man who knows everything, he who knows the family secrets.[40] Forget about him. Don't tangle with him over anything at all. People like this are demons that leave Hell to torment everyone. Don't even think of tangling with him. This Sota de Oros is the devil, he is the Asmodeus of the family. Your Papá has many people like this around him and Estrada is the one with the silver tongue who gossips the most.

At the end of this long and deeply emotional letter to her son, Francisca added:

> I had already read your letter many times, so I knew it by heart. It seemed to me that you didn't write anything negative about your Papá. Seeing him so angry with you on account

---

38. California, U.S., Wills and Probate Records, 1850–1953 (database on-line). Provo, Utah, USA, Record of Wills, Vol. A-B, 1857–1873, 386, accessed through Ancestry.com; José Vallejo to F.B.C.V., February 11, 1867, C-B 441, box 6, folder 7, TBL.

39. This conversation, continued below, is from Andrónico to F.B.C.V., April 8, 1862, C-B 441, box 6, folder 3, and F.B.C.V. to Andrónico, no date, C-B 441 FILM, reel 4, 185–87, both in TBL. Francisca made the same point about Mariano Guadalupe in a letter to Platón written around this same time. She said, "It's all because of your Papá's bad temper, which prevented him from knowing how to handle his children in the past, as well as now, and even into the future. It breaks my heart to say this, but it is the truth." F.B.C.V. to Platón, April, no month or year, C-B 441 FILM, reel 4, 210–14, TBL.

40. The Sota de Oros is a Tarot card with the figure of a knave. It is a derogatory slang term implying that the person is a libertine.

of the stories, intrigues, gossip, or whims, I thought it would be a good idea to show him your letter, for many reasons, but especially because you had not spoken ill of him. I gave him the letter and he read it. He became so angry that it weighed on me that I had given it to him. But you already know what your Papá is like. He gets mad whether you say something to him or not. It's enough to drive a person crazy. Dear son, I don't know what to do.

After Francisca showed her husband Andrónico's letter, he composed a reply, which she sent under her own name: "It doesn't seem prudent to me that you went to San Francisco without any money or a job to help you pay for what you need. Come back home. You always will be welcome here and can have whatever we might have without feeling that you owe us anything. Your Papá misses you very much and he has told me so. You know that he loves you. If you have thought that he's angry with you, he says he doesn't know the reason why."[41] Francisca then most likely consulted Epifania in Vallejo, who took Andrónico in and allowed him to find his own way by teaching music and Spanish. Epifania wrote Platón in January 1863, "Andrónico lives here at the house. He gives music and Spanish lessons. They pay him forty pesos a month, which is enough for him to buy clothes. He doesn't like to work very hard. He is very heavy and very healthy."[42]

During the 1860s, finances became a continuing and increasing problem for Francisca and Mariano Guadalupe. After the U.S. District Court confirmed Vallejo's claim to Rancho Suscol, squatters appealed that decision to the U.S. Supreme Court. During his 1860–61 visit to the East Coast, Frisbie attempted, unsuccessfully, to do some lobbying in Washington, D.C., on behalf of his father-in-law. In March 1862 the Supreme Court invalidated Vallejo's claim. In doing so, it also invalidated sales of parcels of the Suscol land that Vallejo had made to others. In 1863, Frisbie, who had himself purchased some of those parcels, went east again and persuaded Congress to pass a law legitimizing those sales. The fact that Governor Leland Stanford had appointed Frisbie commander of the California State Militia undoubtedly helped his lobbying efforts. But in the meantime Vallejo feared that he might have to return the money he had received from those sales. Also, both he and Francisca resented the fact that Frisbie did not seem to be suffering financially as much as they were, even though they believed that much of his success was because of the money their family had given him.

They apparently shared these opinions with other members of the family. For instance, she told Platón: "You already know what the Americans are like when it comes to keeping the property that belongs to the Californios. They are all alike. Isn't it true that you didn't believe the Captain would be capable of treating your Papá so horribly? Well, he is the worst one of them all. At least the other Americans didn't know us, but this one is married to one of my daughters. He is an ingrate,

41. F.B.C.V. to Andrónico, June 4, 1862, C-B 441, box 6, folder 5, TBL.
42. Epifania to Platón, January 26, 1863, C-B 441 FILM, reel 3, 22–23, TBL.

Andrónico Vallejo.
*Courtesy of California
State Parks, Sonoma
Barracks. No. 243-x-3486.*

a disgrace, but he is an American and the only thing we can expect from him is deceitful behavior."[43]

Toward the end of 1862, Francisca communicated some of these thoughts to Epifania. She replied to her mother, "I don't know what to say or what to think regarding what you wrote in your letter to me. It's very difficult for me to believe that John stole Papá's property. If you could see how hard he works to make a living, you wouldn't accuse him of such serious and baseless crimes. If Papá says that his property was stolen, then why doesn't he come and take it back if he knows that John has it. Tell him to come and take it back himself." She continued, "With regard to the money you want me to send you, I don't know how I can do that. John doesn't have any money, not even for himself. He says that he will do everything possible to help in any way he can." The next month, Epifania told Platón, who was on the East Coast, "If you were to hear what they say about John, it would frighten you."[44]

With the expenses Vallejo was incurring educating his children and renovating Lachryma Montis, he did not have sufficient funds. He therefore had no other choice than to mortgage Lachryma Montis. San Francisco real estate businessman Thomas Madden purchased the mortgage, but Vallejo was deeply concerned that he would not be able to meet all of the interest payments when they came due.[45] In addition, the disputes over Rancho San Cayetano dragged on without resolution, and this distressed Vallejo whenever he had to go to the Monterey area to try to straighten matters out. His letters to Francisca, who was spending time in Vallejo

43. F.B.C.V. to Platón, April, no date, no year, C-B 441 FILM, reel 4, 210–14, TBL.

44. Epifania to F.B.C.V., December 10, 1862, C-B 441, box 4, folder 12; Epifania to Platón, January 26, 1863, C-B 441 FILM, reel 3, 22–23, both in TBL.

45. Langley, *San Francisco Directory, 1871*, 416.

with her young children Luisa and María as she helped Epifania take care of her four young daughters, were filled with loneliness, anxiety, fear, and foreboding. This greatly troubled Francisca, and she urged him to take good care of himself. In the same letter, she practiced writing his name to accommodate his desire that she write to him in her own hand.

San Francisco
July 19, 1862[46]

Francisca,

I'm sending on the steamer the items you asked me to get for you: sugar, coffee, tea, soap, ordinary candles, and decorative ones. Everything was paid for on credit to the <u>man with a moustache.</u>

I have to contend with many difficulties in order to pay Mr. Madden, but in the end I do owe him the money and I need to pay him. I'm going to renegotiate the mortgages on Lachryma Montis and Quiquiriquí for one year, with the option of paying them off before the end of that time.[47] The interest I'm being charged is twelve percent, compounded monthly. I'll send you the mortgage papers on Monday so you can sign them. After this I need to work and sell the other properties I still have, and then pay Madden as quickly as possible before the interest increases the amount owed. We need to economize as much as possible.

If Natalia and Jovita want to come on Monday, they can do so. I'll be at the dock. They will stay here for a few days and return as soon as possible. I haven't been able to sleep for several nights in a row.

Tell the children to take care of everything, especially the fences, so that no cattle or horses will get in.

My regards to the loved ones.

M. G. Vallejo

San Francisco
July 21, 1862[48]

Francisca,

I have attached the mortgage papers in favor of Mr. Madden, and the papers include all the property in Sonoma. Sign the mortgage papers and the note and

46. BANC MSS 76/79c, box 1, folder 25, TBL.
47. Quiquiriquí was the name of the vineyard near Lachryma Montis.
48. C-B 441, box 1, folder 4, TBL.

deliver them to Mr. Wheaton so he can have them filed.[49] As soon as all of this is finished, I'll return.

Regards to the children.

M. G. Vallejo

San Cayetano near Watsonville
February 13, 1863[50]

Francisca,

Two years ago, on the night of the 10th, about twenty miles from here, I became ill with the brain fever and it has happened again, but it wasn't as strong.[51] I was quite ill, alone, and without the comforts of home I'm used to. I think that you left Sonoma for San Francisco on that same day, and you managed not to drown. Two years ago today you arrived in San José, where you found me very ill. Señora Pico, who was there, wanted to medicate me with an enema.[52] Do you remember? I certainly do. Despite the fact that my head felt so heavy, the specter of Señora P. kept pursuing me. I would see her in my dreams armed with that awful <u>thing</u>, lifting up the bed sheets, pulling down my underwear, lifting up my shirt, sticking her hand up . . . my . . . backside, <u>not finding</u> the right spot to insert that wretched <u>thing</u>. I wanted to die from embarrassment, anguish, and fear. But in my dreams that woman seemed like a wild beast to me. She had Herculean strength and would pick me up as if I were a child. I would defend myself heroically, sweating, and out of breath. She would say (it seems like I'm hearing her now), "Come on, sweetheart, let it go in." "Hey, you, Petra, come here and push the syringe in as far as it will go. Stick it inside him and then jump back. Get out of the way, his bottom is wiggling."

Jesus Christ! How I suffered! What a horrible dream! God help me! It was just a dream but believe me, I woke up tired and sweating. I called out to Enrique to ask him if a woman had entered the house. When I came to, I felt so violated that I felt my body up and down. I finally got better. I'm telling you all of this exactly as it happened in the dream. That damn dream also reminded me of the little story called "Open sesame," and I couldn't stop laughing.

According to Don Pepe's letter, they applied two more small tubes of medicine on you. I hope the medicine helped relieve your pain. Feel better, don't worry, be patient, and you'll see that your good health will return.

Regards to the girls, Ula, and Napoleón, and don't forget Señor Don José.

M. G. Vallejo

49. The mortgage was $17,500. See Emparán, *Vallejos*, 108. William R. Wheaton was a lawyer who worked for the U.S. Land Office. 1870 U.S. Census, 11th Ward, 2nd District, San Francisco, 1; *Sonoma Democrat*, July 8, 1876.
50. C-B 441, box 1, folder 4, TBL.
51. The "brain fever" was a severe headache, possibly a migraine.
52. "Señora Pico" is María del Pilar Bernal, who was married to Antonio María Pico and had a daughter named Petra; 1860 U.S. Census, San José Township, Santa Clara County, 151; Northrop, *Spanish-Mexican Families*, 2:207.

guadalupe Guadalupe Gue Gu gu e Ga
guu

querido y sienper ~~adorado~~ de mon?

querido. esposo. y conpañero. y amigo.
no se como ~~te~~ yamarte si es poso. o conpanero. o amigo.
o Guadalupe. o General. o mariano. o señor Vallejo.
tengo la cabesa tan trastornada que no se casa te
yamar ~~quitado la familia esta~~ porque tu mismo me as
dicho que no quieres que te de el tratamiento de marido o es
esposo. entonces te dire don Guadalupe Vallejo
estaba soñando que tu me desias muienogado que no te
digera marido ni esposo. y que yo te desia que me digeras
como te abia de te yamar y tu desias dime don de
demaniel don diablo pero no me digas marido.
asi estaremos peliandonos al tienpo que luisita
entro y me recordo y me dio una carta leia yo mui
asustada la abri y me puse a tirla. y boiviendo
que tu lancreias acias soñado. nomas que los sueño
eran diferentes. tu soñabas que la Señora pico y su
hija petra te echaban seringa. a ti y tu me
la echabas a mi con estarme reganando. pues
tenia tanta pena y araba tanto que el corazon
parecia que se me queria salir por la boca
un sudor frio tenia en todo el ~~que~~ cuerpo.
asta que poco a poco se me fue quitando: y
bolvi a ter tu carta en la que me dises que te ~~at~~
biste culado la piebre cereblar. O Dios......se me
quito el. udor y me dio fiebre. por que queria
ya ir a berte. dises que ~~m~~ estas aliviado cuidate tu
~~no~~ no vayas a trabamar ~~a~~ te caias a enfermar tan
legos aun estanes. no estoi mui alibiada del pecho per
todavia no pudo salir del quarto porque las nudisinas
son mui peligrosas y la ansia me da todas las noches
~~no~~ no me da tan fuerte como antes pero todavia no
sani. dime dias te nido notisias de platon. toda la fa
milia esta de buena. napolion y luisita y mare lita
te mandan un millon de abrasos cada uno. don pepe
~~s~~ a estado aqui y me ~~acia~~ a echo mui buena conpani
natalia ~~es~~ y jovita y ula ~~s que te an escrito~~ ~~to~~
todos estan buenos.

B

1863 [sometime after February 13, 1863]⁵³
Guadalupe guadalupe, gua gu gu yuu [written at the top of the letter]

Dear and always ~~adored~~ demonic husband, companion, and friend,⁵⁴

I don't know what to call you. Is it husband or companion or friend or Guadalupe or General or Mariano or Señor Vallejo? I'm so confused that I don't even know what your name is. You yourself have told me that you don't want me to treat you as a husband or spouse, so I will refer to you as Don Guadalupe Vallejo. I was dreaming that you very angrily were telling me not to call you husband and that I was asking you to tell me what I should call you. You said I should call you Don Demonio or Don Diablo, but not to refer to you as my husband. We were fighting like that when Luisita entered the room and woke me up to give me a letter from you. I was very scared. I opened it and started to read it. I saw that you, too, had been dreaming, but your dreams were different. You were dreaming that Señora Pico and her daughter Petra were inserting a syringe into you and you were angry with me and scolding me, because I was crying so hard. But it was because I felt so sorry for you. It seemed as if my heart wanted to try and come out through my mouth. A cold sweat took hold of my entire body but little by little it went away. I read your letter again, in which you told me that you had suffered a brain fever. . . . Oh my God . . . I stopped sweating and then became feverish because I wanted to go and see you. You say that you already feel better. Take care of yourself. Don't work and then get sick, especially when you are so far away from where we are. I feel so much better from the chest problem but I still can't leave my room because the medicines are very dangerous. The anxiety I feel every night is not as strong as it previously was, but I'm still not cured. Tell me if you have received any news from Platón. The whole family is fine. Napoleón, Luisita, and Marillita each send you a million hugs. Don Pepe has been here and Natalia and Jovita have been very good company for me. Everyone is well.

IN THE MIDST OF THESE DIFFICULTIES, VALLEJO RECEIVED A LETTER from his daughter Natalia informing him that she was engaged to marry Attila Haraszthy. In a letter to Francisca, he sourly remarked that he had heard via the grapevine that another daughter, Jovita, was engaged to Attila's brother. The fact

---

53. C-B 441 FILM, reel 4, 188–89, TBL.
54. The word *adorado* (adored) has a line through it, and *demonio* (devil, demonic) is written to its right.

(*left*) Count Agoston Haraszthy. *Courtesy of California State Parks, Sonoma Barracks. No. 480-x-578.*

(*below, left*) Drawing of the home of Agoston Haraszthy, on the Buena Vista ranch in Sonoma, 1850. *Courtesy of the Sonoma County Library Photographic Collection. cstr_pho 043141.*

(*below, right*) Lachryma Montis Vineyard wine label, 1858. *Courtesy of the California Historical Society. MS 2204_001.tif.*

that he was learning about this while in the Monterey Bay area seemed to him to be a replay of how he had heard five years earlier about Adela's desire to marry Levi Frisbie.

Both Haraszthy brothers, Attila and Arpad, were sons of Hungarian immigrant Agoston Haraszthy, who had come to the United States in 1840. After some time in Wisconsin, Agoston moved to California in 1849. He first settled in San Diego, where he served as marshal and county sheriff. After serving a term in the California legislature, Agoston moved to San Francisco, where he was the first assayer of the U.S. Mint. Sparked by the possibility of engaging more directly in the viticultural activities in which he had dabbled in San Diego and San Francisco, he moved from San Francisco to Sonoma in 1856.

Indeed, the main thing that attracted him to Sonoma was the fact that Vallejo's two active vineyards in the region demonstrated that the North Bay could become a wine-producing area. Haraszthy purchased some land, which eventually became known as the Buena Vista winery. Attila served as vineyard foreman, and Arpad, who had spent a few years studying at Éparney in the Champagne district of France, was cellar master. Agoston Haraszthy and Vallejo both won prizes for their wines at the 1860 Sonoma County Fair. The families were close, and a double wedding witnessed by a Catholic priest was held at Lachryma Montis on June 1, 1863, with Natalia and Attila exchanging vows along with Jovita and Arpad.[55]

San Cayetano
Pájaro Valley
April 15, 1863[56]

Francisca,

I'm enclosing a letter for Natalia. It's my reply to one that she recently wrote to me saying she was engaged to marry Attila Haraszthy. But she says nothing as to whether she has consulted with you or has even told you about such a thing.

As you will see in my reply, I can do nothing more than give my consent to what she requests, because she is of age and of sound mind to choose a man to be her husband. I believe that it is my duty to send you the letter so that you can read it before giving it to her. Perhaps there is something I may not be aware of, or maybe someone wants to surprise me. If that isn't the case, you should give her the letter.

It's very strange that whenever I come to Monterey the girls always want to get married, and other people always announce it before I find out. I've been assured that Jovita also is engaged to one of the other Haraszthy young men. I haven't been informed about this directly, but rather through hearsay. We'll see how it all ends up. Señor Haraszthy has said nothing to me about that family matter. He should have had the courtesy to tell me about it unless he doesn't know anything about it either.[57]

Natalia told me that you are now well. Regards to all of the children.

M.G.V.

55. Biographical information about the Haraszthy family is taken from McGinty, *Strong Wine*.

56. C-B 441, box 1, folder 4, TBL

57. Haraszthy wrote to Vallejo on March 9, 1863 (written in English). He said, "I have the honor to ask by this letter from you the hands of your daughters Miss Natalia Vallejo for my son Attila, and Miss Jovita Vallejo for my son Arpad. All that is required to make the parties perfectly happy is the much desired consent of your paternal approval to their happy union." Vallejo had apparently not received the letter yet. He did receive it later in April and responded to Haraszthy on April 29, 1863. DLG-V 24, letter 1.

General Andrés Pico, January 3, 1878.
*Courtesy of The Bancroft Library,
University of California, Berkeley.*
POR: *Pico, Andrés: 3.*

AS THE SAN CAYETANO MATTER DRAGGED ON, VALLEJO SPENT AN increasing amount of time in San Francisco and Monterey. In San Francisco he consulted regularly with his lawyer, Benjamin Brooks, and visited family members and friends who were visiting the city. In letters to Francisca, he lamented his reversals and loneliness and passed on to her information he happened to hear about her relatives and friends. He remained concerned about making sure his children received the kind of education that would enable them to prosper in this new world he was finding increasingly difficult to negotiate. The tone of Vallejo's letters to Francisca indicates that she was urging him to remain calm while she herself was struggling with ways to keep the children still at home well fed and well clothed.

San Francisco
June 10, 1863[58]

Francisca,

I've just seen Federico Pickett, Don Andrés Pico, and some other men who have come from Los Angeles.[59] They say they just left your brother Ramón Carrillo at his ranch. He is healthy and safe and everything that has been said about him is

---

58. C-B 441, box 1, folder 4, TBL.

59. Charles Pickett, a lawyer, arrived at Sutter's Fort in 1846 after a three-year stay in Oregon. Pressed into service as a guard, his sympathy and kindness to the prisoners held by the Bear Flaggers impressed Vallejo, and they remained close from that time on. He was often called "Philosopher Pickett," and Vallejo's unfamiliarity with that English term may have been why he referred to him as Federico, a Spanish name that began with the same sound. See Powell, *Philosopher Pickett*, 20, 34–40.

(*left*) Ramón Carrillo. *Courtesy of the Autry Museum of
the American West, Los Angeles. No. 2002.1.5.39.*
(*right*) Ramona Carrillo de Wilson. *Courtesy of
The Bancroft Library, University of California, Berkeley.*
POR: *Carrillo de Wilson, Ramona:1.*

false.[60] Right now I'm going to visit Doña Ramona.[61] She lives near Larkin's house
on Stockton Street. Have Uladislao tell Dr. Fauré to send me the samples of aguardiente tomorrow on the steamer to see if I can sell some of it.[62] It would be good if
Ula himself could send them to me, entrusting them to the officer on the steamer.

M. G. Vallejo

B. S. Brooks' Law Office
San Francisco
July 2, 1863[63]

Francisca,
    Yesterday I visited Ramona and the visit lasted from eleven o'clock in the morn-
ing until seven o'clock in the evening. Ramona is in very good shape, very pretty,

---

60. Ramón Carrillo was accused of complicity in the 1862 murder of John Rains, the owner of Rancho Cucamonga,
    where Ramón worked. He was arraigned but discharged. See McGinty, "Carrillos of San Diego," 290.
61. After the death of her husband, John Wilson, in 1860, Francisca's sister Ramona spent an increasing amount of
    time in San Francisco. See McGinty, "Carrillos of San Diego," 132.
62. Víctor Fauré, a native of France and a physician by training, managed the production of wine from the grapes
    grown on Vallejo's property. McGinty, *Strong Wine*, 300, 302–3, 317, 319.
63. C-B 441, box 1, folder 4, TBL.

and as always very nice and filled with kindness. At first she was somewhat bitter, but after conversing with her for a while I was able to bring her around and she is very happy with me.

She says that your Aunt Chepa died, so did Emigdio Véjar and his son Lázaro.[64] They all died of smallpox. Her daughter Juanita is very ill and, even though she has improved somewhat, she doesn't expect her to live much longer.[65] The doctors say she only has part of one lung and the other one is failing. She still looks very ill to me, based on the way she looked yesterday when I saw her. The news from Mexico is always bad.

My regards to the children.

M. G. Vallejo

B. S. Brooks, Counsellor at Law
Office 11 and 12 Metropolitan Block,
Corner of Montgomery and Washington Streets
San Francisco, Cal.
July 16, 1863[66]

Francisca,

Yesterday I saw Ramona and she already had moved herself to another house. But the sick woman couldn't leave so they carried her upstairs to her sister's room, which is in the same house. Ramona leaves her room to keep the sick woman company. Yesterday they took over the rooms downstairs and moved all the furniture around, which made a lot of noise. The sick woman suffered greatly, and Ramona said she almost died.

I haven't been able to get my hands on even one peso in silver. This is killing me. It saddens me and I just can't go on. I think I'll go to the house on Saturday. If they assassinate me, what can be done about it? It's a cruel alternative but the circumstances are so demanding and distressing. I don't like to write sad letters, but I just can't go on.

My regards to everyone.

M. G. Vallejo

---

64. José María de Jesús Emigdio Véjar was born in 1809 and died in January 1863. His brother Lázaro was born in 1811 and died in February 1863. Mutnick, *Some Alta California Pioneers*, 3:1212–15; *Find a Grave*, accessed through Ancestry.com.

65. Juanita was born in December 1838. She married Juan Castro in 1856 and died in August 1863. Santa Bárbara Presidio Baptism 1299; *Sacramento Daily Union*, August 8, 1863.

66. C-B 441, box 1, folder 4, TBL.

Lachryma Montis
November 14, 1863[67]

Francisca,

I hope you will be very happy and will feel better in Vallejo, but I'll have to leave day after tomorrow, Tuesday, for Pájaro. I want to know if you'll be going or not, so that I can determine how I should leave things at the house. My departure is very urgent. It's possible that I might receive some money, at least enough to buy some clothing for the boys and some shoes and more stockings for me.

Give my regards to the whole family.

M. G. Vallejo

B. S. Brooks Law Office
San Francisco
November 23, 1863[68]

Francisca,

I still can't leave here because the people with whom I'm supposed to arrange my departure for Pájaro have been away. But today at eleven o'clock we will get together to coordinate what should be done. I'm anxious to leave here, for besides not having anything to do I'm running out of the little bit of money I brought, and I haven't been able to get even a single peso from anyone. Friends remain loyal as long as you have a lot of hard cash and credit but never faithful when they see you are in short supply. That is the way of the world, and it will always be like that. I'm thinking about selling all the property I have left in different areas for a reduced price. If I can collect a considerable amount of money, I'll pay my debts, establish myself in San Francisco, buy a plot of land, and build an establishment there that will cover the family's expenses. Then we can enroll the children in school so that they will learn something. In that way I'll fulfill, as soon as possible, the obligation I'm so anxious to realize. Then, if I can, I'll spend a year seeing the world. Then I'll return home to die, which will be very soon, perhaps even before I return.

I'm tired, bored, and feel hopeless from having to live with so much work and anxiety. This is not the life I lived ten years ago. I've been robbed by greedy men, unworthy of the trust I placed in them. On the other hand, I can no longer tolerate living among people who only think about acquiring, through dishonest means, that which belongs to other people. I don't have any peace of mind. After working my entire life in order to live with some degree of comfort, I haven't managed to do that at all.

---

67. C-B 441, box 1, folder 4, TBL.
68. C-B 441, box 1, folder 4, TBL.

Ida Haraszthy Hancock.
Courtesy of Allan Hancock College,
Santa Maria, California. GAM 418.

Give my regards to Nap., Lulú, and María, and if Don Pepe is at home, also give him my best.

M. G. Vallejo

San Cayetano
March 22, 1864[69]

Francisca,

I saw in the newspapers that Ida Haraszthy arrived in San Francisco, and it's very possible that she had a chance to see Platón in New York.[70] I'm anxious to know if Platón is dead or alive. It's been eight months since I received a letter from him, and that silence has me very worried. In the last letter I wrote to him from Sonoma, I remember that I was scolding him because he wasn't writing to me. It's possible that he didn't like that scolding and that's why he hasn't written to me again. Nevertheless, he shouldn't be so sensitive or so easily hurt, unless he now thinks like an "American," by that I mean flaunting his independence. This wouldn't surprise me, despite the fact that he's always been very obedient. Nevertheless, if you could find out something from Ida, ask her how Platón is doing. Give her my regards and congratulate her on a safe arrival to the family home. Also, give my regards to Señora Haraszthy.

---

69. C-B 441, box 1, folder 4, TBL.

70. Ida Haraszthy was Agoston Haraszthy's daughter. At this time, she was unmarried, but the next year she wed Henry Hancock. McGinty, *Strong Wine*, 424.

No matter how much I have done to resolve the business that brought me here, I haven't been able to do so because of brother Fortoul. He has filed his lawsuit regarding the division of the land, and I still don't know when it will be over. I've worked very hard to sell my part, but since they have offered me so little money for the land I haven't wanted to sell it. They offered me 10,000 pesos for land that is worth 30,000 pesos. I find it very hard to sacrifice the last hope I have here. After so much expense and so many delays, it's also very hard for me to return home without any money, not only for expenses but also for the outstanding accounts I have in Sonoma. I don't know what to do. I'm waiting for the storm clouds to dissipate a bit and for the financial horizon to clear. I've been hoping that Frisbie, who is in Washington, would have finished the business regarding Suscol, which was introduced again in Congress. The squatters have resumed their strong efforts to invalidate the land title, and Frisbie went to see what he could do. You already know that this was half completed last year, but the devil seems to meddle in everything. When I was in Vallejo, Frisbie told me that, despite the reversals and expenses, my share would be 75,000 or 80,000 pesos and he would get the same amount. But he felt it would be a good idea to wait a while in order to sell at a higher price. So I've been anxiously waiting for the moment when he returns to find out the result. I'm getting tired of all of this. Besides, I'm getting very old very fast. I'm already more bald than Don Juan Cooper. I do like it though, because baldness is in fashion, especially when I go to church because I can sit in the front pews.

I've also lost about ten teeth and four molars, which is also in fashion. When you see me you won't recognize me. I'm quite the spectacle. Sometimes I feel like dying or running away. It is very nice to be fashionable, but being bald, old, and without teeth is intolerable. The children aren't going to recognize me, neither will you. The only thing left is for me to become one-eyed and gimpy to look like a great . . . . What are people going to say? Look how old age ruins a man! What can I do? There is a remedy—a wig, false teeth, etc., but there is no remedy for old age because it can't be beaten out of a person. Damn years.

You haven't written to me, not a single word since I've been away. It bothers me a lot because you know how much better I feel when I receive letters from the family while I'm away from home. But what can be done about it? That's the way everything happens. The more a person wants for things to be better, the less support he receives. The whole family has written to me except for Fannie and Andrónico. It's already obvious that they are very independent. They approach life on their own terms and at their own risk. It troubles me greatly, but such is life. You know me and you are aware that I don't believe in the doctrine that the sacred bonds of nature are broken when a person gets married. A person's father and mother come before a spouse in terms of family ties and affection. It is the law of nature and God commands it. Isn't that right?

Mariano Guadalupe and his son Platón.
Courtesy of California State Parks,
Sonoma Barracks. No. 243-1-371.

I was in Monterey a few days ago, where I saw your sister Doña Ramona and her daughter Doña María Ignacia.[71] They are well, and Doña Ramona says that after Holy Week is over she's going to San Francisco and plans to live there. From there she can then go and pay you a visit. I hope I'll be there to have the pleasure of welcoming her in the manner she deserves. I owe her so many family favors which I'll never be able to repay. Even though she isn't able to remember those favors, it is a debt that one must not fail to repay in some way.

Regards to Ula, Nap., Lulú, and María, also to Natalia and Jovita and don't forget their husbands.

M. G. Vallejo

IN THE SPRING OF 1864, FRANCISCA SUGGESTED THAT THEY THINK ABOUT increasing their income by renting out their family bath house, which functioned very well because of the abundant springs on their property. Her husband was

71. María Ignacia was born in May 1840. She married Domingo Pujol in 1858. Santa Bárbara Presidio Baptism 1381; Northrop, *Spanish-Mexican Families,* 2:329.

furious at the suggestion. He feared that such a strategy would advertise their financial insecurity to a wider public and thereby hurt both his and the family's images as people of property and substance. He probably also thought that he, as the traditional head of the family, should be the only one to make such suggestions.

San Cayetano
April 26, 1864[72]

Francisca,

I wrote to you three days ago. I suppose you have received my letter and it probably seemed to you to be a bit serious and not very pleasant. When I was answering your letter, I was furious with the entire world, with all men, with the human race, with fate, and with everything ever written under the sun. I was in such a state when I received the letter you had written to me that, without pausing for an instant to reflect on it, I picked up my pen to answer it <u>truly believing that you had posted an advertisement in Sonoma so that the family bath house could be used by the public</u>, which made me go crazy. However, after rereading your letter, I saw that you were consulting with me and were waiting for my decision in order to do it or not, which tempered my rage. I was determined to write to you, but if there is anything in the letter that is <u>personal</u>, do not take offense, for I am repentant. This is not the time to aggravate the horrible circumstances in which we currently find ourselves. Useless complaints would only make matters worse, and this would lead to the total ruination of a family that is so dear to me and that should be as dear to you as well.

I have ended up poor because people have stolen from me. It is not because of any bad decisions on my part, even though people have wanted to assert that. It is just bad luck, and it has not been in my power to remedy this. It almost seems like I was destined to suffer those strokes of bad luck. As you know, it was not humanly possible to correct them because this was the direct result of a grand public movement that was supposed to drag down the fortunes of men like me who made themselves more visible.

Ending up poor because the most powerful government in the world has <u>taken over</u> my most valuable properties is not my fault. It is just that I have not been able to fight for them successfully due to a lack of material force ($$) to counteract it. A capitalist manages one or two million pesos and conducts his business in China and Europe. He sends three or four clipper ships to those places in search of valuable cargo and as soon as everything is on board he sets sail. While sailing back to San Francisco in large and expensive ships they get caught in a hurricane in the middle

---

72. C-B 441, box 1, folder 4, TBL.

of the ocean and they perish . . . ships, cargo, and men. Who is to blame for this? A farmer, who is a speculator, plants a large amount of wheat, barley, potatoes and uses all his money, and even his credit, on this enterprise because wheat, barley, and potatoes bring a very high price at market. However, after having made such an expenditure, the seedlings begin to appear, but not a drop of water falls in the winter. Who is to blame for this? Or if the harvest was good and a fire destroys it all, or if the market goes down and the items in question are no longer worth anything? Who is to blame for this? Or if someone plants grapevines, orchards, etc., and the wine or the grapes aren't any good? Who is to blame for this? Enough said with regard to taking a philosophical approach to things. But referring to our situation, it is true that lately we have suffered shortages up to a certain point, painful shortages that we were not prepared to experience. However, I have spent three years hoping to find a way out of the predicament of that damned business at Suscol, which in the end has humiliated me tremendously, causing me to be in debt to those who have been working for me, and it is the reason for the mortgage on the property. I came here to handle the business regarding this property with the hope that I could come out with at least $15,000, but I have not been able to accomplish this due to some complications that were not within my power to resolve. If I had been able to foresee this, I never would have come. I have suffered greatly, both physically and emotionally. I have been alone, totally alone, working hard to sell and get some money to bring back home. But that <u>damned money</u> has disappeared from the country, everybody is <u>hopping mad</u>, crying out, and wailing for it. I was in Monterey several days ago and believe me, that place is pitiful. There are many families in the same situation, and if it were not for the fish they would have died of hunger. I said to myself, "Thank God that there are geese, ducks, hens, and all types of vegetables to eat at my home." I was making comparisons between the two places, and it did give me some consolation in my heart. I even wanted to share with them what my family had, which seemed like an abundance of food compared to what they had.

The greatest consolation I have received while being away is receiving mail from the whole family and holding it in my hands. Their letters do my heart good, they distract me, and they are a salve that has cured me somewhat. If only you had written to me as well, how happy I would have been! What satisfaction I would have received! How relieved I would have felt! I have been very carefully searching for what one could call <u>happiness</u> among some people. I have not been able to find it anywhere. I have asked (without people paying me any mind), heard, and discovered that in this detestable world everyone runs away from happiness. Gossip, scandal, murmurings, slander, lies, and evil itself reign everywhere. In the end, I have been nothing less than horrified by what I have discovered here. But God is great, God is good, the God of Napoleon!!!!!!!, that all-seeing and all-knowing God

Lachryma Montis, 1877. Residence of General M. G. Vallejo.
The bath house is to the right of the main house, close to the curved front fence.
In Sonoma County Atlas. *Thos. H. Thompson and Co., 84.*

who <u>should take into account</u> our actions and how we have used our language!!!!!
That God—and our own conscience, I hope!—will punish those who maliciously
or innocently have done wrong. I wish I hadn't known so much!

This is not a sermon; it is a letter written from the heart. I want you to read it
with an open mind. I need to pour out my feelings with someone who (<u>putting
aside biased passion</u>) understands me. How happy I would be if, in the end, after
so many years of <u>loathing and animosity toward me</u>, you could free yourself of that
deep-rooted hatred you feel for me and for the members of my family. Hatred and
rancor produce nothing more than countless evils. I realize that loathing is natural, but even so, I follow the maxims of the men who have said, "One should seek
peace and reconciliation when there are families that suffer because of the lack of
reason on the part of their parents." My sons and daughters give me, up to a certain
point, the greatest pleasure of my life. They know it and so do you. They express
it in their letters along with the trust they have. Whether absent or present, they
realize this, and it pleases me to say it. I am tired of living without receiving any
letters from you while I am away from home. It is an emptiness that I feel when I
receive letters from Fanita, Adela, Natalia, Ula, Jovita, and Nap., but I don't see
a letter from you. Do you understand? Andrónico has not written to me either.

I want to return soon. Give my regards to Ula, Nap., Lulú, and María, and many more to Don Pepe.

M. G. Vallejo

WITH THE SAN CAYETANO MATTER STILL UNRESOLVED, VALLEJO continued to be lonely. He told two of his daughters, "Estrada and I are alone in a house that is on top of the hill. From there we can see the ocean and the pueblo of Watsonville, where everyone stops their wagons or other carriages. There is also a river in front. The pueblo of Santa Cruz and the pine groves of Monterey can also be seen. We always hear the loud sound of the waves crashing on the shore." But the picturesque scenery did not lessen Vallejo's sense of isolation and suffering. He continued:

> Your poor Papá! It's very hard for me to speak because a few days ago many of my teeth fell out and my face is very bruised. Estrada laughs at me a lot and he is always asking about you and María. He also says that you will laugh at me when you see me. The only clothing I put on are socks, a white undershirt, and the red robe I had in San Francisco when I was ill. On my head I wear that cap with the small beads. I also wear the green tie Ula loaned me for this trip. That's what I look like all day long. Since no one comes here, there's a good chance that I will spend from morning until night without being interrupted.[73]

His loneliness was evident in his frequent complaints that his adult children were not writing to him as often as he thought they should. Platón finished his studies at Columbia in April 1864 and ranked second in his graduating class. He returned to California shortly after graduating. His first position was as an assistant surgeon on board a storeship stationed at Mare Island. His own Civil War experience, along with his father's continuing contacts with some of the officers at the naval base, certainly helped him obtain that position. But matters were different with Uladislao, whose situation was not so accomplished or settled. After leaving Fordham he returned home and was unable to settle on any significant career path. He worked for a while at a department store in San Francisco but spent much of his time at Sonoma lacking any direction.

Although Platón and Uladislao were very much on his mind, Vallejo also often referred to the three youngest children, Napoleón, Luisa, and María, whom Francisca was raising at home. His major fear was that he might not be able to provide for them as well as he desired. Napoleón had left Santa Clara and was now in the Sonoma public school, along with Luisa and María. But Vallejo wanted them to receive a better education than he thought the public school could provide. He

---

73. M.G.V. to Lulú and María, March 28, 1864. C-B 441 FILM, reel 4, 99–100, TBL.

Francisca Benicia Carrillo de Vallejo holding
a photograph of her son Platón. *Courtesy of
California State Parks, Sonoma Barracks.
No. 243-1-1394.*

told his daughter Adela, "If I end up poor, I won't be able to provide the same
education to my youngest children as I did for my older children. Poor Napoleón,
Lulú, and María! But what can I do?"[74] The oldest of the three, Napoleón, would
occasionally be allowed to travel to San Francisco or Monterey to visit his father.

When Vallejo was not at San Cayetano or in the Monterey area, he was spending
a considerable amount of time at the San Francisco office of his lawyer, Benjamin
Brooks. In her letters to her husband, Francisca was, as usual, very forthcoming
about not appreciating his frequent absences away from her and, especially, their
children. She also urged him not to allow himself to become so absorbed in what she
suggested was unjustified self-pity. Francisca was more direct in a letter to Platón:

> There are so many things I want to tell you but you can see that I can hardly write. In a
> few words I will tell you that your Papá has lost everything in some way or another. There
> is no hope of resolving any of this because he has such a bad temper, which is intolerable.
> There are times when he is in such a good frame of mind that you wouldn't believe he is
> your Papá, but then he quickly becomes so angry that nobody can believe this is the same
> man. There are times when I will want to speak to him about something or ask him a
> question and he responds with such an angry tone and with such bad words that it scares
> me. He changes from one moment to the next, from one extreme to another. Just imagine,
> Platoncito, how sad I feel.[75]

When Vallejo wrote Francisca from San Cayetano at the beginning of May 1864,
he remarked to her that he had just learned that Plácido Vega had recently arrived
in San Francisco. Vega had served as governor of the northern Mexican state of

74. M.G.V. to Adela, May 6, 1864. C-B 441 FILM, reel 4, 109–110, TBL.
75. F.B.C.V. to Platón, April, no date, no year, C-B 441 FILM, reel 4, 210–214, TBL.

Sinaloa in the early 1860s. He had organized a military company intended to support Mexican president Benito Juárez in the face of the French intervention. After Juárez had to abandon Mexico City in May 1863 and retreat north to San Juan Potosí, he appointed Vega as a special agent to go to California to secure arms that would help his Republican forces resist the French forces, who eventually named Austrian archduke Maximilian emperor in April 1864.

Vega arrived in San Francisco in March 1864 and quickly found a mixed reception. Many Californios, such as Vallejo, welcomed him and contributed some funds for the purchase of the armaments he was seeking. But San Francisco public officials, often in league with the French consulate in the city, refused to allow those armaments to be exported. Vallejo quickly decided that defending Mexico against foreign interference might give Uladislao a sense of direction and purpose. He also hoped that Vega would be able to arrange for Uladislao to travel to Sinaloa's capital, Mazatlán, and join the Republican forces there. These forces were headed by Jesús García Morales, Vega's successor as governor.[76]

San Cayetano
May 6, 1864[77]

Francisca,

You finally wrote to me in your own hand and it's a very long letter. I can assure you that it is very well done, except for the <u>scolding</u> you gave me. When you want to and put your mind to it, you also write well, but you are a bit lazy. You should try to write in the new style, which isn't just beautiful penmanship, but also a letter that is composed well. You probably already know that Platón has graduated and is now a doctor. He performed quite brilliantly on the exams, surpassing more than seventy young men who graduated at the same time. I'm very happy about that, and also because in all the newspapers they speak very highly of him, and in some they even express admiration. If only we could see him soon. Poor Platón, he left a boy and will return a man with a distinguished and respected profession. I wonder what he will say when he finds out that Jovita, who was in school when he left, is now married and has a baby?

You have done the right thing by sending the vegetables to the hotel and the eggs to the bakers. You know very well that it is quite normal to do that. Let's not think about the bath house again. When I get home, we can talk.

I'm very aware of what you told me about Don Pepe, but I wanted you to write

76. On Vega and California, see Miller, "Californians against the Emperor;" Miller, "Plácido Vega"; and Miller, "Arms across the Border."

77. C-B 441, box 1, folder 4, TBL.

Plácido Vega.
*Courtesy of The
Bancroft Library,
University of California,
Berkeley.* POR: *Vega,
Plácido:* 1.

to me in your own hand. There are some things a person desires. Why shouldn't you write to me when the whole family does so? We are friends again, but please try to be happy when I arrive home.

Kiss all of the children and receive the affection from

M. G. Vallejo

Over[78]

General Vega is in San Francisco. He is quite the gentleman, has a very good reputation, and is very rich. I have made some arrangements regarding Ula, so that he can go to Mexico under the protection of the general, who has promised me that, if the fortunes of war against the French and for the independence of Mexico are favorable to him, he will send Ula back to me with the rank of general. General Vega wants to take Ula with him. I've written to him and said that he will find Ula to be a young man who has been very well educated in the American style. Even though Ula is young, he has the biggest heart on earth. He is brave and wishes to fight in defense of his ancestors' homeland and the original homeland of his parents, whose blood courses through his veins. I'm waiting for a letter from Señor Vega. We shall see what happens. Poor Ula! I can already see him wearing the sash of a general. War is dangerous, but it is the profession of brave men. If the outcome is favorable, there is much to hope for. The enemy fires the bullets, but God determines where they land. When fighting for a holy cause, one shouldn't think about the risks. If a man doesn't test his mettle, he will never experience satisfaction, for "Nothing ventured, nothing gained."

---

78. Vallejo wrote this to be sure Francisca read the back of the page.

LADIES', GENTS', MISSES'. BOYS' AND CHILDREN'S BOOTS, SHOES AND BROGANS.

Receipt for Mrs. Genl. Vallejo, November 23, 1858, from Holcomb Brothers. *Courtesy of California State Parks, Sonoma Barracks. No. 243-x-4274.*

Sonoma
May 7, 1864[79]

Guadalupe,

You can't imagine how grateful I am to you and to Platón for the gift you sent me. As soon as I received the twenty pesos I went to Sonoma to pay for Lulú's and my shoes. And I even had enough money left over to buy one peso's worth of soap. That is how I spent the twenty pesos. I was very pleased to be able to pay for the shoes.

If you are involved in something that benefits you, me, and the children, don't hurry back. Do things with care and clarity. I suppose you already have as much experience with men as you do with women. Men are the reason we're poor. Don't be sad or troubled, for God gives things and God takes them away. That's how I think. Help General Vega as much as you can. By helping General Vega you are

---

79. C-B 441 FILM, reel 4, 223, TBL.

helping all the good Mexicans. You said that my letter was very short. It's because I can't write well.

Take good care of yourself and live peacefully. Come home when you can, but don't be gone too long, because that frightens me. I'm already imagining that you aren't going to come back. No, no, I don't want to think like that. Isn't it true that I shouldn't think that way? . . . Guadalupe, there are times when I'm very sad and spend too much time thinking.

If you see Doña Carolina Días, give her my regards.

Benicia Carrillo

San Cayetano
May 10, 1864[80]

Francisca,

Lorenzo was here the day before yesterday, and I had him take some small rolls for the girls and Nap. They are the ones I have here for when I drink chocolate. Lorenzo promised me he would take them to the house and tell you that he saw me and that I'm here alone in my mother's house. If only I had been able to send you some money. Then you could have come here to see me. I'm not suffering as much from the absolute solitude in which I find myself as I am from thinking about my business affairs and from not being able to see my family. You know very well how much I love the children. I can't bear being away from them. I'm not going to say anything to you because you wouldn't believe me. You should have no doubt that you are never far from my heart, because you are the one who made me a father by giving me such good sons and daughters. What a pity that you haven't understood me for such a long time! Isn't that true? Yes, I'm a very strange man, but that is the way I am and only death will take away the tendencies I was endowed with by nature. Perhaps it was providential that we got married—two people with such different temperaments. Without delving into the principles of physiology, which society has adopted as good, it is said that to always produce fine children married couples must possess different temperaments. With regard to children, the principle is correct, but I don't like seeing you suffer on my account. I'm tormented by your suffering, which results in your <u>abhorrence</u> of me, after I made you happy by giving you such a fine family. I hope the children will always be good and won't cause us any heartaches! Poor children! They each write to me every day. You could say that even the girls' husbands write to me because, when I send them my regards by way of their wives, they know it is appropriate to reciprocate.

---

80. C-B 441, box 1, folder 4, TBL.

All my friends write to me congratulating me on Platón's brilliance as a student at Columbia University in New York. They say he performed very well, and the diploma "Doctor in Medicine" was well deserved. I'm very happy and I even dreamed that he was in California. Last night, to be exact, I dreamed he was traveling on the steamer that will arrive in eight days (next Tuesday, May 17) and that Fanita, Adela, Dr. Frisbie, and the captain had taken Platón to Sonoma. You were crying because you were so happy. If only my dream were reality! I very much would like to see you cry, because when you cry you always feel better. <u>Do you remember the times when you cried and then got over your bad feelings?</u> Another thing, when you cry, you love me, isn't that so?

I'm waiting for Mr. Brooks so I can finish up here. Then I can go see you. Would you like that? Tell me so and I'll go and see you soon. What do you say? Will you be happy? Will you give me . . . a kiss . . . with all your heart? I'm waiting for your answer, from your head as well as your heart.

Kiss the children.

M. G. Vallejo

San Cayetano
May 14, 1864[81]

Francisca,

I'm enclosing the letter I just received from General Vega so that you and Ula can read it. Show it to Ula and tell him that I have very little left to do to complete my plan with regard to him. Perhaps I'll leave here next week.

It's necessary that this not be made public, because the <u>French who are in Sonoma</u> will tell everybody. I don't want them to know about my plan, for if it doesn't turn out well, they will make fun of me. Tell Ula that I'm still hopeful, and that "<u>I don't give up the ship</u>" yet.[82]

Be careful with the letter.

Kiss Nap., Lulú, and María.

M. G. Vallejo

---

81. C-B 441, box 1, folder 4, TBL.
82. In English in the original letter.

Sonoma
May 14, 1864[83]

Guadalupe,

There are so many things I want to say to you, but it's better to keep quiet. As soon as you are back in Sonoma, then I'll tell you. And you will have to respond to what I have said to you. I have received four letters from you, but I didn't answer them because I'm very busy. Since I can't write quickly, I put off writing. Come and see the children. They think about you so much. Poor innocent little ones. Come and stay here for a week or two, or however long you want. Come so you can converse with them. Come if your business affairs allow you to. Come if you feel like seeing the mother of your children. If I give you a kiss with all my heart? With all my soul? Will you come now? Yes, you will come?

Benicia de Vallejo

San Cayetano
May 18, 1864[84]

Francisca,

Your last letter, dated May 14, arrived yesterday evening. You can't imagine the effect it had on me. This is perhaps the first time you have written to me with tender feelings, perhaps the first time your heart has spoken to you on behalf of the man who, even though he has flaws (something we all have) they are not as serious or exaggerated as slander and envy make them out to be. Neither is he guilty of the flaws attributed to him by aspersions cast by others.

Your letter seems to be one of peace and affection. It has been a soothing balm that calms me. First, my soul took a breath, then it found consolation, and then tears paid homage to the solace my heart was feeling. I've suffered so much in so many ways. My business affairs, in the hands of rather unfortunate people, have been in a continuous state of flux and are constantly at risk of being wiped out. But each day I always have hope. The only consolation I have had these last six months has been the exchange of letters with the family (except for Andrónico, who doesn't write to me). Fani, Adela, Natalia, Jovita, Uladislao, and Napoleón are the ones who have served as my angels. I've written many very long letters to them, based on what the circumstances required. All of them have written enough to satisfy my pride as a father of an educated family. I'm not ashamed to say that they have been educated as I have seen fit.

83. BANC MSS 76/79c, box 1, folder 17, TBL.
84. C-B 441, box 1, folder 4, TBL.

Alone, totally alone, withdrawn from all of society, with nothing more than memories of my mother's home, I sleep in her bed with no other living soul around except for Estrada. I have lived through some very cruel days. Every day since I arrived here I was hopeful that I could settle everything. But a thousand unexpected obstacles have prevented that from happening. I wanted to return to Sonoma with money, but I haven't been able to acquire any. Besides, you know they have wanted to assassinate me. I've also been in a very bad mood because of the debts. I'm ashamed. I need to pay or die.

I very much want to see you, as well as the children, because I love them very much. Perhaps they love their poor Papá. I'll be leaving soon. I take you at your word for what you said to me in your letter. Do you remember?

Lorenzo was here and told me he would go by the house to give you some small rolls I sent you.

I suppose that on Monday you received the letters I sent you from General Vega. He is a very refined man. It seems to me that Ula will be fine by his side. If Ula is lucky and fate looks somewhat favorably on him, I believe he will make this his career. Mexico is at war with a very strong nation but should come out victorious in the end. Besides, a young man like Ula can become a general there and aspire to even greater things. It is said that Señor Vega possesses an immense fortune.

I started this letter with the sole purpose of writing loving things to you, but I had so much to say.

If Señor Brooks provides me with a little bit of money, I'll leave here next Monday, May 23. I would like you to send me Señor General Vega's letter right away so I can answer it immediately.

I want to see everyone. And . . . make you fall in love with me?

M. G. Vallejo

As he waited for Vega to agree to take Uladislao to Mexico with him, Vallejo continued to be concerned about many things. The monthly mortgage payments for Lachryma Montis continued to weigh on him. And his uncertainty about whether he could afford to pay for the education of his three youngest children gave him continued anxiety. He obtained some relief and closure when Vega arranged for Uladislao to depart for Mexico at the end of July.

San Cayetano
May 22, 1864[85]

Francisca,

Don Pepe wrote me a very sad letter, lamenting that his illness is very serious and that he is suffering terribly in so many ways. He even bid me farewell. His letter is very tender, and it fills me with sorrow. As I was reading it to a friend, my friend told me, "I know of a remedy that immediately cures those who are suffering from bladder problems."

Prescription:

A rather strong potion is made from elderberry stalks and mallow roots. The potion is then chilled. Have the patient drink a good amount of it and he will immediately pass a stream of urine.

My friend says that he has a lot of faith in this medicine. Have the remedy prepared and send it to Don Pepe.

Poor Don Pepe. I hope I can see him.

I'll leave for San Francisco tomorrow, Tuesday, or at the latest on Wednesday. Don't mention this, because from there I plan to go to Vallejo to see Frisbie.

Give my regards to Platón, Ula, Lulú, and María.

M. G. Vallejo

Brooks & Whitney
July 1, 1864[86]

Francisca,

I'm sending you two small boxes of the pills you asked me to get. I didn't see Mr. Green until today, so that is why I hadn't sent them to you earlier.

What you told me about María Ignacia made me very sad. I'm sad for you as well, because of what I told you about Rosalía.[87]

The time to set things straight will arrive. Yes, it will arrive. I truly hope that you will live to old age and that you will make peace with the people whom you believe are your enemies.

---

85. C-B 441, box 1, folder 4, TBL.

86. C-B 441, box 1, folder 4, TBL.

87. María Ignacia Pujol died two years later on July 18, 1866. *Find a Grave*, accessed through Ancestry.com. Rosalía's husband, Jacob P. Leese, was becoming more involved in schemes to purchase land and mineral rights in Mexico, notably in Baja California. He had recently returned from a trip there. His schemes eventually amounted to nothing, although in pursuit of them Leese traveled east in 1865. He did not return, effectively abandoning his family. Perhaps Rosalía was already being troubled by her husband's behavior. Valadés, *Historia de Baja California*, 187–97; *Daily Alta California*, June 5 and June 28, 1864; Beebe and Senkewicz, *Testimonios*, 24.

General Vega can't leave now because of the countless difficulties that have arisen. Ula is well, but very anxious to leave.

Kiss Nap., Lulú, and María. And you, receive the affection from

M. G. Vallejo

Brooks & Whitney
San Francisco
July 7, 1864[88]

Francisca,

The reason I've been detained here is because I'm waiting for General Vega to leave for Mexico. I've already been here for a month, and I'm filled with anguish and a sense of desperation because I don't have any money to pay Ula's and my expenses. I've tried to sell whatever seemed marketable to me, but I've had no luck. There is a terrible shortage of money and who knows what will result from such a crisis.

I am 56 years old today. This is one of the saddest days of my life. I have no money, my health is poor, and I can't even be with my children, who are my <u>only reason</u> for living. Yes, if Nap., Lulú, and María were educated, I wouldn't have to live another day. I abhor life, this hateful life filled with all sorts of bitterness that makes me want and hope to bring it to an end. May God give me patience to tolerate my life until the children no longer need me.

General Vega has encountered many difficulties in obtaining his weapons, and as a result he hasn't been able to leave.[89] I hope I can always be of help to him. May he land on the beaches of his homeland without any difficulties.

Give my regards to Don Pepe and tell him that soon I'll be spending a few days in Sonoma. Kiss Nap., Lulú, and María. And you, accept my heart and soul in good faith and unconditionally. Do you want to receive that birthday present of mine?

M. G. Vallejo

---

88. C-B 441, box 1, folder 4, TBL.

89. On Vega's difficulties in sending weapons to the Juárez forces from San Francisco in 1864, see Miller, "Plácido Vega," 138–41.

San Francisco
July 20, 1864[90]

Francisca,

The more I work and the more I worry about finding the means to obtain money to pay Madden's mortgage and other pending accounts that you are aware of, the less hope I have in succeeding. So seeing that it is necessary to make a quick and decisive decision to save the house and the lands of Lachryma Montis before Mr. Madden and his mortgage absorb it all with the interest he has accrued up until now, I believe it's timely and absolutely necessary to sell Quiquiriquí with its orchards and houses. It pains me but it's necessary to quickly pay off the debts before things get even worse. I can see a frightening crisis approaching and it's necessary to be prepared in anticipation of its arrival. If I could wait longer and see the business improve somewhat, I would wait. But nothing is clear, nothing. On the contrary, the entire future is dark, with a monetary storm on the horizon. Nevertheless, I want to protect you and the family because I want to feel at peace having fulfilled my duty as a man and a father. There isn't even one peso here, let alone the opportunity to obtain one.

This letter is for you alone.

Kiss Nap. and María and wait to kiss Lulú until I return.

I am your,
M. G. Vallejo

San Francisco
July 27, 1864[91]
Confidential

Francisca,

Tell Jim, confidentially, to keep a careful eye on the <u>barracks</u> during the day as well as at night.

It seems that Mr. Madden doesn't want the doctor to remain there. We shall see about that. It bothers me up to a certain point, but they say that "he who owes money either pays up or begs."

Ula left on Saturday. May God guide him.

Give Nap. and María a kiss.

M. G. Vallejo

---

90. C-B 441, box I, folder 4, TBL.
91. C-B 441, box I, folder 4, TBL.

THE FINANCIAL DIFFICULTIES AT SONOMA PERSISTED. FRANCISCA URGED her husband to be frugal and to avoid involvement in any monetary schemes that might be offered to him in San Francisco.

Brooks & Whitney
San Francisco
July 27, 1864[92]

Francisca,

Send for Jim and ask him if he can send me one hundred gallons of the good brandy he has set aside in a large barrel. Tell him that, if there's enough to fill a one hundred gallon cask, he should go and ask Pedro for the cask and have Pedro tell him when he can send it.

I'm so mortified. If the brandy arrives, a man is going to buy it for five pesos per gallon, which adds up to $500. From that amount, $125 will be paid to the government. What is left will be applied to some other accounts. I'll also buy some shoes.

Give Nap. a kiss.

M. G. Vallejo

Brooks & Whitney
San Francisco
October 21, 1864[93]

Francisca,

I bought the following from Mr. Green's steamer at the embarcadero:
    2 large boxes of candles
    3 large boxes of soap
    1 barrel of white sugar
    5 gallons of coal oil[94]
    1 box of tea (common)
    1 box of a variety of teas
    25 pounds of rice

92. C-B 441, box 1, folder 4, TBL.
93. C-B 441, box 1, folder 4, TBL.
94. "Coal oil" is in English in the original letter.

Merchants' Exchange building, ca. late 1860s, by Lawrence and Houseworth. *Courtesy of The Society of California Pioneers. LH0209.*

If I can, I'll buy the material for sheets this afternoon. I'll be leaving in a hurry tomorrow, Saturday, headed for Monterey. Who knows if I can tolerate the journey.

I haven't even been able to buy a shirt. I'm sending the cart with Jasy by way of Vallejo. I paid 50 pesos.

M. G. Vallejo

Sonoma
[no month] 28, 1864[95]

Guadalupe,

The little girls and I are fine. We don't need anything. Mr. Pickett is here, and he is keeping us company.

Jim couldn't rent the house to Dr. Waslet because he says that six pesos for one room is too much. I told Jim not to lower the price because twelve pesos is not a lot to pay for two very good rooms, a kitchen, a well, common rooms, and a very large veranda.

Guadalupe: remember what I told you about your <u>money</u>. . . . conduct your business well. <u>Don't trust anyone, anyone at all</u> . . . and take care of yourself.

Let me know if you have had any news about Ula. Give Napoleón my many regards.

Benicia de Vallejo

ULADISLAO ARRIVED AT MAZATLÁN. THE SITUATION THERE WAS VASTLY different from what he and his father had expected. The Republican forces had splintered into hostile factions. In the middle of October, Governor García Morales's forces were attacked and defeated by one of his rivals, General Ramón Corona, and García Morales was arrested. Uladislao was a member of the Morales force and was also arrested, but he was sent across the Gulf of California to Baja California.[96] Vallejo was fearful that Uladislao might go back to the Mexican mainland to continue fighting. To prevent this, he decided to try to get money to his son so that he could return to Sonoma.

95. C-B 441 FILM, reel 4, 179–80, TBL.
96. Ortega Noriega, *Breve historia de Sinaloa*, 223–38.

Uladislao Vallejo in 1868.
*Courtesy of the Autry Museum
of the American West, Los
Angeles. No. 2004.22.11.22.*

San Francisco
November 10, 1864[97]

Francisca,

The news I have regarding Ula is that in the last military action in Mazatlán against the government he performed very well and with bravery, taking sides with the government. After the battle, he was taken prisoner alongside Governor García Morales, and Ula was exiled to Baja California.[98] As soon as I found out, I hurried back from Pájaro so I could pay for his return passage to Sonoma. I've arranged everything so that, no matter where he is found, the steamer will bring him back.

As you probably have seen in the newspapers, the pronouncement of Mazatlán was by the liberals themselves.[99] This has upset me tremendously because they did this at a crucial moment when they should have remained united in order to save the country. I'm writing Ula a very long letter. If he hasn't left La Paz or Cabo San Lucas yet, he probably will be here on the 20th of next month. I fear that Ula, with his restless and undaunted spirit, could have gone to join up with Señor Juárez, but I hope not. He didn't go to fight against the Mexicans but rather against the French, but fortunately it was in defense of the Constitutional government.

97. C-B 441, box 1, folder 4, TBL.

98. Vallejo would have learned about the battle from dispatches from the field that arrived in California, such as "Our Letter from Mazatlán" in the *Daily Alta California*, November 3, 1864, and "Revolution and Fight in Mazatlán" in the *Sacramento Daily Union*, November 4, 1864.

99. A pronouncement (*pronunciamiento*) was a formal written protest, typically drafted as a list of grievances or demands, that was often employed by various Mexican military figures against their opponents in the nineteenth century. See Martínez, "Inventing the Nation." The text of the pronouncement of the Corona forces against García Morales can be found in Buelna, *Breves apuntes*, 38–41.

Give my regards to all the children and wait patiently for Ula to return, as will I.

Yours,

M. G. Vallejo

Sonoma

November 15, 1864[100]

Guadalupe,

I received your letter dated the 10th. I've seen the newspapers and was thinking that you might be able to do something to help Ula. When you write to him, tell him to come back. God willing, nothing has happened to poor Ula.

Everyone here at home is fine. There is nothing new to report. Luis was here for about a month, and he returned to Napa with Levi, Enrique, and Juan Montenegro. Enrique came back by himself fifteen days later and I asked him about Luis. He told me that Luis was at Luz's home. Enrique kept telling me every day that he was headed for San Francisco. I will find out and have someone let you know.

Tell Estrada that, yes, he did forget the potatoes.

Benicia F. de Vallejo

San Francisco

November 17, 1864[101]

Francisca,

I have returned here again to consult with Brooks about several matters and also to send $110 to Ula. He asked me for the money. I sent the money with Don Ramón de Zaldo because I know that Ula likes him.[102] If Ula can return, he most likely will do so either with Don Ramón or on the next steamer.

If you receive this letter in time, send Napoleón to me so he can tell me everything and also take some sweets for the girls.

Give everyone a kiss.

M. G. Vallejo

---

100. BANC MSS 76/79c, box 1, folder 19, TBL.

101. Madie Brown Emparán Research Collection, 9-42-243, Sonoma State Historic Park.

102. Ramón de Zaldo was a native of Spain who was involved in a variety of legal activities assisting the attempts of Californios to defend their land claims in the 1850s and after. Shuck, *Bench and Bar*, 545.

San Francisco
November 19, 1864[103]

Francisca,

I received your letter and I'm happy that you are doing well with the boys. Napoleón arrived and he'll be going to El Pájaro for a week. Tell Jim to lease the house to Dr. Waslet, as best he can, and to take care of the family until Nap. returns.

I think I'll be able to sell El Pájaro for 14,000 pesos. I'll have to use half of the money to make payments in Sonoma, and the rest of the money is for some business with Madden in order to save the vineyards at Lachryma Montis and Quiquiriquí, if that is possible.

Give the girls a kiss.

M. G. Vallejo

Fortunately, the San Cayetano matter was being resolved, and Vallejo hoped that the resolution would give him access to greater funds. In the meantime, he stayed in contact with Vega, who remained in San Francisco. Uladislao finally returned in December.

San Cayetano
November 27, 1864[104]

Francisca,

I arrived at this place eight days ago, which is to say, I left San Francisco with Napoleón. Tomorrow we will leave for Monterey, weather permitting. As soon as I finish settling the accounts of Juan Antonio's estate, I'll leave Monterey and return home. I wrote to Ula from San Francisco and told him to come back with Don Ramón de Zaldo, who took some of General Vega's papers with him and plans to go and see Señor Juárez. The general was specifically charged with seeing Ula and bringing him back. I also spoke with the owners of the steamer. They told me they would bring Ula back if he wanted to return to California. The other day I sent Ula's letters to Platón so that he can send them to you and the girls.

Today, Saturday, there was a very strong south wind that practically blew the house away. It has caused so much damage everywhere. It was a south wind that brought rain. The rain has caused the river to swell tremendously, but everyone is very happy because it finally has rained.

---

103. C-B 441, box 1, folder 4, TBL.
104. C-B 441, box 1, folder 4, TBL.

Juan Antonio Vallejo.
*Courtesy of California State
Parks, Sonoma Barracks.*
No. 243-x-3452.

Estrada really wants to send the potatoes but unfortunately the steamer *Salinas* is not making trips to San Francisco at this time because it is being repaired.

So that you wouldn't be all alone at home with the family, I begged Mr. Pickett to spend a few days there. Since Nap. is returning with Mr. P., I'm sending more sweets with him and I'm sending you <u>a little yellow ring</u>.[105]

Yours,
M. G. Vallejo

P.S. How is Natalia? Give my regards to her, and also to Jovita, Lulú, María, and Jim. It's raining, the river is swollen, and it's already Sunday so the letters can't be put in the mail.

Sonoma
December 5, 1864[106]

Guadalupe,

I've just received your letter in which you tell me that you have entrusted my compadre Don Ramón de Zaldo to look for Ula. God willing, he will find him. Natalia and Jovita aren't in Sonoma. They left for Vallejo over a week ago and Platón hasn't sent me any letters. Luisa and María are fine. As always, I'm having chest problems. I've had the pain for a week, but as they say, the old ox is never

---

105. Probably a gold ring.
106. Madie Brown Emparán Research Collection, 9-42-243, Sonoma State Historic Park.

lacking any ticks. It's necessary to put up with the pain because we are all going to die from some illness or another. It is known that Sergeant Berreyesa has died.[107]

Everyone in Sonoma is very happy because it's raining a lot. The ravines are filled with water, so is the creek. Everyone is waiting for the rain to stop in order to begin plowing. Jim says for you not to worry because he's taking good care of everything. He told Pedro to give the vines a good pruning and not to leave too much fruit on them because it will go to waste.

I received the yellow ring, as well as the sweets. Pickett is very happy here. Lulú, María, and I send you many hugs and kisses as a thank-you for your nice gifts. When you and Napoleón return, don't come on the steamer because it's very windy now. Tell Estrada that as soon as you finish the business in Salinas not to forget the potatoes, because he has told me that the potatoes from Pájaro are so good. He also told me that the beans are very delicious and that just mentioning them made his mouth water. I haven't been able to forget that.

School for the girls has finished. I promised to take them to Napa so they could play with their Aunt Luz's girls. If you don't want me to go, let me know, because they are coming for me this Saturday. Avril was here for a few days keeping me company. I asked him about Luis Leese, and he told me that Luis was at your niece Marina's rancho. I don't know what the name of the rancho is now. Luis is already here.

Napoleón: I am so happy that your Papá bought you some clothes. Take good care of them. Take good care of yourself and don't fall into the ocean. I can already picture you as you sink into the ocean. Be careful because the tide can rise all of a sudden and the place where you were standing just moments ago can now be filled with water.

Benicia de Vallejo

Sonoma
December 10, 1864[108]

Guadalupe,

Everyone here is fine. Napoleón arrived here without any problem, but he has some very bad news. Platón and General Vega are very ill. Tell me what has happened. Don't hide anything from me. I'm very sad about Platón because he is my son and I'm sad about General Vega because he is our beloved friend. I love the general as much as if he were one of our sons. Give him my best regards.

---

107. José de los Santos Berreyesa, who had been a sergeant at San Francisco and Sonoma, and who was then living in Martínez in Contra Costa County, died on October 30, 1864. Bancroft, *History of California*, 2:718; *Find a Grave* index, accessed through Ancestry.com.

108. Madie Brown Emparán Research Collection, 9-42-243, Sonoma State Historic Park.

And you, how are you? Are you well?
If you see Doña Carolina, give her my love.

                                                            Benicia de Vallejo

San Francisco
December 12, 1864[109]

Francisca,

  Napoleón already told you the reason why I returned to San Francisco. General
Vega was very ill, and he was extremely anxious to see me before he got worse so
that he could entrust me with taking care of some private matters. Even though
he was much improved when I arrived, he was still determined to trust me with
the responsibility of taking care of some very valuable property he has in the state
of Sinaloa. I'm supposed to arrange the best possible terms of sale regarding the
property while ensuring the best possible advantages for both of us. I'll have to take
possession of the property, which includes the land as well as personal property,
houses, horses, cattle, etc. The land needs to be measured by a surveyor. Maps
of the boundaries need to be prepared. Any other property that needs to be sold
will also require that type of assessment by a surveyor. As soon as the land titles
are formalized, if I can't go back, it's more than likely that I'll see if Platón can go
and fulfill two objectives. The first would be to take possession of the land, and
the second to see if he would like to settle in one of the many beautiful cities in
that state. Everyone assures me that within three or four years Platón could make
a fortune there. He could also establish his reputation as a doctor since there are
very few doctors in that country. In any case, it would be very good for him and
for me, too. Everyone who is familiar with the property I'm referring to says it is
extremely beautiful. But it requires an energetic and intelligent person to make
the best use of it under the present circumstances in which the country finds itself.
Undoubtedly, the prosperity of the country will take off in an extraordinary manner
in the areas of agriculture and mining. Because immigration will greatly increase, it
will be necessary to prepare the land before the influx of families coming to settle
there can begin.[110]

  It is very probable that Uladislao will be arriving in three or four days on the
steamer coming from Mexico. Don Ramón de Zaldo was entrusted with bringing
him back. I'm almost certain that he'll be coming this week if he didn't accompany
Uladislao to where President Juárez is located, which could have happened. In any

---

109. C-B 441, box 1, folder 4, TBL.
110. Neither Mariano Guadalupe nor Platón went to Sinaloa.

event, if nothing has happened to Ula, he will arrive on another steamer with D. Ramón. Poor Ula, he so hoped to wear the Mexican uniform. But at least he has gained some experience and will have seen that the world is very demanding and that dreams are not realized that easily.

Take care of the children, give everyone a kiss, and write to me.

Yours,
M. G. Vallejo

San Francisco
December 14, 1864[111]

Francisca,

Day before yesterday I wrote to let you know about Ula's arrival from the coast of Mexico. I've kept him here for two days because I wanted to know about the goings-on in that part of the world. But the poor boy is so weak, so ill, and so crestfallen that I was afraid he might get worse if he stayed here any longer. So I sent him home by way of Vallejo so that Platón can give him some medicine and also to give him the opportunity to visit with his sisters. In addition, he wouldn't be able to receive the appropriate care here. The extremely damp weather in San Francisco would be very harmful to him.

The setbacks and misfortunes he suffered for the cause of Mexico and her forefathers, as well as the calamities and hardships he suffered during that five-month period, are very profound and more than enough for him to have acquired necessary worldly experience. He left here strong and healthy, filled with illusions and patriotic zeal, and capable of causing wonderment in the minds of the coldest souls. But his hopes were dashed by the treachery and evil of monstrous men capable of corrupting not just simple people but also even the most corrupt and clever of individuals. Ula, nevertheless, has conducted himself as a man of honor. He has stood on the side of justice, honor, duty, and patriotism, setting an example of bravery and good sense, which above everything else brings him much honor, now and always. His sacrifice and selflessness are public and well known. After engaging in battle he was taken prisoner and deported. He now is returning to his family home, practically at death's door. Poor Ula! Good Ula! I now love him more than ever. I believe you will feel the same way.

My best to Mr. Pickett. Give Lulú and María a kiss.

Yours,
M. G. Vallejo

---

111. C-B 441, box 1, folder 4, TBL.

A few days ago I was counting up the change I received whenever I bought something. I think I sent that money to María and Lulú with Napoleón, but I can't quite remember. Ask Nap.

Brooks & Whitney
San Francisco
December 16, 1864[112]

Francisca,

Right now, at 12 o'clock, I received your letter dated the 11th. General Vega is now well and he sends you his best. Platón is also fine, even though I haven't been able to see him. But I do keep looking for him. I'm in semi-seclusion, that is to say, I'm in a room known only to a few friends. We are making arrangements with General Vega regarding the property that he and his family have in Sinaloa. Some people, big talkers who never seem to be lacking, think this is a bad idea. But everything is as it was before.

I imagine that Ula is probably back in Sonoma by now. I already wrote to you about this. I sent him by way of Vallejo. Mr. Pickett sent me a complaint that was lodged against you. He says that he has protested over and over again because some orange trees have been removed and placed in other areas. He says that the people who removed the trees also took some of them.

Take care of Mr. Pickett. He is a very good friend of the family. Kiss the children and give my best to everyone.

Yours,
M. G. Vallejo

---

112. Madie Brown Emparán Research Collection, 9-42-243, Sonoma State Historic Park.

CHAPTER 3

New Family Horizons
and Challenges
1865–1870

*I*n January 1865, Vallejo left California with John Frisbie on a trip to the East Coast. The precise purpose of the trip is unclear, although it apparently related to a business venture Frisbie was hoping to develop. There also was some urgency to the trip, for Frisbie's wife Epifania was six months pregnant when she left to accompany them on the trip.

Vallejo had never been out of California, so the trip was eye-opening for him. The twenty-seven-day ocean voyage was, in and of itself, an experience. In a letter to his children from New York, he told them, "When I return home I will tell you about the many things I saw, especially about the man who fell into the ocean and was immediately eaten by sharks right before our very eyes. The sharks follow the steamer and circle around it waiting for something to fall into the water so they can eat it. They are very large and very fierce."[1]

The trip was extensive. When they arrived in New York toward the end of January, Vallejo's reaction was typical for a Californian arriving in the northeastern part of the United States in the middle of winter: "The cold in this country is intolerable." He continued, "The only way to come to terms with it is by having the pleasure of watching a large number of men and women ice skate in Central Park. This frozen park is loved by everyone."[2] On January 31, Vallejo and Frisbie

1. M.G.V. to Napoleón, Lulú, and María, March 23, 1865, C-B 441 FILM, reel 4, 160–61, TBL.
2. On Sunday, January 29, the *New York Times* reported, "The week ending Saturday has been the coldest week of the season, and Friday night the coldest night of the week. The thermometer at Delatour's stood, at 7 1/2 o'clock yesterday morning, at five degrees below zero."

(*above*) *Central Park, The Lake*, ca. 1862, by Currier and Ives. Vallejo complained that the lake was frozen during his 1865 visit to New York City.
Courtesy of the Library of Congress. No. 90715718.
(*below*) U.S. Capitol building, 1865.
Courtesy of the Library of Congress. No. 2016852433.

took a train to Washington, D.C. This was his first time traveling by train, and he was amazed at the speed by which trains traveling in opposite directions on adjacent tracks passed each other. He told Platón, "Along the way we encountered many trains that were headed to New York as if they were 'bats out of hell.' It's frightening to see such things. Fifty miles per hour! To find myself a foot away from something that produces a noise I only heard for an instant and then it was gone in a flash!" In Washington he visited the Capitol and said, "I can't help but admire its grandeur. I sat on the same chairs that Washington and all the great men of the United States sat on."[3]

Vallejo remained in New York for the better part of two months while Frisbie was attending to business. Though none of his larger plans seem to have worked out, Frisbie was able to use some of his contacts to help Platón obtain a position with the Pacific Mail Steamship Company, which he believed would give the youth better employment opportunities than if he continued to work on a storeship of the U.S. Navy. Vallejo's impressions of the large cities of the East Coast were much like those of many other people on first encountering them. These urban centers seemed to be unbelievably noisy and crowded and full of unsociable people focused entirely on themselves. And the cold continued to bother him. In a letter to his children toward the end of March, he said, "I don't like this country because it is very cold. The sea turns to ice and so do the rivers. Ships and boats get wedged in and can't sail until the weather gets warmer."[4]

Washington, DC
February 6, 1865[5]

Francisca,

I have written to everyone, except you. Naturally, as is to be expected, they all probably showed you my letters so you know what I wrote to them. But I can't resist the temptation to paint you a picture of the way I've had to fend off the extreme cold in this country. You already know that I have never been able to tolerate, under any circumstances, wearing socks or undergarments made of wool. But now, in order to leave my room (which is a veritable sweat lodge) Frisbie has suggested that I adopt the following manner of dressing: two pairs of thick woolen socks, two thick woolen undershorts, and two thick woolen undershirts, all worn at the same time. And on top of these clothes I must wear heavy pants, a heavy winter coat, and extremely thick boots. Dressed in this manner I'm forced to stand in a

3. All quotes in this paragraph are from M.G.V. to Platón, February 2, 1865, C-B 441 FILM, reel 3, 30–31, TBL.
4. M.V.G. to Napoleón, Lulú, and María, March 23, 1875, C-B 441 FILM, reel 4, 160–61, TBL.
5. DLG-V 45, letter 4.

perpendicular fashion, which makes me feel like a sword in a sheath. Frisbie says this is what is fashionable here. The funny thing is that I don't even recognize myself. I feel like I'm one of those people in the circus who stand on top of giant balls and try very hard to keep their balance. In addition to this ensemble I must add a stovepipe hat. I either go out dressed in this manner or stay in my room where I'm burning up from the heat of a coal stove. Can you imagine how mortified I feel and how ridiculous I look? I am this giant bundle that seems to be possessed by the devil. That is how I'm adapting to everything. But it infuriates me that I look like a loaded-down pack mule. It hurts my pride!

In addition to the thick boots, I wear rubber shoes on top of them so I won't slip on the ice in the streets. If I only wore the boots I would be in danger of continuously falling flat on my face, which happened to me before I adopted those rubber shoes. Doesn't this seem very odd to you? Do you think this is the price I have to pay for some sin I committed in the past? And who in God's name convinced me to come to this country in the winter? In the end, I'm just so . . . f***ed.[6] Forgive my use of that word, but I can't find a more appropriate one. So old, so foolish, so conceited, and so proud (up to a certain point). I look like some sort of rotund mound without any body shape. Who is making me do this? Nobody. I am to blame.

If truth be told, I have seen a lot in the short amount of time I've been here, especially during this winter season. But I still haven't seen anything that impresses me as much as the <u>Capitol</u> building, Central Park in New York, and how cold it is in this country. Everyone admires this country, saying it is the leader of invention and of great businesses. I, too, admire this country but for other <u>reasons</u>, which I cannot put down on paper. I will explain it to you some day. From a distance I have seen the Supreme Court judges, who caused my ruin by rejecting my claim to Rancho Suscol, without justice or an ostensibly honest reason. What a disgrace! What cruelty! <u>But this is the price to pay for the progress of invention and for great businesses</u>.

It's possible (if I don't die) that as the weather improves I will be able to tell you a thousand wonderful things about this country. Even though everything is completely frozen, I can see that the countryside, the rivers, bays, and cities must have a grandiose appearance. The throng of people from New York to Washington is frightening. Based on that I'm assuming that in the spring it will be worse. California's climate, however, is that of the gods, and those who live there are blessed. This comparison can only be made by experiencing both regions.

I feel very confident knowing Platón is with you. Do the best you can. Don't be envious of me because I have come here. Take care of our children, don't be jealous of me. I can assure you that I don't feel like doing anything because of the <u>figure</u> I cut. And I will add my integrity and manhood to that.

---

6. Vallejo uses the word *pendejo.*

Give my regards to everyone. Take good care of yourself so that when I return you will give me a kiss filled with love and peace at Lachryma Montis in California. Do you like that idea?

I am always your,
Guadalupe

5th Avenue Hotel
New York
March 20, 1865[7]

Francisca,

I am still alive, but I don't know how I have been able to tolerate how cold it is in this country. However, a few days ago the temperature improved, and I feel like going outside for a few moments to get some fresh air, but I must stay bundled up, otherwise I would be exposing myself to the illnesses that are so easily acquired here.

This city of New York is an immense place where everybody walks up and down the streets without knowing one another and without speaking to anyone. The hustle and bustle and the confusion are such that the noise level is extremely loud. You have to speak by shouting, and even then, you cannot hear each other. I am tired of the trains. They run constantly, day and night, and are so crowded with people. One is scared to ride on the trains because so many people are killed in the collisions that occur every day. Sometimes, when the trains travel on bridges over estuaries, the bridges collapse, and the passengers drown in their seats. At other times, two trains meet up as they are going down the same track. It is horrible to see how the people and the cars are ripped to shreds. This happened on a train that was going to Washington and, fortunately, I was spared. I have learned my lesson.

I have thought a lot about you and the family. However, when I realize it is necessary to travel on a steamer from San Francisco to here, six thousand miles in the middle of the ocean, and remembering that you get seasick so easily, I am happy that you are in our little house in Sonoma. I am extremely sorry that I have come here. I fear having to return by way of that damned ocean. It is so vast and the trip is so difficult. The only reason I made the decision to go so far away and leave my family behind was because I needed to see if I could arrange my business dealings with Frisbie and work together with him. I hope everything will work out for me, and if not, I will skin that mean bastard.[8] At least I will have seen something I can tell you about. But I don't want you to think that I am very impressed by what I

---

7. C-B 441, box 1 folder 5, TBL.
8. *Pelo mi indina rata.*

The elevated railways of New York, by Charles Decaux.
Courtesy of the New York Public Library, Miriam and Ira D. Wallach
Division of Art, Prints, and Photographs: Picture Collection. ID b17095064.

have seen, which is more than I expected before coming here. The country is an immense plain with ravines that are lower than the plain itself, without a single hill or mountain, filled with towns. It's true! I don't know why the sight of such a large plain is offensive to me. All the trees in the entire country are very small, similar to the two little oak trees in front of the henhouse. It looks like an orchard. The land is very arid. There are only small pine trees and oaks. The most beautiful thing I have seen is the Bay of New York at night. It is quite lovely because the bay is surrounded by more than two million inhabitants. It is a very small bay. All the cities are illuminated with gas lights that reflect on the water. In addition, thousands upon thousands of steamers also travel with lights. Just imagine that you are looking at a sky filled with stars on a dark night and there are also stars below, on the water. This is truly very beautiful. The fruit here has no taste. The grapes taste like boiled eggs.

The steamer leaves today and I would like to leave as well. I don't like this place, nor do I like the climate. It's true that there are very impressive things here, but I don't like them. Everything here boils down to being money hungry. I think the people are insane. It is a terrible state of confusion. Friendship is only out of self-interest, and I didn't think of it like that before. Just thinking about that makes me unhappy. The madness they exhibit with regard to money is rabid <u>desperation</u>.

Take care of the children and take care of yourself as well. I sent quite a bit of money for you with Platón. I hope it has been of use to you.

Platón already has a good position. We still have poor Ula to worry about. In a long letter I wrote to him, I gave him a lot of advice, primarily on the matter you told me about when I was home.[9]

Goodbye, see you in about sixty days.

M. G. Vallejo

VALLEJO VISITED NIAGARA FALLS AND BOSTON TOWARD THE END OF March and the beginning of April. He was back in New York around the second week of April. The surrender of Lee's Confederate army on April 9 and the assassination of President Lincoln on April 14 disrupted Vallejo's and Frisbie's plans. They were still in New York when Lincoln's funeral procession passed through the city on April 26, and Vallejo watched the spectacle from the window of the Fifth Avenue Hotel where he was staying. The experience overwhelmed him, as he wrote in a letter to his daughter Natalia:

> In the end, when Sr. Lincoln's body was brought to the city, he was given funerary honors such as the like no other person in the world has received. The funeral procession was twelve miles long and 8,000 men were marching in formation. The number of spectators was between 900,00 and 1,000,000 souls. It was stupendous and magnificent. What stood out most was that there were no disturbances among such a multitude of people. As the catafalque passed by, everyone removed their hat in silent respect. Countless numbers of bands played funeral marches. And there was a profound silence among the men and women who wore a black armband as a symbol of mourning. Flags were at half-staff and cannons were fired every thirty seconds. Everything, everything was very solemn. The procession passed in front of the Fifth Avenue Hotel and lasted six hours.[10]

The news of Lincoln's assassination reached the West Coast by telegraph. Adela, married for less than two years, found herself sympathizing with Mary Todd Lincoln. She wrote her mother: "The flags are still at half-mast in honor of Lincoln; the assassin and his companion have already been killed. When Papá returns just think of all the stories he will tell us about what he saw and heard at that time. It is unbelievable to think that Papá would have been there and would have seen such

---

9. In a letter to Platón, Vallejo said, "Tell Ula that he has never been on my mind as much as he is now and that I am hopeful regarding things in Mexico. I believe that his second trip to Mexico might be very favorable." M.G.V. to Platón, February 2, 1865, C-B 441 FILM, reel 3, 30–31, TBL.

10. M.G.V. to Natalia, May 15, 1865, C-B 441 FILM, reel 4, 111–13, TBL.

a tragedy. I doubt that he regrets his trip to the United States. Poor Mrs. Lincoln. She is very ill, almost out of her mind, and frightened. She still has not been able to leave the White House."[11]

Frisbie's business hopes apparently did not materialize. He most likely indicated to Vallejo that the chaotic nature of public affairs stemming from the end of the Civil War and the assassination of President Lincoln were largely responsible for his lack of success.

New York
April 10, 1865[12]

Francisca,

From Fanita's letters I have learned that you have been a bit ill, but that it isn't anything serious. I hope you are completely well by now. When you receive this letter, I will already be in Panama on my way back to California. My plan is to leave here on the 23rd of this month. Since I will be leaving soon, I don't want to go into too much detail. I will just say that I have visited many large cities and I have seen many things I have liked and admired. I will tell you all about it when I see you.

Take care of the children and give them my regards. Tell them I will see all of them soon if I don't drown during the voyage.

I am,
M.G.V.

5th Avenue Hotel
New York
April 30, 1865[13]

Francisca,

Finally, on May 15 I will be leaving for California, returning from visiting this country that I admire but do not love with my heart because the weather, just like the people in general, have treated me very badly and have been the cause of my ruin and that of my family. You already understand what I am saying.

So many things have happened since I wrote to you from Washington that I would need a ream of paper to tell you everything. And since I will be leaving soon, I will wait until I get home.

---

11. Adela to F.B.C.V., April 28, 1865, C-B 441, box 4, folder 1, TBL.
12. C-B 441, box 1, folder 5, TBL.
13. C-B 441, box 1, folder 4, TBL.

Funeral Honors to President Lincoln, from *Frank Leslie's Illustrated Newspaper*,
May 13, 1865, 120–21. *Courtesy of the Lincoln Financial Foundation Collection.*

I hope that you and the children are well. Wishing you all good health, I am your
M. G. Vallejo

Give my greetings to Don Pepe.

5th Avenue Hotel
New York
May 28, 1865[14]

Francisca,

It is now going on one month since we should have left here for California, but
so many significant things have happened with regard to public issues that everything has been turned upside down, paralyzing the business matters, which when
we first arrived had every sign of being handled successfully. But the war and the
assassination of President Lincoln have caused everything to be delayed, thus

14. C-B 441, box 1, folder 5, TBL.

Fifth Avenue Hotel, New York City, 1892, by Strohmeyer & Wyman.
Courtesy of the Library of Congress. LC-DIG-stereo-1507698.

detaining us longer than I wished to be here. Nevertheless, perhaps I will be able to leave by the first of June. I am tired and even more bored with this country. It is true that the weather has changed and the countryside looks better, but I don't like this climate. The air is bad and the people worse, which makes me tired of everything. I can no longer take care of my health.

I have hopes that I will be leaving here soon. If I should have the need to return some day, it will be in a very different manner: <u>you soon will understand why I am saying this to you.</u>

John Bidwell. *Courtesy of
the Library of Congress,
James Wadworth Family Papers.*
LC-MSS-44297–33–066.

I need to write to Natalia; her letter is waiting to be answered.
Kiss the children.

M. G. Vallejo

P.S. I wrote to Don Pepe quite a while ago and he didn't answer me.

WHEN VALLEJO RETURNED HOME HE FOUND THAT PLATÓN'S POSITION
as a ship's surgeon with the Pacific Mail Steamship Company was secure. Uladislao,
however, was still recovering from his ill-fated trip to Mazatlán and spending most
of his time at Lachryma Montis. Frisbie and Vallejo tried to lobby Congressman
John Bidwell to obtain a position in the U.S. Army for Uladislao, but nothing came
of those efforts. Vallejo maintained contact with Plácido Vega, who was still in
San Francisco attempting to raise arms and funds for the Juárez government in
exile. Vallejo told Andrónico, "I have been helping General Vega with his business
affairs here and in Mexico."[15]

Most important, Vallejo found that the interest payments on the mortgage of
Lachryma Montis were quickly becoming more than he could afford. In January
1866 he had to deed Lachryma Montis and its vineyard to Thomas Madden. He

15. Platón to F.B.C.V., October 3, 1865, C-B 441, box 6, folder 12; M.G.V. to Andrónico, March 17, 1866, C-B 441 FILM,
reel 4, 114, both in TBL.

Pacific Mail Steam Ship Company's steamer *San Francisco*, 1853.
Reproduced by permission of the Huntington Library, San Marino, California.
John Haskell Kemble Collection. prij HK 00469.

was very unhappy with this arrangement. Money also continued to be a concern for Francisca, who was caring for Napoleón, Luisa, and María at home. Although Platón was doing decently well as a ship's surgeon, the constant voyages that were part of his job meant that he was more absent from home than present and consequently unable to provide much in the way of financial assistance. By the end of 1866, Vega had gone back to Mexico and Uladislao had accompanied him. They traveled to El Paso del Norte in Chihuahua,[16] which was serving as Juárez's temporary capital after he had been forced progressively farther north by French advances. Uladislao enlisted in the Republican army.

Napoleón, along with Luisa and María, was in public school in Sonoma. In March 1866, J. M. Sibley, a teacher at the public school, wrote Vallejo to inform him that Napoleón had been "suspended from the public school for a period of two weeks." Sibley continued, "The cause of this suspension is his infringement of two cardinal rules of the school that forbid fighting and profanity." Sibley told Vallejo that, since this was Napoleón's first offense and since there had been some provocation, this punishment was "as lenient as possible."[17]

---

16. El Paso del Norte was renamed Ciudad Juárez in 1888.
17. J. M. Sibley to M.G.V., March 15, 1866, C-B 441, box 5, folder 46, TBL.

Vallejo
February 9, 1866[18]

Francisca,

Ever since I left Sonoma and arrived here, I've been sick with that damned rheumatism in my left shoulder and pain in my ribs. It's gotten to the point that I can barely move. Adela and Fannie have been taking care of me and applying a potion of very strong medicines to take away the pain. But the potion burned me and some skin has fallen off on the side where I have the pain. I'm finally feeling better, so much so that I was thinking of leaving for Sonoma today with Eleazar Frisbie.[19] If it doesn't rain tomorrow, it's possible that I'll leave with Eduardo.

Platón was here for two hours and returned to San Francisco in a hurry. He will return in thirty days, and by then it would be good if Jovita were here.

Benicia continues to improve.[20] Frisbie will leave today for New York. He is taking Fanita with him.

Señora Blackman will go to New York when Platón returns.

I have a banana tree root that can be planted in a wet and warm spot. I hope it bears fruit.

Adela, Fannie, and all the little ones send you greetings.

Take care of the children. Give my regards to Andrónico, Ula, and Nap.[21]

M.G.V.

Sunday
April 29, 1866[22]

Guadalupe:

Wherever you are, wherever you are living, I haven't received any news from you since you left home, not even once. Perhaps you haven't written to me at all, or maybe the letters got lost. Or it may be because you no longer love me. You need to come home so we can talk for a bit. If you can't come, let me know so I won't be waiting for you. Whenever you can come, please come. The house is completely changed. We have taken all the furniture out of your room and replaced it with other furniture.

---

18. C-B 441, box 1, folder 5, TBL.

19. Eleazar is a brother of John B. Frisbie who had come to California with the New York Volunteers and settled in the North Bay region. Bancroft, *History of California*, 3:750; Munro-Fraser, *History of Solano County*, 349.

20. Probably a reference to Cynthia Benicia Frisbie, an eight-year-old daughter of John and Epifania Frisbie.

21. Andrónico would periodically offer piano lessons at Lachryma Montis to young students in the Sonoma area. Emparán, *Vallejos*, 251.

22. BANC MSS 76/79c, box 1, folder 17, TBL.

The rest of your things are in the room. The other rooms are set up and ready to receive visitors. We now have a little Fanita. Jovita is here. She is the one who manages everything in the house from top to bottom so that I don't have to do anything.

Napoleón and María were sick but they are fine now.

Guadalupe: I don't want to trouble you about anything, but I am forced to do so. I don't have any money to buy what we need. You know that no one can be without shoes and other things. Napoleón is practically naked.

Guadalupe: I had written this letter several days ago but I didn't send it to you because I thought you would be coming home but . . . you were very busy.

San Francisco
April 30, 1866[23]

Francisca,

This Sunday morning, I received the letter you wrote yesterday. In spite of it being so short, the letter is very significant to me because I understand it. In the first place, I am here just as the magnetic force is always attracted to the pole. I came to San Francisco with a specific objective, or rather, to receive about four hundred pesos that a man from Pájaro owes me. He has not sent me the money, nor has he come or written to me. I planned to come for three days, and I have already been here for more than sixty. I came all dressed up and I am still that way. Of course, every day I am thinking about heading back to Sonoma, and each day there are new obstacles. General Vega has begged me to help him expedite his departure to Mexico, and I can't abandon him. It is true that nothing can be done without money, even though there is some hope this week. That is how I have been existing for a day, a week, a month, two months. Every day is filled with anguish, afflictions, increasing distress. My soul suffers as much as it can endure. When I see you, I will tell you a thousand things that, even though they might seem incredible, are true.

Platón arrived while I was reading your letter in my room. I was very sad. He gave me twenty-five pesos for me to send to you, and I can confirm that it is a gift from your son. Poor Platón is very busy, and he feels bad that he has not paid you a visit. There are so many sick people to care for, which makes it very difficult to travel up to Sonoma. He said he can barely go to Vallejo, not even for a short time.

I have not had the heart to abandon General Vega during his time of difficulties, nor can I refrain from helping him as much as I possibly can.

I will see you and the children soon.

Your,
M.G.V.

23. C-B 441, box 1, folder 5, TBL.

P.S. Take my books and papers up to your room even if that means piling them up in a closet.

On February 12, 1867, the Casa Grande on the Sonoma Plaza was destroyed in a fire. Even though the family had not lived in the house for several years, it contained a large amount of documentary material that Vallejo had collected from his father as well as through his own extensive military and political activities since the 1820s. In the house there also was a manuscript that Vallejo was composing on the history of California before the U.S. takeover.

During the first decade of American rule, Vallejo had become acutely aware of the generalized disdain for Mexico and Mexicans that the newly arrived Americans to California felt for them. He therefore decided to compose a history of pre-U.S. California. This was his first attempt at writing such a history. He mentioned to a friend that he was doing this so that the Americans might realize that "when they took over this country, there was a civilization and men who belonged to a race equal to, if not better than theirs."[24] The manuscript and a good amount of documentary material that stemmed from Vallejo's father were destroyed in the blaze. Francisca described the conflagration in a letter to Adela:

> On Monday, at 3:30 in the afternoon, the Casa Grande in Sonoma burned down. I cried as if one of my own children had died. [It was] the house in which we lived for so many years, the house that your Papá built with his own hands so that we could all live in it together. That is where you were raised, where you all left your marks and scribbles on the walls when you were little, along with your first attempts at handwriting. You remember that, don't you? As the house was burning I went to see it to say goodbye. I watched it burn for four hours. Napoleón and I were the only ones watching the fire burn down the house. Your father and your uncle Salvador refused to go. People from all over the valley were in the plaza. It seemed like a feast day and it got rowdy when they salvaged a barrel of brandy. The people were dying of thirst. Everybody drank the brandy, got drunk, and then they would race into the burning building. It was frightening to watch. They worked so hard and managed to save Laiden's store. It was a miracle that the barracks were spared. The people carried water to put out the fire and used one of those pumps that can throw water really far, but it was of no use. Some people got burned a bit and others twisted their knees, but it was nothing serious. The families who lived in the house were not able to take out anything of value, except for a few trinkets that weren't worth anything. Those are the types of things people save when they are scared.[25]

The fire forced Vallejo to discontinue his historical work.

---

24. M.G.V. to Anastasio Carrillo, December 19, 1866, DLG-V 54, letter 1.
25. F.B.C.V. to Adela, February 20, 1867, C-B 441 FILM, reel 4, 223–26, TBL; *Sonoma Democrat*, February 16, 1867.

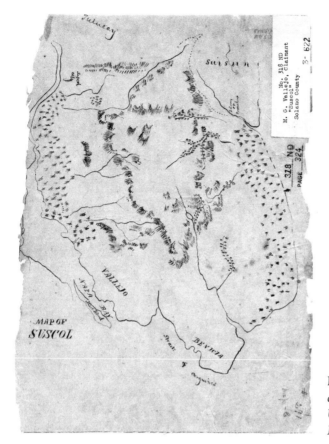

Map of Suscol, 1850. *Courtesy*
of The Bancroft Library,
University of California, Berkeley.
Land Case Map B-622.

In April 1867, Frisbie received a patent, or deed, from the federal government for the sections of Rancho Suscol he had purchased. This made his own financial situation somewhat more secure. But his reluctance to use that security to assist his father-in-law irritated Vallejo, who poured out his feelings in a letter to Frisbie's brother Levi. He undoubtedly hoped that Levi would pass that message on to his brother. Vallejo wrote:

> I saw in the newspapers that Frisbie and others have received patents, but Frisbie hasn't said a word about it to me, which is very strange. Perhaps one of these days he will remember that I do exist and that there is a "General Vallejo" who always has remembered him under any and all circumstances. He knows how much my family suffers. He conducts business, receives money, and totally forgets that "the fruits of one's labors" should be shared with the poor who have helped produce those fruits. But as such, that is the way of the world.[26]

26. *Napa County Reporter*, April 27, 1867; M.G.V. to Levi Frisbie, April 24, 1867, C-B 441 FILM, reel 4, 169–70, TBL.

Mission and College of Santa Clara, 1856, by Henry Miller.
Courtesy of Santa Clara University Archives and Special Collections.

Francisca shared these sentiments. In 1868 she wrote Frisbie: "You promised to give me 25 pesos each month. If you would do me the favor of taking 80 or 100 pesos out of the account and give them to Adela, that way she can pay a few small bills she is aware of and send me a few things that I greatly need. If you don't want to give me the money from that account, don't give me anything. Take the money, instead, from General Vallejo's account. There is no woman who suffers more than I do." Around the same time, she stated in a letter to Jovita, "Frisbie has finally shown his true colors. He owes your poor Papá money. We are at the point where we might lose the house. If that happens, who knows where we will live." In another letter to Platón, she called Frisbie "such a liar."[27]

In the meantime, Napoleón, who had told his mother a few months earlier that he was "teaching the same as first two classes in Catechism of the Vallejo Sunday School," entered the upper division at Santa Clara College.[28] Although Vallejo was happy that his son was receiving a good education, he was concerned about the type of religion the Italian Jesuits who staffed that institution were inculcating in the students. But Napoleón seemed to be enjoying himself. At the end of 1867 he sent his mother a letter in which he proudly stated that he had a leading role in a student drama production, which he termed "a grand display of our abilities on the stage."[29]

27. F.B.C.V. to Jovita, F.B.C.V. to Platón, and F.B.C.V. to Frisbie, all no month, 20, 1868, C-B 441 FILM, reel 4, 223–26, TBL.

28. Napoleón to F.B.C.V., March 31, 1867, C-B 441, box 6, folder 11, TBL (written in English). He described his excitement at getting ready to go to Santa Clara in that letter and in another letter to her the next day, April 1, 1867, C-B 441, box 6, folder 11, TBL.

29. Napoleón to F.B.C.V., December 15, 1867, C-B 441, box 6, folder 11, TBL.

(left) Platón Vallejo. *Courtesy of the Autry Museum of the
American West, Los Angeles. No. 2002.1.5.69.*
(right) Lily Wiley. *Courtesy of the Autry Museum of the
American West, Los Angeles. No. 2002.1.2.34.*

The family did have reason to celebrate, for in November 1867 Platón married
Lily Wiley, a native of New York whose sister was married to a Sacramento River
boat captain. The wedding was held at Trinity Episcopal Church in San Francisco,
with a subsequent Catholic ceremony in Vallejo. Platón resigned his position with
the Pacific Mail Steamship Company, and he and Lily moved to Vallejo. There he
opened his own medical practice.

Lachryma Montis
Sonoma
June 5, 1867[30]

Francisca,

   Day before yesterday the heat was intense, suffocating, and intolerable. Today's
heat is almost deadly. I don't know how every living thing here hasn't died, or how
everything that has died by virtue of the sun's rays hasn't caught on fire. As for me,
I'm telling you, I thought I would end up dead today, before having the chance to

---

30. BANC MSS 76/79c, box I, folder 25, TBL.

Trinity Episcopal Church, San Francisco, by Carleton E. Watkins.
Courtesy of the California Room, California State Library, Sacramento, California. FL *166589.*

write this letter. My head, blood, and heart (made worse by my other problems) are driving me crazy. And it is all because of today's terrible heat. In the end, I hope that it hasn't been the same in Vallejo and that everyone who is gathered together there can be of comfort to each other. Even the bath water is hot, so hot that I wasn't able to bathe, which is unbearable. It seems that there's been some sort of revolution on the part of the Geysers or Calistoga.[31]

31. The Geysers are a large geothermal field about fifty-five miles north of Sonoma that produced a series of hot springs in the North Bay region around Calistoga. The *Petaluma Weekly Argus* for June 6, 1867 noted, "The drying winds which prevailed for more than a week during the latter part of May seem to have taken all the moisture from the earth. And as a consequence, grains seems to be drying out and presents a rather sickly appearance." This warm and dry weather apparently made the hot springs too warm for Vallejo.

I'm here waiting for a response from Frisbie to the brief letter I wrote him. He should answer right away. I wrote him the other day, when I went to San Francisco. He had Madden ask me to write the letter. Frisbie told Madden and Fevis to buy this property in his name since I wouldn't be able to do it. I wrote the letter as a test. If Frisbie doesn't do what he is supposed to do and behave like a gentleman, <u>it will be necessary to take appropriate steps, and the first one will be for you and the entire family to be ready to leave Frisbie's house immediately</u>. Until that happens, it is necessary to begin preparing Nap., Lulú, and María so that they won't think they will be returning to school for the time being. We will return here as soon as <u>each person pays</u> the debts he owes.

Very bad habits do exist. When a man is a swindler and a thief, he habitually does both things. Sometimes he even believes he isn't doing anything wrong.

There are men who habitually lie. They even believe that the lies they have fabricated are true. There are women who believe they are pregnant because <u>they slept with a man</u>. They swear they can feel the child's movements from the first month until the ninth. They make preparations for the baby up until the moment they are supposed to give birth!! They arrange for a <u>midwife</u>, a bed, and more. But when the <u>moment of truth</u> arrives, there . . . is . . . nothing. There are some men who are entrusted with considerable amounts of property, for a very long period of time, with no questions asked. They become so familiar with the property that they believe it belongs to them. Can you believe it? Have you ever seen such a thing? Well, I've seen it many times, so much so that I actually doubt my own existence. Such is the power of experience.

A crazy man said,

> "I had nothing,
> I have everything
> Because of an obsession.
> What could it be?"

I now want to die. In any case, my life is getting shorter (July 7, [I will be] 59 years old), but I won't die of old age.

Give my best to everyone.

M.G.V.

July 1867[32]

Guadalupe,

Jim says that he's sending Pedro with the pipes, along with the 100 gallons you told me about in your letter of July 7. Jim says he will take care of everything else you told me about, in confidence, in the other brief letter.

---

32. BANC MSS 76/79c, box 1, folder 17, TBL.

Uladislao Vallejo, Jovita Vallejo
Haraszthy, and Napoleón Vallejo in
1868. *Courtesy of the Sonoma County
Library, Photographic Collection.*
cstr_pho 007333.

He already left. May God accompany him. Napoleón, María, and I are fine.

God willing, everything will go well for you in your business dealings. Don't worry so much. Do things with passion but also with joy.

Lachryma Montis
Sonoma
July 7, 1867[33]

Francisca,

I've just received a letter from Uladislao, along with his photograph, and some printed material. I'm sending it all to you so that everyone can read it. Ula complains that no one in the family writes to him. And he most likely has every reason to complain. When someone is far away from relatives and loved ones, it is very gratifying to receive letters from them. I only wish that Fanita, Adela, Napoleón, Lulú, and María would all write letters, beautiful letters, of course. They can send the letters to me. I will then send them to Ula. How happy he'll be to receive them! How proud he'll be to show them to his friends because he is so proud of his family! If only Frisbie could or would want to write to him, and the doctor, too. Each one could write him a brief letter.

I'll make sure that Attila and Natalia write to him as well.

Give my best to everyone.

M. G. Vallejo

---

33. C-B 441, box 1, folder 5, TBL.

I'm about to burst from anger. I've been quite ill today. My head feels like a volcano because of hunger, rage, and desperation. I don't know what to do. I very much fear that I'm going crazy. The fruit has shriveled up, toasted by the heat of the sun. The heat is intolerable. Jim hasn't appeared yet. He received the money for the barrels and pipes on the first of the month, but I haven't seen him. That's all that is needed to complete the project.

Lachryma Montis
Sonoma
July 9, 1867[34]

Francisca,

I've written you several letters, which were delivered by Adela, but I haven't received a response to any of them.

I haven't heard from Napoleón. Maybe he'll be staying in Santa Clara. I fear that there is some sort of intrigue with that boy. Nap hasn't written to me and I find that strange. Who knows if he is being advised by the priests or someone else in matters pertaining to religion, matters that I may not agree with or that may not be to my liking.

Perhaps my last letter to Nap frightened the priests. You know full well that religion is good when there is no fanaticism, unless it is for men who want to become priests or for those who want them to become priests. In that case, fanaticism is mandatory.[35] You haven't written to me, nor have Adela or Lulú. If I can leave tomorrow or day after tomorrow, I'll bring you the clothes you left on top of Lulú's bed.

Give my best to everyone.

M. G. Vallejo

VALLEJO WAS CONTINUING, AS HE HAD BEEN DOING FOR SOME YEARS, TO spend a considerable amount of time in San Francisco seeking a variety of ways to raise money. They all proved unsuccessful. His absences left Francisca at home with the children. With finances very uncertain, she developed and implemented plans to supply vegetables and eggs to various businesses in Sonoma as a way of

---

34. C-B 441, box 1, folder 5, TBL.

35. Napoleón became aware of his father's attitude toward the Santa Clara Jesuit priests. In a letter to his mother describing his father's visit to Santa Clara, he mentioned the priests and said "Papá can't stand the sight of them." Napoleón to F.B.C.V., April 20, 1868, C-B 441, box 6, folder 11, TBL.

raising money. She implemented these projects without consulting her husband and sought his approval only afterward. She also encouraged him, as strongly as she could, not to allow himself to become so consumed with the myriad business dealings he was trying to arrange in San Francisco.

Pine St. #318
San Francisco
February 6, 1868[36]

Francisca,

The day after I arrived from Sonoma, I had a very dangerous accident. As I was going down the stairs, the heel of my boot got tangled up in the fringe of the carpet and I tumbled backward, "body and soul," with a deadly force. I dislocated my left arm, elbow, knee, and hip bone. I've been in bed for eleven days. Yesterday I got up feeling much better.

Let me know if the butcher gave you the 50 pesos.

Give my regards to everyone.

M.G.V.

Napa
April 9, 1868[37]

Francisca,

Yesterday morning I received a telegram saying that Ana Bale was very ill and that she wanted to see me, so I traveled to Napa on the steamer. She passed away ten minutes before I arrived at the home of Don Luis Bruck.[38]

She will be buried tomorrow in the Napa cemetery.

Platón's wife Lily is quite ill with rheumatism.

The Vallejo family, in Vallejo, has recovered very well from the measles.[39] Frisbie is sick. Fannie, Adela, Jovita, and Lulú are well.

---

36. C-B 441, box 1, folder 5, TBL.

37. C-B 441, box 1, folder 5, TBL.

38. Ana Guadalupe Bale, born in 1849, was the daughter of Antonia Soberanes and English surgeon Edward Turner Bale. In the mid-1840s, Bale was involved in a dispute with Salvador Vallejo, who whipped him and was in return shot by Bale. He died in 1849. Louis Bruck owned the farm next to the Bale farm in Napa. San Francisco Solano Baptism 1698; Bancroft, *History of California*, 2:708; Vallejo, *Recuerdos*, 2:1133–36; Northrop, *Spanish–Mexican Families*, 2:271; *Napa County Reporter*, April 18, 1868.

39. Jovita described the measles the various children caught in a letter to her mother. Jovita to F.B.C.V., March 28, 1868, C-B 441, box 4, folder 28, TBL.

I was unable to go to Santa Clara, but I sent Napoleón four nice shirts, three undershirts, three undershorts, a dozen socks, a dozen handkerchiefs, a dozen collars, six ties, and some money.

Guadalupe Cooper broke his leg and is quite ill.

The court gave me permission to come and I will return soon.

Tell Salvador that if the rain ruins the corn we planted, it would be better to replant it.

Give María my regards.

M. G. Vallejo

Sonoma
December 2, 1868[40]

Guadalupe,

The letter that I asked Don Pepe to write for me was not intended to humiliate you, as you seem to think. My intentions were very good and pure. If I asked Don Pepe to write it for me, it was because I was very busy. And, you know full well that I don't know how to write very fast. I also never thought that what I said to you in the letter was to be kept secret from Don Pepe because you, yourself, in my presence, have said the same thing to him about the bath house. He is an old man who has known the family for many years, and he probably knows other secrets . . . and I will tell you again, there are no secrets in the letter I wrote to you, nor any bad intentions on my part, as you said in your letter. Because you are my husband, I was asking you for your advice, in case you wanted to give it to me or it made you happy to give it to me. At the same time, I also was trying to be of help to you in some way or another. That was my intention. It pains me, Guadalupe, that you greatly disapprove of even the slightest comment on my part or if I tell you that I want something. It never would occur to me in my wildest dreams to offend you or humiliate you. Guadalupe! Guadalupe! What little regard you have for me after living together for so many years. It is very obvious that you look at me with indifference, [even] after so many years that I have spent attending to you as a wife, a friend, and a companion. Do you believe that I wanted to humiliate you or do something that would be an insult to your honor or mine? Never! Never! If telling you about things that are needed and what the family is lacking is offensive to you, then what am I supposed to do? Always the same issues, always the same difficulties: I think one way and you think otherwise. I want to do things correctly, and you tell me I'm doing things wrong. So, which one of us right? As soon as I

---

40. C-B 441, box 1, folder 5, TBL.

realized that you didn't like my idea about the bath house, that is, that it didn't seem like a good idea to you, I didn't give it another thought. That was the end of it.

I am also going to tell you about the vegetable garden. I am delivering vegetables to the hotel, and eggs that the hens lay are going to the baker. I am informing you about this in this letter so that you will let me know whether or not you approve. I hadn't told you about this before because I didn't believe it would be necessary, but since you were so offended by the news about the bath house, that is why I am informing you now. If you don't like it, tell me, so I can stop making deliveries. I don't want you to think that I am also doing this to humiliate you. Don't think that I am so stupid, because if I wanted to humiliate you, there are any manner of ways in which I could so. But I am not planning on doing that, nor do I want to do that, because that is not who I am.

You tell me in your letter that you would like me to write about happy things and how I seem to want to make our life unbearable. But you are the one who makes your own life unbearable, and you do the same to mine. You blame me for any little thing I do, think, or want. Guadalupe: you need to view me in a different manner and not believe I am such a bad person. Don't disparage me so much, because you are only hurting yourself. It makes me so sad to think that you are so ill-disposed and angry with me for no reason. I am tired, sick, and angry because of this, and I can't find any solution. Let's leave all of this in God's hands, don't you think? When you come home, don't return angry. Come back happy because that is what I desire. Even though we are poor, if there is something you don't like, tell me so that I can do it the way you want. But don't mistreat me for no reason at all, because I can't put up with it. You are killing me; my heart is aching. I would rather die than see you angry.

Don't worry so much, manage your business dealings well, and don't get so upset if you can't get what you want. When you are able and your business dealings permit it, come and spend some time here, so that you can attend to the business matters here. It will also serve as a bit of a distraction for you. I think this would be good for you.

FAMILY ISSUES CONTINUED TO COMPLICATE THE RELATIONSHIP BETWEEN Mariano Guadalupe and Francisca. She often went to Benicia or Vallejo to help her daughters take care of their own children. By the end of the 1860s, Epifania was in Vallejo raising eight children and Adela had given birth to one girl. In 1866, rising indebtedness forced Agoston Haraszthy to surrender the leadership of the Buena Vista winery. In 1866, Arpad became the chief winemaker for the wine cellar of

Isidore Landsberger in San Francisco. He and Jovita moved there that year, but they seem not to have settled in one particular location for long. Their first residence was a house on Mason Street, but they moved into different houses and hotels several times over the next decade. Jovita bore two children. The 1867 birth of a boy whom they named Carlos was difficult, but Arpad assured his mother-in-law that "Jovita sits up every day a few hours, and in a few days will be able to move about again." In 1869, Arpad was hospitalized for smallpox, but he made a complete recovery. Agoston moved to Nicaragua in 1868 and accidentally drowned there the following year. Natalia and Attila and their three children continued to live at the Buena Vista vineyards in a residence that Natalia always called "Champagne." Natalia told her mother in November 1869 that the bad harvest of that year had so depressed Attila that he was thinking of abandoning the vineyard and moving to San Francisco or Vallejo. The bad harvest was due to an infestation of phylloxera, which forced them to close the winery in the 1870s.[41]

In addition, Andrónico was struggling to put his fledgling music teaching career on a solid footing. He gave lessons in both Vallejo and Sonoma. Adela reported to her mother at the beginning of 1869 that "Andrónico gives music lessons and teaches Spanish." But when he was in Sonoma his relationship with his father, who was himself struggling financially, was anything but pleasant. Francisca told Jovita in 1868:

> Your Papá and Andrónico are always arguing. It seems that a dark spirit has come between the two of them, so instead of winning an argument, they lose. . . . You already know that your Papá is very quick-tempered. And Andrónico, who is obstinate and arrogant, loves to scold everyone with very crude language. Every chance he gets, he says that things are not like they used to be. He has completely turned against the family. This horrifies me and causes me great sadness. It is so hard to deal with such quick-tempered people who can't interact with anyone because of their bad attitude. I do everything I can to put up with it, but it is hard.[42]

In 1868, Plácido Vega returned to San Francisco. The factionalism in the Juárez forces that had been apparent in Mazatlán in 1864 had persisted, and he ran afoul of some important leaders who accused him of keeping for himself some of the money he had raised in San Francisco. He was briefly jailed but was able to escape to San Francisco, where he still had many friends, such as Vallejo. He spent about a year there before returning to Mexico and eventually allying himself with Porfirio Díaz.

During this time, Uladislao remained in the Mexican army. In 1869 he wrote to his mother, " Madre, I am doing very well here. I am in need of nothing except for a house, which is what really bothers me. I am in love with a Mexican woman, but I am certain that I won't be marrying her because she is poor. She isn't incredibly

---

41. McGinty, *Strong Wine*, 430, 460–72; Arpad to F.B.C.V., June 11, 1867, C-B 441, box 4, folder 27; Adela to F.B.C.V., February 10, 1869, C-B 441, box 4, folder 8; Natalia to F.B.C.V., November 11, 1869, C-B 441, box 4, folder 29, all in TBL.

42. Adela to F.B.C.V., January 25, 1869, C-B 441, box 4, folder 8; F.B.C.V. to Jovita, no month, 20, 1868, C-B 441 FILM, reel 4, 223–26, both in TBL.

poor, but I need a woman who has much more money." However, by the next year he had tired of army life and let his family know that he wanted to return home. He eventually did so in 1870. When he came back to Sonoma he was ill and experiencing chills. He spent some time with Natalia at her Buena Vista home, and she was able to nourish him back to health.[43]

B. S. Brooks
Counsellor at Law
Nos. 11 & 12 Exchange Buildings,
San Francisco
May 14, 1869[44]

Francisca,

General Vega finally left yesterday, at three o'clock, for the coast of Mexico on a very swift sailing ship. May the Heavens look down on him so that he has a safe journey and everything turns out well for him. I decided not to go because, after the difficulties that arose regarding his departure, I had to remain here to finish up some business dealings during his absence. His departure was dependent upon this. But as soon as I hear news of his arrival, I'll head for home right away.

I don't know if I can leave tomorrow, Saturday. But I think I'll be ready to leave by Monday, if I can finish up some very interesting documents.

Give my regards to everyone.

M. G. Vallejo

International Hotel No. 137
San Francisco
June 30, 1869[45]

Francisca,

I'm including Mr. Aguillon's receipt for the rent of the barracks.[46] Send it to him.

I've been trying to find some money to send to Ula, who asked me for money so he can return home. I finally arranged it in such a way to make it possible for

43. Lerma Garay, *El general traicionado*, 111–65; Nakayama, *Realidad y mentira de Plácido Vega*, 133–71; Uladislao to F.B.C.V., February 9, 1869, C-B 441, box 6, folder 16; Natalia to F.B.C.V., March 20, 1870, C-B 441, box 4, folder 29, both T B L.

44. C-B 441, box 1, folder 5, T B L.

45. C-B 441, box 1, folder 5, T B L.

46. Camille Aguillon, a native of France, settled in the Sonoma region around 1860 and became a leading wine maker in the area. Tuomey, *History of Sonoma County*, 2:896; 1870 U.S. Census, Sonoma Township, Sonoma County, 20; Emparán, *Vallejos*, 374, 386.

Ula to receive $150 in time for him to return by way of Guadalajara. From there, a gentleman will take him to San Blas and General Vega will take care of the rest.

General Vega wrote to me that he [Ula] arrived safely in San Blas. We'll see what happens next.

I've managed to sell the wine from Quiquiriquí, but they won't pay for it until three months have passed.

I've been very sick for a week with rheumatism in my arm, but I'm much better now. I've gone to Jovita's house every day and she is fine. A ship set sail today for the coast of Mexico and I've been writing to General Vega. If everything goes well for him, I expect that we'll end up with something decent and then be able to get out from under so many worries. I have to get my hands on about five hundred pesos that Mr. Brooks is supposed to give me. That is the real reason that has kept me here. If he turns the money over to me soon, it will be used to enroll Lulú and María in the Colegio de Santa Clara.

Don't worry about me. I'm too astute to be taken advantage of. I am very, very, very angry here.

I haven't seen any of the family from Vallejo, nor have I seen Frisbie. Nobody wants to buy the wine that Dr. Fauré makes. I don't know what the hell is wrong with it, but I'm going to see if I can get rid of it.

Give my regards to the girls and give them a kiss. Also, to Salvador and Doña Carolina.

Take care of everything.

M. G. Vallejo

International Hotel No. 137
San Francisco
July 1, 1869[47]

Francisca,

Tell Lulú that among the books that are in the storeroom there is a fairly large one, bound in blue linen. It is the history of the war with Texas in the year 1836, written by General Green.[48] Have her look for it and send it by Express to:

W. W. Chipman, Esquire
Exchange Building No. 17
San Francisco[49]

47. C-B 441, box 1, folder 5, TBL.

48. Green, *Journal of the Texian Expedition against Mier.*

49. William Worthington Chipman (1820–73), an attorney, purchased the Encinal de San Antonio from Antonio María Peralta in 1851 and became one of the founders of the city of Alameda in the East Bay. Bancroft, *History of California*, 6:478.

Vue de la Maison de M.M.C. Aguillon et Robin, Sonoma, Cal., 1878.
Courtesy of the Sonoma Valley Historical Society.

Mr. Chipman will pay for the Express here.
Give my regards to everyone.

M. G. Vallejo

International Hotel No. 137
San Francisco
July 2, 1869[50]

Francisca,

I'm sending $20 pesos to you, by way of Mr. Aguillon.[51] I'm also sending a large box of cookies on the steamer from Petaluma via Lakeville.

I'm attaching the receipt for Mr. Aguillon, for when he pays you on August 1.

50. C-B 441, box 1, folder 5, TBL.

51. "$20 pesos" is the way it appears in the original letter. The Californios often referred to U.S. dollars as pesos.

The steamer from Mexico should arrive this week. I'm expecting it to bring news, whether good or bad. I'm anxiously awaiting the steamer's arrival to find out about a thousand things.

Give my regards to Salvador and the girls.

Yours,
M. G. Vallejo

International Hotel No. 137
San Francisco
September 9, 1869[52]

Francisca,

It won't be long before I'll be finished with the business I've been dealing with in Mexico. On Saturday the steamer leaves for San Blas. As soon as it leaves, I will head out for Vallejo. Then we can go to Sonoma to put the house in some sort of order.

A few days ago I received a letter from Uladislao. He asked me to send him $300 so he can return. I'm sending him the money on this steamer. I had already sent him another $300 by way of Acapulco but he didn't receive the money because he came by way of Guadalajara instead. I hope he'll come home soon. Tomorrow afternoon, or day after tomorrow at the latest, I want you and the rest of the family to each send me a brief letter that you have written to Ula. I can then send the letters on the steamer. Tell Platón to be in charge of this and have him send the letters to me.

Jovita is well and so are the little ones. They send you their regards with a thousand affectionate hugs.

If my plans work out well, we'll have something, so as not to be so limited. Then you can make an appearance once in a while on the train. What do you think?

I have a nice little stove for the house and two ladders for picking fruit and olives in Sonoma.

Give my regards to Fannie and her children, to Adela and her children, to Platón and his . . . I mean his wife, to Andrónico and Napoleón, and also to John and Livay.[53]

Yours,
M. G. Vallejo

52. C-B 441, box 1, folder 5, TBL.
53. Vallejo's way of spelling "Levi."

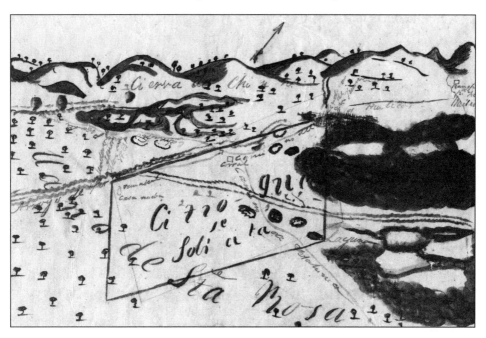

Diseño del Rancho Cabeza de Santa Rosa.
Courtesy of The Bancroft Library, University of California, Berkeley. Land Case Map 124.

THE FAMILY CONTINUED TO EXPERIENCE A HOST OF DIFFICULTIES.
Mariano Guadalupe's brother Salvador and Francisca's brother Julio were both
suffering. Salvador appeared to have lost interest in many current affairs, such as
his own financial and social situation. Julio, who lost a good amount of the rancho
property he inherited in the Santa Rosa area when his mother died, was finding
it very difficult to care for the six young children borne by his wife, Teodosia
Bojorques.[54]

Finances remained an issue. Vallejo sent Francisca what money he could, but
it was never all that much. Francisca urged him to rent out more of his land and
his vineyards, but Vallejo's attachment to the property he had spent so much time
developing was too strong. He also probably thought that renting out so much land
would advertise to his contemporaries how serious his financial difficulties were,
and he did not want to do that. He was especially upset when he suspected that,
despite her agreement a few years earlier not to rent out the bath house, she had
taken preliminary steps to do just that.

54. McGinty, "Carrillos of San Diego," 294–300.

(*left*) Julio Carrillo. *Courtesy of California State Parks,*
Sonoma Barracks. No. 243–73–1.
(*right*) Theodosia Bojorques Carrillo. *Courtesy of*
The Bancroft Library, University of California, Berkeley.
POR: *Carrillo, Theodosia (Mrs. Julio):1.*

Lachryma Montis
Sonoma
September 20, 1869[55]

Francisca,

I arrived at the house at noon and found Salvador seated under the trees in front of the house, "chatting with a friend," as he says. Everything was clean and well swept, which I wasn't expecting. Jef was out hunting. It's now four o'clock in the afternoon, and Jef still hasn't returned. I need to send him to Sonoma to get some provisions for us to eat. Of course, I haven't had anything to eat yet, despite the fact that Salvador offered me a bit of rabbit broth he has in the kitchen. The whole house is open and very clean. Your room is also airing out and it's exactly the same as how you left it. The one thing that is noticeable is the silence. But we have watercress in the irrigation ditches and apples. We are managing somehow.

Salvador seems like the god of the jungle or Adam in Paradise. He is very philosophical about everything. He doesn't even want to have the dream of our first father, which made him Eve's companion. Such a peculiar man! He gets along fine on his own. He eats what he wants, drinks what is available, and sleeps without a

---

55. C-B 441, box 1, folder 5, TBL.

care in the world. He says it's the great life! He fears no one, owes nothing to anyone, and has a good relationship with God and nature. Damn, damn, damn, I say.

Palomo died. Jef had tied him up to the wagon with a rope. Palomito jumped and was strangled by the rope.

It is eight o'clock at night and Jef still hasn't returned. I haven't even had lunch, but Alberto is arriving with some sugar. We are going to heat some water.

Give my regards to everyone.

Yours,

M. G. Vallejo

Lachryma Montis
Sonoma Valley
November 6, 1869[56]

Francisca,

Today I sent for Vicente and I spoke to him very carefully about what you asked me to do with respect to the Indian Bernabé, his son. After he went to consult with Teresa, Bernabé's mother, he came back to tell me that the mother didn't want her son to leave.[57]

Julio was here yesterday. He came with two of his young daughters. He told me one of them is named Felicidad.[58] He said he was going to send her to Vallejo and that you would assume responsibility for her. He left her at Natalia's house so that he could possibly send her by stagecoach. I offered to take her myself, but since it was something that had been arranged beforehand I didn't insist. She is a very pretty girl. Even though I knew nothing about your taking charge of her, it seems to me that it's good to help friends who need assistance, even though we are poor. Poor Julio. I feel so sorry for him because he has lost all his property and he has a large, young family to support.

Julio was seated in my room for about an hour. He asked me many unusual questions. Among them was one that went something like this:

"What kind of work do you all do?"

"Whatever we can do, or whatever I can do. As you can see, right now I'm reading. At other times I write letters and sometimes I write poetry."

"And to whom do you write letters and for whom do you compose poetry?"

---

56. C-B 441, box 1, folder 5, TBL.

57. Vicente and Teresa were Indigenous servants. It is unclear what Francisca wanted their son to do.

58. Julio is Francisca's brother, who lived in Santa Rosa and had donated to the city the land on which the county courthouse stood. He had a reputation as a habitual gambler, which may have contributed to his financial and emotional difficulties. Julio Carrillo's and Teodosia Bojorques's daughter Felicidad was born in 1859. McGinty, "Carrillos of San Diego," 294–300; 1860 U.S. Census. Santa Rosa, Sonoma, California, Roll M653_69, 404.

"I write letters to the people with whom I have business relations, or people who are my friends, to my male friends or my <u>female friends</u> (I emphasized this), to my many relatives, and to people who have treated me kindly. I write verses to the muses of poetry, or I write about what the muses have inspired me to compose. I write about the sun, the moon, the dawn, good weather, rain, Minerva and Midas, beautiful women, and important men."

"Yes, but what type of work do you do?"

"As you can see," I responded, "I need an intellectual job. With regard to physical labor in general, <u>I don't want it and I don't need to do it.</u>"

"So, what do you live on?"

"A man works so he can have a room or a home where he can eat and sleep. What more does he need? Well, I have both a home and food to eat, I don't bother anybody, I don't get drunk, and I don't frequent taverns. In the end, I work when I can, but it's been a long time since I've done that."

"Yes, but you have been a big spender."

"True, quite true, but it's always for something beneficial," I responded. "And if you don't believe that, take a look at my family and you'll see that I'm right. I'm a proud man and it doesn't bother me to say so. <u>When there is a storm, a flood, cataclysms, or a worldwide deluge, wouldn't you say that a successful man is one who can escape with his family even though he has nothing left?</u> Well, that is what has happened to me. Noah foresaw the flood and built the ark. He escaped in it even though he was somewhat poor. The rest of the world . . . drowned . . . but Noah was saved."

"And Don Salvador, why doesn't he look for work?" he asked me. "With a horse and a small two-wheeled cart he could earn a good living cleaning stables."

"He can't," I responded. "He's broke and he's already old. Besides, he's living at home with his brother.[59] He doesn't incur any expenses; he hardly eats at all. He's the only one who can answer for that. But I want you to know that he would blow his brains out before going around cleaning stables."

"So, why do I have to do it?"

"Well, every person knows what they are capable of doing," I responded. "I can do everything, but there are some people who are their own worst enemies. That's the way of the world."

We ended the conversation and it seems that he left very satisfied.

We gave him a good lonch, wine, brandy, sardines, bread and cheese, a stew made with poplar leaves, tomatoes, and a lot of red chili, and a very nice grape leaf salad with olive oil.[60]

Give my regards to all the children.

M.G.V.

---

59. Salvador Vallejo spent much of these last years of his life at Sonoma. McKittrick, "Salvador Vallejo," 328.
60. With "lonch" Vallejo was replicating the way he heard the English word "lunch."

Lachryma Montis
Sonoma Valley
November 6, 1869[61]

Francisca,

Today, Saturday, I received your letter dated the 3rd of this month. I will respond by saying that I found the house very clean. That's how it should be because you were here. So that nothing damages the house, every day I open the windows and air it out. I don't touch anything. I've left it just the way you did. You know very well that I don't ever like to disturb where things are placed, or stick my nose into what somebody else has done, even if I should. I don't want to, I have no desire to do so, nor do I have the slightest intention of doing so. In the afternoon I close the windows in your room and go down to my room, where my only objective is to read and write or <u>compose some verses, as always</u>.

You tell me that you "<u>imagine that I am settling the business affairs regarding Lachryma Montis, and you plead and beg me to work with Mr. Aguillon or with Attila or with Mr. Baciñang or with the Robines boys, renting all the land and the entire vineyard to them, everything except for the house, because you say that I would like to rent it to someone who knows how to take care of it....</u>"[62]

I will begin my response by saying that I came to L. Montis (property that I still consider to be mine) to live in my house, alone, not to arrange what already has been arranged for quite some time. At least here I have a room where I can sleep, I have water to drink, and some fruit to eat. My expenses are so much less, no more than four reales a day, and there are three of us living here. You know who they are. I suffer here and put up with a lot, but it's my port in the storm and my fate. In the past I spent as much money as I could to turn this property into something decent, because I knew beforehand about the financial catastrophe that would befall me. When I was going to lose the property the last time (at auction), in order to save it I sold all the property I inherited on my father's side at El Pájaro and turned over the $15,000 pesos to Mr. Madden. However, it is still at risk, but I think it can be saved.

With regard to renting the property, nobody better than I knows men who are able to do it. Without your having to remind me, I don't believe there is anyone here who can do it adequately. Aguillon openly says he doesn't want to do it. On the contrary, if it were possible he would like to rip up the agreement he has for

---

61. C-B 441, box 1, folder 5, TBL.

62. Emil Robin came to Sonoma from his native France in 1854 with four of his sons. He worked as a vintner and died in late 1869 or early 1870. Wilkins, "1852 Sonoma County Census—The Robin Family," 1–3; Bascom, "Report on the Robin Family," 4–7, both in Sonoma Valley Historical Society; Emparán, *Vallejos*, 419.

Quiquiriquí. Baciñang is a consummate scoundrel, and an inveterate trickster by nature. The Robines boys!!! . . . !!! Their father is my friend, he is an old man, and I respect him. Therefore, I don't want to say anything negative about his sons.

Attila wants to sell his vineyard and his house as soon as possible and go to San Francisco or Vallejo to open up a wine establishment. So of course he doesn't want to take on a small vineyard like Lachryma Montis.

The only thing needed to make this work is money to spend on this place again, so it can return to being the paradise it was before. But if that can't happen . . . to hell with it all. I want to live the last four or five years of the life that I have left without people tormenting me. I want to have some money for my daughters and sons. I want to live in a little house where I'm the person in charge, or set it on fire and look for another house.

I'll see Vicente today about the matter regarding the Indian boy Bernabé. I'll let you know what happens.

There are two cords of wood in the storehouse. Some Indian women are lingering around these parts: Simona, Caridad, Isidora, Teresa, Rosario, and Crispina.

Give my regards to Platón, Adela, Andrónico, big Lili and little Lili, and Salvador. Give my regards to everyone.[63]

Yours,
M.G.V.

John Frisbie was elected to the state legislature in the fall of 1867 and engineered a bill that strengthened the position of the California Pacific Railroad, of which he was a vice-president. The railroad actually existed more on paper than it did in reality. The real purpose of the legislation was to give it a more secure legal standing. The officers of the California Pacific Railroad calculated that the larger Central Pacific Railroad, which was constructing the transcontinental railroad along with the Union Pacific Railroad, would not want to be confused with this almost fictional "California Pacific" entity, whose main accomplishment was a single rail line between Sacramento and the city of Vallejo.[64] They hoped that the Central Pacific would eventually purchase the California Pacific as a way of getting rid of it. This did not happen over the next few years, since the Central Pacific was more interested in completing the transcontinental project. So in 1869 Frisbie moved his wife Epifania and their eight children to his hometown of Albany, New York.

---

63. "Big Lili" was Platón's wife, Lily Wiley. "Little Lili" was Adela's ten-year-old daughter, Francisca Adelayda. Vallejo spelled their names both "Lili" and "Lily" from time to time.
64. Hittell, *History of California,* 4:486.

St. Catherine's Academy, Solano Square, Benicia.
Courtesy of the Library of Congress. HABS CA-1542.

In the fall of that same year, Mariano Guadalupe and Francisca's two youngest children, Luisa and María, entered Saint Catherine's Academy in Benicia instead of John L. Ver Mehr's Saint Mary's Hall in San Francisco, which Jovita had attended. That school had burned down in 1860, and Ver Mehr had moved to Napa. Even though Mrs. Ver Mehr offered to give Luisa and María private tutoring there, Vallejo and Francisca decided to send the girls to an established institution.[65]

Saint Catherine's Academy was run by Dominican sisters, and some of Epifania's daughters had attended the school. Since this was the first time Francisca's girls would be away from home, she took it upon herself to become acquainted with the Dominican sisters so she could let her own children know how to behave appropriately at the academy. She told them, "Both of you, take care of yourselves, behave well with everyone, and be humble and obedient with your teachers, especially Mothers Luisa and Tomasa, and Sisters Raymunda and Jacinta. Try to do your very best. Don't go out into the garden alone; only go accompanied by one of the nuns. Read this letter every day so you won't forget what I have told you." Vallejo made a similar appeal to María in March: "I encourage you to apply yourself to your studies so that you can shine in the class you are enrolled in at the beginning of your upcoming examinations." Napoleón, fresh out of Santa Clara and now working for Frisbie's California Pacific Railroad, added his own encouragement

---

65. Ver Mehr, *Checkered Life*, 415; Mrs. Ver Mehr to M.G.V. March 4, 1867, DLG-V 58, letter 7.

Casa de López, Old Town, San Diego, California. State Historical Monument No. 60.
This was the home of Juana López, the mother of Prudenciana Vallejo López de Moreno.
Reproduced by permission of the Huntington Library, San Marino, California.
Helen Long Collection of Moreno Documents, box 19.

to his young sister: "Be a good girl and study hard so that when you are older you won't be embarrassed to write."[66]

During this time, Vallejo had to confront an episode from his past. The person who forced him to do this was María Amparo Ruiz de Burton. As we have seen, she and Vallejo had been in contact since the early 1850s, and Vallejo had visited her in Staten Island during his 1865 visit to the East Coast. During her stay in San Diego in the 1850s, María Amparo had become friendly with a single mother named Juana López and her daughter Prudenciana. Since María Amparo had largely been raised by a single mother herself, they undoubtedly talked about their circumstances. In the course of those conversations, she learned that Prudenciana's father was Mariano Guadalupe Vallejo.

Juana López was actually a cousin of Francisca Benicia Carrillo, for López's father and Francisca's mother were siblings. Prudenciana was conceived a few months after the wedding of Francisca and Mariano Guadalupe.[67] It is not clear when Vallejo became aware of her birth and whether or not Francisca ever became aware of this. But we suspect that the close family relationships made it likely that she was aware of Prudenciana's existence.

---

66. F.B.C.V. to Luisa, no date, C-B 441 FILM, reel 4, 197–98; M.G.V. to María, March 5, 1870, C-B 441 FILM, reel 4, 101–102; Napoleón to María, February 9, 1869, C-B 441, box 6, folder 16; Napoleón to M.G.V., February 8, 1869, C-B 441, box 6, folder 11, all in TBL.

67. She was born at the end of May 1833, San Diego Baptism 6552. Francisca and Mariano Guadalupe had been married on March 6, 1832. San Diego Marriage 1770.

María Amparo Ruiz de Burton was a very direct woman, and when she found out that Vallejo was Prudenciana's father she urged him to acknowledge her.[68] By this time, Prudenciana had married José Matías Moreno, who had been Pío Pico's secretary in 1846, had a rancho in northern Baja California, and served as *jefe político* for northern Baja California in 1861–62.[69] When María Amparo's husband, Henry S. Burton, died in 1869, she returned to southern California.

Vallejo eventually took her advice. In 1869, José Matías Moreno and Prudenciana visited San Francisco. They stayed with Miguel Pritchard, who was secretary of the Mexican consulate. Vallejo met with her and acknowledged that he was her birth father. When she returned to the San Diego area, she wrote him a letter thanking him for this, and he responded with a letter of his own. He combined heartfelt sentiments with a calculated attempt to maintain contact with her without any letters from her being noticed by Francisca. He also told María Amparo that he had seen Prudenciana, and he received a reply from María Amparo. Prudenciana and Mariano Guadalupe stayed in touch through third parties like Ruiz de Burton and José Arce, a relative of her grandmother.[70]

Sonoma Valley
September 24, 1869[71]
Señora Doña Prudenciana Vallejo de Moreno

My dear and beloved daughter,

I have just received your heartfelt letter, dated the 19th of last month. That you have written to me has pleased me so very, very much, and I reply by congratulating you on your safe journey and arrival in San Diego. The fact that Don Matías's health is improving each day gives me great satisfaction. May God will that he completely recovers his strength, and may he continue, as he has up until now, being the protector and father of such a fine and large family. Be good, my daughter, and always help your husband to take care of everything, and even more so now that he is ill. Be loving and kind to him, for he is such a worthy and good father. That way, you will fulfill your responsibilities as a wife and as a mother, and you and your children will receive blessings from Heaven and also from your father who sincerely loves you with all his heart.

Through you I am sending my warmest regards to Don Matías. Tell him not to fear because the climate and tranquility will help him recover his health soon. And

---

68. Sánchez and Pita, *Conflicts of Interest*, 102–3.

69. A *jefe político* was a political leader.

70. Sánchez and Pita, *Conflicts of Interest*, 436, 459, 468, 479–80; José Arce to Prudenciana López de Moreno, July 26, 1872, HLG 936, Huntington Library, San Marino, Calif.

71. HLG 905, Huntington Library, San Marino, Calif.

(left) Prudenciana Vallejo López de Moreno, 1857.
Reproduced by permission of The Huntington Library,
San Marino, California. Helen Long Collection of Moreno Documents, box 19.
(right) José Matías Moreno.
Reproduced by permission of the Huntington Library,
San Marino, California. Helen Long Collection of Moreno Documents, box 19.

<u>now more than ever</u> he should count me among his many true friends, because his children are closely related to me, and you, dear Prudenciana, even more so. Tell him that I will help him however I can.

Shortly after you left San Francisco I paid a visit to the Pritchard family, where you were guests. They remember you fondly and asked me to give you their regards, which I am now doing with pleasure. Doña Avelina, in particular, sends her regards to all of you.

I don't want you to go to the trouble of sending me the "Cenzontle."[72] I am as grateful to you as if I had received it; but if you insist on doing so, send it to this address:

> Gen. M. G. Vallejo
> Port St. Orleans Hotel[73]
> Care of Mrs. A. Haraszthy
> San Francisco

72. A *cenzontle* is a mockingbird.

73. Jovita was living at this hotel with her husband, Arpad Haraszthy, and their two young children. McGinty, *Toast to Eclipse*, 75.

Dr. Víctor Fauré.
*Courtesy of California
State Parks, Sonoma
Barracks. No. 243-x-5270.*

As soon as I return to the city I will remember your shoe size, no. 3, and also your glove size, no. 6, and that you do not have legs like a "Yankee." I will ask Doña Avelina about the last point <u>in case she knows something about it</u>. Or if she doesn't, what can we do? I will just guess.

Give my regards to your husband and kiss all the family for me. And you, receive the love and esteem of your father who loves you and gives you his blessing.

M. G. Vallejo

P.S. I am frequently away from here, and it would be better if you addressed my letters as usual but put them inside <u>another envelope</u> that says: "Víctor Fauré, M. D." Sonoma.

He will give them to me or send them to wherever I am.

September 14, 1869
Staten Island, New York[74]

. . . Good for you for having gone to see Doña Prudenciana. That is what you should have done thirty years ago! Doesn't it horrify you to think that for so many years you deprived her of all that affection which was hers by the laws of nature? . . . I don't want to preach to you, but honestly, of all your sins, my son, this is the

---

74. Sánchez and Pita, *Conflicts of Interest*, 302–3.

worst one I have noticed in you . . . but better late than never . . . and since she surely has forgiven you, I hope that God will also forgive you! I was very moved by that part of your letter, and I also cried with both of you, even though from far away. . . .

M. A. de Burton

WHILE FRISBIE AND HIS FAMILY WERE IN NEW YORK, FRANCISCA SPENT a good amount of time caring for their house in Vallejo. She often took her daughters María and Lulú with her. Her husband generally remained in Sonoma and looked after the house and the employees and servants as best he could. Since the 1860s, the vineyards at Lachryma Montis had been under the care of Pietro Giovanari, and he had brought members of a number of Italian families to Sonoma to help him work these vineyards. Prominent among this group were members of the Caminata and Fosati families. Some of these family members also rented land from Vallejo.[75]

Lachryma Montis
January 3, 1870[76]

Francisca,

   Neither you, nor Andrónico, Adela, Platón, big Lily, or little Lily have written one single letter to me. Even Jovita has forgotten about me. Well, fine. I've always heard it said that "One father for one hundred children, but never one hundred children for one father." I've always resisted accepting that a saying such as that is a hard and fast rule, but that's how I feel. I like to think that there are no rules and no exceptions, but sometimes the power of <u>reality</u> takes hold of me and almost undermines my ability to philosophize. What can I do? You know very well that, for me, receiving letters from my family, wherever I may be at the time, has always been a consolation that nourishes my soul. But perhaps they have forgotten about me because they are close to you and far away from me. Well, such is the world. I'll suffer because I can't do anything about it. "May God help them!" I hope that when they are old their children will be as loving to them as they are to me now. They always have written to me in the past, but now they don't. I miss their letters very much, more so now that I am alone, so alone, here in this lovely place. On to something else.

75. McGinty, *Toast to Eclipse*, 36–39; McGinty, *Strong Wine*, 401–2; Emparán, *Vallejos*, 105, 145, 213, 419.
76. C-B 441, box 1, folder 6, TBL.

Reservoir at Lachryma Montis, by Carleton E. Watkins.
Courtesy of The Bancroft Library, University of California, Berkeley.
BANC PIC 1974.019:069-ALB.

The Italians are working very well. It seems to me that they are hardworking men. Today, after planting some vegetables, they finished the trench from the white door along the side by the roses of Castilla up to where the water comes out of the reservoir. Oh what a trench! It is wide, deep, and well made. At least the property is improving each day and it's already starting to look like it did when I had a lot of money. Of course, you should see how clean I'm keeping the area outside of the house. I dug a circle around your flowers by the fountain in front and put a good amount of manure in there. I then covered it back up. The flowers look nice. The entire house has been well swept: the kitchen and dining room, too. The only thing that makes me mad sometimes is Jef's lack of initiative and Salvador's selfishness. But I'm <u>starting to show my claws</u>. After we finish lunch, the dishes are washed, and then I take <u>everything</u> to the sewing room: bread, sugar, cheese, stews, and lard. That way, <u>more than four</u> [people] find themselves with no other recourse

Fountain in the olive grove at Lachryma Montis, by Carleton E. Watkins.
Courtesy of The Bancroft Library, University of California, Berkeley.
BANC PIC 1974.l019:063-ALB.

than to follow the rules, since there is not much advantage in not doing so. As the saying goes, "I do for you what you do for me." In the end, "I've won this game."

Isidora is washing my clothes. Tomorrow she will iron everything except the shirts.

If you were here, you would be pleased to see how well, well, well the vineyard has been pruned.

When I got to this point in the letter, a gentleman appeared, and I suggested that he let me finish.

Give my regards to Doña Margarita.[77] Tell her to be a good girl for her mother and also have her write. Give my regards to everyone.

M. G. Vallejo

77. Margarita Angulo de Navarrete. See Biographical Sketches.

Sonoma Valley
January 28, 1870[78]

Francisca,

The Italians are already here working and planting some vegetables, taking advantage of the good weather. They seem to be good men and I think they will do well for themselves. We will benefit as well.

Everyone in Sonoma always has had the habit of taking or asking for anything we have here. But now, when those people come asking for things from me, they leave with nothing, because I send them to Señor Barbieri. Therefore, the steady stream of beggars has stopped.

Everything is very clean. I entertain myself by fertilizing the orange and olive trees and by trimming the grass and sweeping around the whole exterior of the house. So if you pay me a visit on one of these very beautiful days, you will find that everything is in good order. The house has been well swept and ventilated.

Give my regards to Adela, Jovita, big Lily and little Lily, Doña Margarita, Andrónico, and Platón. And don't forget Lulú and María, if you should happen to see them. And believe in me as you wish,

M. G. Vallejo

P.S. Today I'm sending a small box of oranges to Lulú. She requested them in a letter she wrote to me.

Lachryma Montis
Sonoma Valley
February 14, 1870[79]

Francisca,

I am including two letters for you, one from Fanita and another from her daughter Benicia. Read them and show them to Adela, Jovita, Andrónico, and Platón. Tell each one of them that I said it would give me great pleasure if they each would write a letter to Fanita and Benicia. I know how eager poor Fannie is to receive letters from the family. I answered her letter with one that is eight pages long, which will alleviate her loneliness, that is, being far away from her loved ones. You, of course, must write to her as well. In one of the paragraphs of my letter I painted

78. C-B 441, box 1, folder 6, TBL.
79. C-B 441, box 1, folder 6, TBL.

a very graphic description of the night of the fire and I told her about countless incidents. I even brought up the one about that old woman and the silver. I hope you are content and happy. Remember that we are going to die soon. Be good, like always, and think of me as your best friend.

M. G. Vallejo

Lachryma Montis
Sonoma Valley
February 24, 1870[80]

Francisca,

Today I received your little letter dated the 20th, in which you inform me about the fire in Vallejo on Sunday. It's necessary to be careful with chimneys and to always be on the alert. Now you can see that fire is always a threat to a home. There is a saying, "When you see your neighbor's beard being shaved, get yours wet." I'm always careful, because some fires are <u>good for business</u> for those who <u>insure</u> their homes, which almost always burn down. It would be good if only those insured homes burned down, but unfortunately others suffer because of the malice of those owners.

The Monday when I took the chilis (Platón gave some to you), I also went down to Gilroy. I returned the following day. And here I am, with nothing new to report. When I went down on the steamer, Arpad told me about the fire.

Give my regards to Doña Margarita. Tell her to be a good girl, because if she isn't I'll get mad and will inform her mother and father. I must give them good reports about her and also about Juan. Enrique Blackman told me yesterday in San Francisco that Adela and Lily were on the steamer *Antelope*. They were going to the grand concert by Urso.[81] I think I saw them as the steamships passed each another on San Pablo Bay.

It is four o'clock in the afternoon and Juanito just returned from school. I gave him your message and the poor boy immediately went to check on your flowers. Even though the flowers were very tidy, he started to tidy them up again, because his aunt asked him to do so.

Salvador is becoming more and more careless. You could say that he is watering the room with a watering can without actually using one at all. He sends you his

---

80. C-B 441, box 1, folder 6, TBL.
81. "Enrique" is Henry Blackman, a relative of John Frisbie who worked for him. 1870 U.S. Census, Vallejo Township, Sonoma County, 70; *Solano and Napa Counties Directory for 1871–72*, 39. The concert was a benefit event for the Mercantile Library Association, and it featured French violinist Camilla Urso. *Daily Alta California*, February 22, 1870.

regards. He always says that even from far away you <u>meddle in everything</u>, and that you would make a good alcalde. Right now he's making popcorn using lard and red corn. Everything is greasy and the stove is filthy.

Give my regards to Jovita and always believe that I am your,

M. G. Vallejo

Are you still angry? Be happy; write me a beautiful letter . . . and I'll go running <u>to see you</u>.

Lachryma Montis
Sonoma Valley
March 30, 1870[82]

Francisca,

I'm cleaning all around the inside edges of the little fence in the front, because the Italians are digging on the other side of the fence and planting tomatoes. Perhaps tomorrow I can begin to clean up the paths to the spring of the orange grove. They are covered with grass because of so much rain. Then that side of the house will begin to look very tidy. The weeping willow, the one in the small patch of green grass, is very, very, very pretty. It provides lovely shade, as do the other trees. The alameda is beginning to turn green.[83] The orange trees are beginning to produce new leaves. Then come the orange blossoms.

Salvador is fine, the same as always. He sends his regards to everyone. He is so lazy when it comes to writing that I feel bad telling him to write, even though he receives letters from the girls. You know how he is.

Tell me if I should send you the sewing machine, because if you aren't going to use it it would be silly to send it to Vallejo and just leave it there.

If there were a train, I would send you some stew made with chili and dried meat. The meat I brought back is so delicious. Salvador prepared a very tasty stew yesterday and he thought of you.

Everything is fine here except for ME: I am having heart problems; it beats very fast, maybe because I'm old. The molar is also causing me problems. I'm rotting away and it's beginning in my bones.

Give my regards to the children and pray for the old people. Don't forget your . . .

M. G. Vallejo

82. C-B 441, box 1, folder 6, TBL.
83. An *alameda* is a tree-lined walkway or promenade.

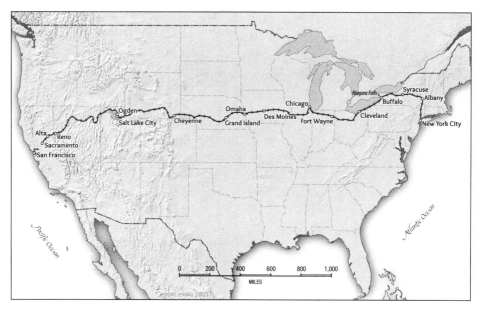

Route of the transcontinental railroad, ca. 1870. *Drawn by Tom Jonas.*

JOHN FRISBIE RETURNED TO CALIFORNIA IN APRIL 1870. BUT HE SOON returned east, inviting Francisca to accompany him on the newly constructed transcontinental railroad so she could visit his family. She had spent considerable time helping Epifania over the years. Inviting her to visit her eldest daughter and some of her grandchildren may have been Frisbie's way of attempting to decrease the family tensions resulting from the 1867 Suscol property patent he had received. Francisca had never been out of California, and for her the trip was a unique experience, which she reported to her husband in a long and detailed letter.

Albany, New York
May 5, 1870[84]

Guadalupe,

We were having lunch with the whole family. I have been with Fannie for a few days. Guadalupe, ever since I left home I had wanted to write to you, but I couldn't do it. You know how long it takes me to write a letter. I wish I knew how to write well and quickly so that I could tell all of you about what I have seen and heard.

---

84. C-B 441, box 6, folder 5, TBL.

(*left*) Rafaela Cota Temple. *Courtesy of the California Historical Society and
the University of Southern California Digital Library.*
CHS-6503 *and* UC142676.
(*right*) John Temple. *Courtesy of the California Historical Society and
the University of Southern California Digital Library.*
CHS-6509 *and* UC142775.

    The day I left Sacramento I felt a bit sad, but I started to pray to God and to the
Most Holy Mother of Light to give me courage and for all of us to come out safely
from the danger we were about to face. I was already starting to see the hills and
the mountain range, and I was thinking a lot about you and my children, when
John arrived and told me there was a Spanish woman in the car. He wondered if
I had seen her. I told him I hadn't, and it was already late. Then I heard a voice
calling out "Cousin." I was startled and turned around to see who was calling me
cousin. It was Rafaela Tempel and a brother-in-law of hers, as well as a niece and a
nephew, who were this man's children.[85] They were all traveling together to France.
    I then told her to come to my room. I was so happy. We started to chat. At various
times my attention drifted to a mountain I would see. I was looking at everything.
Then a porter came to prepare the bed, and my cousin went to her room to sleep.
And then John came and told me to lie down and sleep and not to be scared. They
gave me a small room, for me, all by myself. A short while later everyone was asleep.
I undressed and put on my nightgown. It seemed impossible to me that I, too, was

85. Rafaela Cota of Santa Bárbara married recent American immigrant to California Jonathan Temple in 1850. After
    his death in 1866 she moved to France, where her daughter lived. Bancroft, *History of California*, 5:744–45.

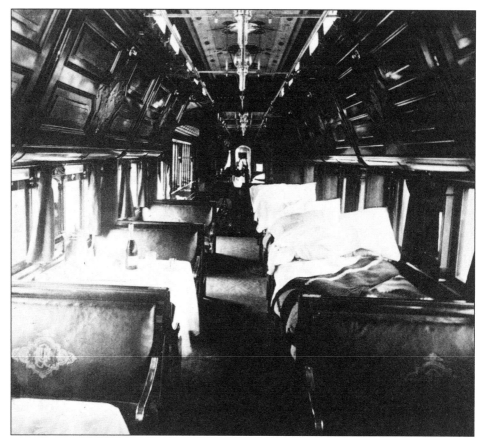

Pullman's commissary car "Gem," 1860–1870, by Lawrence & Houseworth.
Courtesy of The Society of California Pioneers. LH1537.

going to be able to sleep. I prayed and asked the Virgin to help me fall asleep. I couldn't sleep. The train didn't stop moving and swaying from side to side, making lots of noise and going fast. I finally fell asleep.

Then the screeching of the railroad cars reminded me where I was, so I started to get dressed. I was already up when John arrived to tell me to get up so I could see the Sierra Nevada. It was such a beautiful landscape. I didn't get tired of constantly looking at the different hills, mountains, valleys, and water ditches made by the miners. The land had been excavated to make way for the carts to transport the gold.

When we arrived at the top of the Sierra at a place called Alta, John told me, "This is the highest spot. Now we are going to begin to descend the Sierra Nevada." And the train started to travel faster, faster, faster, and faster, and even faster in the afternoon. John told me we still needed to cross the highest mountain range,

Secret Town trestle work, near Gold Run, three miles from Alta, California.
Courtesy of the DeGolyer Library, Southern Methodist University. Ag 1987.0634.

which was called Rocky Mountain,[86] or the mountain of the rocks. It was getting dark, and everyone went to bed and the train kept moving and moving and moving faster. We had very good food: roasted chicken, a great many desserts, cherries and oranges, and anything else one could wish for. As I was trying to remember everything, it seemed as if I were in an enchanted world. I would close my eyes, and it would seem as if some good angels were carrying me. The train was moving so fast it appeared to be flying. I didn't tire of giving thanks to God, to you, and to John for having made this trip possible for me . . . so beautiful, so pleasurable,

86. She spells it "Roquimauntin."

and so grand for me. It seemed that my heart was bursting from my chest because of the happiness I experienced when I would look at the mountains, the hills, and the various places. We traveled four days and four nights through a very ugly and desolate terrain. There was a lot of water all around; small, dried grasses that could grow to the size of one foot; and some small bushes that could barely grow. The ground was the color of ashes, and different colors, too. The water from all the rivers moves everything around, and it seems like someone is stirring it up. It looks so dirty. There is water in abundance all around. The rivers are not like those in Sonoma, Napa, and Sacramento. They come down from the large mountains filled with water up to the level of the ground. Some of the lakes look like seas (filled with boats, docks, the same as in San Francisco). I wasn't able to see very well because the train was moving fast. When we arrived at the river we changed cars there.

We traveled by the area where the Mormons live. On one side there is a very large mountain range and on the other side a salt lake. In the middle there is a very pretty town. It is a new town. Every so often we would arrive at a new town. The next day we began to climb the highest mountain range. When we were at the very top of the mountain range my ears began to pop. I never tired of looking at the mountain peaks, so high and covered with snow. The rocks piled on top of other rocks looked like houses. I never tired of admiring God's splendor and the daring of the Americans. I can't find the words nor do I have the talent to describe how the Americans constructed this route and how God has made sure that it is safe … which is why the trains can cross such high bridges. They place some rocks and some poles together, and the cars run across them. Sometimes the car goes into a dark space; sometimes it seems like the car is flying in the air across the mountainside. Many parts of the route are covered with roofs to keep the snow from falling on the tracks and covering them. The more we traveled along, the more beautiful the countryside appeared to me. The rivers seemed bigger and mountains could be spotted from all directions as we were traveling down the mountain range, or the Rocky Mountains, all day long. Later, we ate dinner and went to bed. The train ran all night long. At dawn we were in a plain that was so large you couldn't see where it ended. The train ran all day, and every so often we would pass by bridges, towns, mountains, land planted with corn, twenty or thirty railroad cars filled with firewood, coal, sheep, people, rocks, soil, iron, poles, planks, ice, sacks, large boxes, and I don't know what else because the cars are closed up like little houses. Some are like small corrals. They are different based on what they are used for. When we arrived at a city that is next to a river, which is called Omaha, we crossed over in a very large steamship and took on other cars.

We traveled all day. I never tired of looking at the mountains, rivers, lakes, towns, and railroad cars. I thought the country that belongs to the Americans was very pretty. When we went on a bridge over the very large Mississippi River, I kept

Dale Creek bridge, near Sherman, Nebraska, 1871.
Courtesy of The Bancroft Library, University of California, Berkeley.
BANC PIC 1963.002:0477:01-A.

saying "Oh, oh, oh, how beautiful, what majesty, oh, God!" John took me by the hand, and we went out and stood to the side of the door of the railroad car. Then Mister Charles came, and he took me by the other arm. When we were about to cross the bridge, it was open because a boat was going to pass through. After the boat went by, the bridge closed, and then we crossed over. Just imagine how I must have been feeling! I couldn't say anything else except, "Sir, oh, how majestic, how beautiful, such a large river, I wonder how they made this bridge." Oh, I asked John thousands of questions. We had already traveled very far and I was remembering everything. I will never forget it. I thought about the boys a lot.[87] If you see any of them, tell them that I saw their rivers, mountains, valleys covered in green grass, and many, many trees and hills. When we arrived in Chicago, I thought the lake was very pretty, as well as the homes, the iron roadways, the ships, the people. Oh, so many things! The train then entered a very large house that was filled with trains pulling six or seven cars. All of the cars inside the roundhouse were filled with people. Everybody was talking; some were going in and others were leaving. We picked up our small suitcases and John said to me, "Follow me, Mother. I am going to introduce you to a gentleman." He told me that the man was an acquaintance of

---

87. She uses the English word "boys" in the original letter.

Bridge over Niagara Falls, 1876. Reproduced by permission of
the Huntington Library, San Marino, California.
Jay T. Last Collection, priJLC-TRAN-001068.

yours. He warmly welcomed us. He wanted me to stay with him so that he could take me to spend time with his wife. John told him that we didn't have time. He then took us to the car, the prettiest one of all. He gave me the main room in the car. We arrived at a town and stayed there. A short time later, John arrived in a buggy and took me to see Niagara Falls.

It is very pretty but it didn't impress me that much. We crossed over the bridge and went to the country of Queen Victoria. I didn't like it very much because the houses are on the edge of a cliff. Then we went up on the train. We traveled all night. We passed through Syracuse at night. The next day we arrived in Albany at seven o'clock in the morning. We were with Fannie and all her little children, hugging them and kissing them. They are all fine. I also am fine. Thanks be to God. Give my best to my children, relatives, friends, and countrymen and take good care of yourself. Goodbye until the next time.

Benicia de Vallejo

I had taken great care in writing this letter, and then I received yours, and the one from my cousin Asunción Montaño Angulo. Tell Margarita to write to me and have her tell me everything about Baja California, and how Tatita and Nanita are doing. Tell her to be good and remember everything I told her. Guadalupe, take care of yourself and take care of our children. Set a good example for them. Tell Ula not to drink any liquor.

ULADISLAO WAS THE MOST WELL-TRAVELED OF FRANCISCA'S CHILDREN, and when he learned of her trip he wrote her a letter from a small house in the garden at Lachryma Montis. He told her, "I imagine that you have seen many things, but I believe there is still much more to see. Tell me how you like traveling by train. What was your impression of the plains, mountains, and rivers? . . . It must be so beautiful."[88]

L. Montis
Sonoma
June 10, 1870[89]

Francisca,

I congratulate you on having arrived well and happy in Albany, where you found your daughter and grandchildren also well. Believe me, I am jealous of the pleasure all of you must have had upon seeing one another in a strange country so far from California, from which you never had left before. I can guess and imagine how you must have felt from the moment you left Sacramento, went up and down the Sierra Nevada, the immense plains up to Chicago, the speed of the trip, and the sound of <u>tatatán</u>, <u>tatatán</u>, <u>tatatán</u>, <u>tatatán</u>, <u>tatatán</u>, day and night, that I told you about, the new and grand cities that you will have seen, etc.

All of this is miraculous, and you should be mindful of that. You should also consider that John's personal manner is nice and elegant, he is always good to our daughter, and he is good to us. This brings to mind the times when I have told you that not all men are alike, neither physically nor in terms of their sentiments or manner. There are some who are simply men and nothing else. And there are others who by their personal manner attract the will of the people, and they even are allowed to hide some of their faults. John is good and we should be proud of him.

I told Fannie in a letter what happened with Lulú and María, who suffered when you left California. They, as well as Andrónico, Adela, Natalia, Jovita, Platón, Ula, and Napoleón, are fine, as am I. We all send you our regards.

---

88. Uladislao to F.B.C.V., June 15, 1870, C-B 441, box 6, folder 16, TBL.
89. C-B 441, box 1, folder 6, TBL.

Don't get sick. Give Fannie and her children a kiss and always believe that I am your

                                                                M. G. Vallejo

Lachryma Montis
Sonoma
June 11, 1870[90]

Francisca,

I forgot to include the attached letter, which was addressed to you by Señora Angulo, Doña Margarita's mother, with my other letter. Señora Angulo's letter arrived with mine on the steamer *Continental*. Since I'm sure you will want to answer her letter, I'm sending it to you.

This morning Salvador, Ula, Juan, and I were chatting in the corridor and I told them, "I'm going to write to Francisca. If you want to write to her as well, do it right away, and I'll take care of mailing the letters." But as of this moment, no one has done it.

It's obvious that not everyone has the desire to write and be communicative like I do.

Give my regards to everyone,

                                                                M. G. Vallejo

San Francisco
July 20, 1870[91]

Francisca,

I'm writing this letter to send my regards to you and all the girls, from Fanita on down to the baby, as well as to John and all his relatives. And I want to tell you that the entire family, from the oldest to the youngest, is in good health. They all hope that you are well, happy, and enjoying yourself as you become acquainted with a new country, big cities, and that perhaps you can visit a few acquaintances from California. I hope this trip will be of benefit to your health, so that when you return you will feel younger and have a greater understanding of the world.

Lulú and María are with Natalia in Sonoma. During the day they stay at home, and at night they go out with Natalia. They are fine and think about you every day.

---

90. C-B 441, box 1, folder 6, TBL.
91. C-B 441, box 1, folder 6, TBL.

Jovita went to visit them about five days ago. She also is fine and is with her children. Adela is always fine and so is her daughter. They all send you their regards. Adela received your letter. I sent it to all the children so they could read it. I told each of them to write to you. That way you will be happy and not worry. Only when a person is in a strange land and very far away from family does that person know how to appreciate correspondence from loved ones, and even from people they don't know. It seems that from a distance the love for one's children multiplies, the soul becomes more tender, the feelings of the heart are more vivid, and a good frame of mind always unites those who left to see the world with those who remained at home. How pure, how sacred is the love for one's children! How divine are the sensations felt by the soul! So much satisfaction from the heart!

Andrónico, Ula, Platón, and Napoleón are all fine.

It seems that the whole family will come during the month of September. That's what is being said around here. I also think the same thing, because the climate of that country is so extreme. The heat is very fierce and the cold during the many months of winter is unbearable. People who are born and raised in a climate as benign as that of California can't tolerate either extreme.

Doña Margarita is still at the convent with her two girls. Her husband goes to visit them in Benicia and then returns to the city for his business. I always remember what you told me before you left. May God help them. I hope this is straightened out once and for all.

Salvador gets fatter each day. I'm very afraid that he's going to come down with a serious illness. He sends his regards to everyone.

Give my regards to John, Fani, and their children, and don't worry about anything. Don't forget John's mother.

M. G. Vallejo

Las Trancas rancho, Salvador Vallejo's home in Napa.
Courtesy of California State Parks, Sonoma Barracks. No. 243-x-3568.

CHAPTER 4

Historian and
Domestic Entrepreneur
1870–1877

W hen Francisca returned from the East Coast in the late summer of 1870, her four married daughters were in the process of raising their own children. Epifania remained in New York with her eight children, but they would return to Vallejo the following year. Adela and her husband, Levi Frisbie, were also in Vallejo, with their eleven-year-old daughter, Francisca Adelayda, whom they called Lily. Natalia and her husband, Attila Haraszthy, were living in Sonoma with their two children. Jovita and her husband, Arpad Haraszthy, were living in San Francisco, also with two children. Arpad was working in San Francisco with Isidore Landsberger and would soon be producing some sparkling wine marketed under the name "Eclipse."[1] In addition, Platón and his wife, Lily Wiley, were living in Vallejo. Three girls would be born to them within the next decade.

Enrique seems to have spent a considerable amount of time in the Napa region. Toward the end of the 1860s, he married María Antonia Carrillo, a daughter of Salvador Vallejo and María de la Luz Carrillo. In the 1870 census they were recorded as living in Napa with their one-year-old daughter, Henrietta. Enrique's occupation was listed as "laborer." However, most of his labor was probably agricultural, for in the voter registration records of 1867 and 1871 his occupation was listed as "farmer." By this time, Salvador Vallejo was spending less and less time at Napa, and Enrique may well have been working some of Salvador's rancho. In 1876, María

---

1. This important story is told in McGinty, *Toast to Eclipse.*

Antonia gave birth to twins, Anita and Camila, but she herself died as a result of that difficult childbirth. Enrique died three years later.[2]

In 1870, José partnered with Susana Higuera. Whether they were formally married in a civil or religious ceremony is not clear. In a letter to Francisca in the 1880s, José complained, "I have not been able to get married because I don't have Papá's approval, even though I am told that I can marry whomever I please." The letter indicates that Mariano Guadalupe was not happy with his son's choice. Genealogy may have had something to do with that. On her mother's side, Susana Higuera was a granddaughter of Ignacio Martínez, who had been Vallejo's commander in the 1820s. In an official report at the end of the 1820s, Martínez reprimanded Vallejo for not having defeated the Indigenous leader Cucunuchi/Estanislao, who refused to return to Mission San José. And Susana's father, Pedro Antonio Higuera, was the sister of Josefa Higuera. She had been the wife of Ignacio Pacheco, one of Vallejo's soldiers at Sonoma. Ignacio's sister, Juana María, was the mother of Vallejo's illegitimate son Enrique. As a result, both sides of Susana Higuera's family brought back episodes that Vallejo did not want made too public.[3]

José and Susana lived in the city of Martínez. In various census and voter registration records, along with newspaper accounts, José was recorded as a farmer, a warehouse worker, and a road worker. In 1886 he was identified in a report from the county board of supervisors as a "poor sick person." He seems to have died at some point after that.[4] Susana lived in Martínez until 1919, when she passed away. A San Francisco newspaper memorialized her as "the wife of José Vallejo, son of General Vallejo," and termed her "one of the oldest inhabitants of Martínez, having resided there continuously for fifty years."[5]

Vallejo's unmarried children were involved in diverse activities. Andrónico was living in Vallejo and developing with intermittent success what would eventually become a successful profession as a music teacher. Uladislao had returned from Mexico somewhat ill from a fever, and he spent some time recuperating at Lachryma Montis. Andrónico's perceived lack of achievement in his father's eyes and Uladislao's lack of direction depressed Vallejo, who was already on the verge of despair over his worsening financial situation. Francisca reported to Epifania that Vallejo was so upset that he was threatening to go and "live somewhere else, he's tired of the family." She convinced him to end his relationship with Dr. Fauré

2. 1870 U.S. Census, Napa Township, Napa County, 78, line 6; Register of Voters, Napa County, 1867 and 1871; McKittrick, "Salvador Vallejo," 326; *Find a Grave* index, Mary Antonia Vallejo and José Enrique Vallejo, accessed through Ancestry.com.

3. José to F.B.C.V., no date, C-B 441 FILM, reel 4, 127, TBL. We date this letter from the 1880s because José mentions his daughter Anita, who was born in 1881; Beebe and Senkewicz, *Mariano Guadalupe Vallejo*, 23–24; Mutnick, *Some Alta California Pioneers*, 2:666; Northrop, *Spanish-Mexican Families*, 1:175.

4. Register of Voters, Contra Costa County, 1877 (farmer); 1880 U.S. Census (warehouse worker); *Contra Costa Gazette*, May 8, 1880, 2 (road worker); *Contra Costa Gazette*, August 7, 1886, 2 (accessed via Newspapers.com); in the 1900 U.S. Census, Susana was identified as the head of the household.

5. *San Francisco Chronicle*, January 18, 1919, 10.

Salvador Vallejo.
Courtesy of California
State Parks, Sonoma
Barracks. No. 243-x-2395.

and put Andrónico and Uladislao in charge of the vineyards and winemaking. She undoubtedly hoped that this would take his mind off his financial troubles and also allow him to establish a better relationship with these two sons. But Vallejo did not follow through on her suggestion. As she reported, "Your Papá did not give another thought to Ula or Andrónico, or to what he had promised them or me."[6]

Andrónico continued to work on his music-teaching career and would eventually achieve decent success. Uladislao went through a series of jobs in and around Sonoma, but nothing seemed to catch his interest. After Napoleón finished at Santa Clara College, he went through successive employments. He first got a job clerking at the California Pacific Railroad, of which Frisbie was a vice-president. He eventually was hired, no doubt at Arpad's recommendation, by Landsberger and Company in San Francisco.

While John and Epifania and their family were back east, Francisca took care of their home. When John returned, Francisca continued to spend a good amount of time managing the Vallejo house for him. Her absences from Sonoma made her husband feel, as he told her in January 1871, "alone, alone, alone," much like Francisca had told him she had felt many times during previous decades. His brother Salvador was the one person who would keep him company, coming over from his own rancho in Napa fairly frequently. But Salvador's behavior continued to puzzle Mariano Guadalupe. In addition to his brother, he counted on the company at Lachryma Montis of the Italian workers and a Chinese house servant. Mariano Guadalupe periodically updated Francisca on events and people at their home.

6. F.B.C.V. to Epifania, August 3, no year, C-B 441 FILM, reel 4, 199–201, TBL.

Lachryma Montis
Sonoma
October 28, 1870[7]

Francisca,

I received your letter and the one from your cousin, Doña Asunción. I can see that you are with the girls and in good company "fixing the country," as Salvador says. I think that Juan is going to be annoyed because Doña Margarita opened one of his letters.[8] It would be good if you sealed it back up. Since you already know what it says, you will be able to see if Juan tells her exactly what was in the letter.

If Doña Margarita doesn't come here to visit, say goodbye to her for me, because if she leaves right away I don't know when I'll see her again, perhaps when I return to Baja someday. Give her a kiss from me because I'm her uncle, another kiss because I was her tutor, and two kisses because I was her father, and my mother gave me permission to be her father. Also, give little Margarita a kiss, and one for each of the Marías and one for Lulú.

So you like Mother Luisa? It's good that you appreciate her. She is a very wise, prudent, and educated woman. I also like her very much. I admire her as a woman, and I value and respect her as a nun. She has appreciable qualities. She has a majestic presence and inspires respect, which is bolstered by a solid education. Now you can see that I, too, like what you like.

Without telling her what I have "said" about her, give her my regards.

Salvador gets up in the morning, leaves, returns, eats lunch, and then goes to bed. He gets up at three o'clock and leaves again. Ula is with Natalia and I'm alone, alone, alone, and still somewhat crippled. The skin on my feet is peeling off. Damn mustard plasters.

Until when?

M. G. Vallejo

P.S. It would be good if you became a nun and changed your name to "Jesusita del Calvario."

---

7. C-B 441, box 1, folder 6, TBL.
8. Juan was Margarita's brother. Martínez, *Guía familiar*, 301.

Lachryma Montis
Sonoma Valley
January 5, 1871[9]

Francisca,

Ever since I came back I've been alone, alone, alone. At times my pain lessens a bit, but I do feel a constant stabbing sensation on my left side. At times the pain is quite sharp. And there is no one here to rub my back. What can I do? Put up with it and suffer in silence. That's life. That's how you suffer when luck has you under its cruel control. I'm now physically ill, poor, isolated, and without resources. I'm also afflicted with mental suffering, which saddens my soul in an unbearable manner. I hope the time will come someday when all of this will be over and I will no longer suffer. I suffer in silence because <u>it is better that way. I would rather lose millions</u> before ever embarrassing our family with an act of violence. I'll suffer for my family, as you recently begged me to do. Do you remember? I only want and hope to make two or three thousand pesos for myself so that I can leave here and look for another way of life where I don't have to depend on anyone. You know how much I'm suffering right now! You know how much embarrassment I feel when I'm with people who think I live in luxury when I'm even without . . .

The weather is very nice, but very cold and dry.

Salvador is fine, as always. He comes and goes from Sonoma every day.

The Italians are working in the garden. The Chinese man makes tea and toast for me twice a day. That's enough. Sometimes Salvador makes a bit of stew the way he likes it. He thinks it's really good, but it isn't to my liking.

It's six o'clock in the evening. The sun disappeared between clouds of fire. The sky was magnificent, especially because the moon, white almost like silver, appeared at the same time from behind some very beautiful clouds of different colors.

I'm entertained by these phenomena of nature, but it always makes me feel sad to be so miserable. Perhaps that's the way of the world.

Give my regards to the whole family, from the oldest to the youngest.

And believe that I am your

M. G. Vallejo

Lachryma Montis
February 5, 1871[10]

Francisca,

I just received Margarita's letter and another one for you, which I have included.

---

9. C-B 441, box 1, folder 6, TBL.
10. C-B 441, box 1, folder 6, TBL.

There is also a letter for Mother Luisa. Margarita wants you to deliver it to her personally so that it will not be opened in the convent. It would be good if you yourself took the letter to Benicia and that you be the one who delivers it to Mother Luisa.[11]

Margarita says that they now are eating green chilis, corn, melons, watermelons, and more. She says that the bay is very large and better than any [body of water] she has ever seen.[12]

Give my regards to the girls and boys, granddaughters and grandsons, and to their parents and grandparents.

Yours,
M. G. Vallejo

Lachryma Montis
Sonoma
April 3, 1871[13]

Francisca,

I've just received, at five o'clock this evening, the letter I'm including, in which you'll see what Margarita has to say. She is at the "Hotel Orleans" on Post Street.

If I could go to Vallejo, I would, but my leg is still bad.

Send Margarita a telegram and she will come to see you right away to speak with you. If she does come, it would be best if you spoke at Adela's house. I believe that that subject is truly beyond her capabilities.

Give my regards to the whole family, on both sides.

Yours,
M. G. Vallejo

---

11. The families of both of Margarita's parents contained people who had married members of the Carrillo family in Baja California. When Margarita and her husband, Pedro, moved to the Bay Area in 1867, they naturally made contact with Francisca, a Carrillo to whom they were distantly related. Margarita enrolled her children in the school Francisca's children were attending, Saint Catherine's in Benicia, where Mother Luisa was teaching.

12. After Margarita's husband's political career collapsed, he did not return to Baja California. Margarita spent a good amount of time in the early 1870s in Baja California, attending to business and land matters involving both of their families. Margarita to F.B.C.V., October 17, 1873; Margarita to M.G.V., October 17 and October 21, 1873, both in C-B 441, box 5, folder 27, TBL.

13. C-B 441, box 1, folder 6, TBL.

Lachryma Montis
Sonoma
April 5, 1871[14]

Francisca,

It has rained from ten o'clock last night until three o'clock this afternoon, a very hard and steady rain.

I'm tired of staying in bed. The elastic stocking constricts [my leg] so much, but I tolerate it as well as I can. Today I didn't put it on, and that damned vein has been hurting me quite a lot. I can't bandage the leg myself.

The Chinese man makes tea for me and then he leaves. He returns, gives me vegetables, and then he leaves. He returns, gives me tea, and doesn't return until the next day in the morning.

Your flowers are doing well. The rooster is very tame. Salvador spent Holy Week reading. I'm either in bed or seated on the big chair.

Give my regards to everybody on "both sides."

M.G.V.

Felicidad is at Natalia's house.

Lachryma Montis
July 6, 1871[15]

Francisca,

I'm so happy that Natalia is better, and that the accident wasn't more serious. A dislocated knee is very difficult to treat.

Doctor Rogers was just here. He came to see if you would be able to let his wife, whom you already know, stay at the house for a while. I defer to you on this. The doctor is very much a gentleman and his wife is a very nice lady. He's planning on living in Sonoma to practice medicine there. The climate of San Francisco is too cold for his wife.

Give my regards to Attila and give Natalia and the "bebeis" a kiss.[16]

Yours truly,
M.G.V.

---

14. C-B 441, box 1, folder 6, TBL.
15. C-B 441, box 1, folder 6, TBL.
16. Vallejo spells the word "babies" as "bebeis." He ends the letter with the words "yours truly" in English.

JOHN FRISBIE'S FINANCIAL SITUATION GRADUALLY IMPROVED. IN 1870 HE was a founder of the Vallejo Savings and Commercial Bank. Like many other California banks, Frisbie's institution invested in silver mining in Nevada during the first half of the 1870s. This proved to be a very profitable investment. In addition, in 1871 the hopes of the officers of the mostly imaginary California Pacific Railroad were realized when the Central Pacific Railroad bought it out. This increased Frisbie's wealth enough that he was able to bring his family back to California. In addition, in December 1871 he was able to purchase Lachryma Montis from Madden and he deeded it to Francisca. Since the California constitution reflected Mexican practice and law and allowed married women to own property in their own name, this was a way of separating Lachryma Montis from any future financial difficulties Mariano Guadalupe himself might experience. Vallejo regarded this as giving possession of the estate back to him personally, and he urged Francisca not to tell anyone what Frisbie had done.

San Francisco
December 15, 1871[17]

Francisca,

I now have the title to Lachryma Montis and this has taken a huge weight off of me. I also have half a million pesos in stocks, which very soon will be worth their face value. Now they are worth one hundred to two hundred thousand pesos. I have several thousand pesos with which to pay some debts in Sonoma. <u>But I'm urging you not to say anything to anyone</u>, because for now it's better that way. And if you do say something to the boys, urge them to <u>keep it a secret</u>.

Since I'm already here, I want to finish up with the man who got in touch with me and get hold of a few more pesos, which we really need.

The girls definitely will be going to school. Lulú is staying with Jovita until Christmas Eve. As soon as I go to the house to put on the roof, you can come if you want to spend Christmas in San Francisco.

I've already paid some debts, but not all of them.

Fannie, Jovita, and Lulú are fine, they send you their regards.

It seems that God is helping us again.

Goodbye, kiss all the children.

M. G. Vallejo

---

17. C-B 441, box 1, folder 6, TBL.

Lachryma Montis, Residence of Gen. M.G. Vallejo, 1857, by Stephen William Shaw.
*Courtesy of the California History Room, California State Library, Sacramento.
In Kuchel and Dresel's* California Views, *vol. 1.2, no. 22,* FL281075.

Lachryma Montis
Sonoma Valley
December 26, 1871[18]

Francisca,

The stagecoach driver told me this morning that they didn't have any problems whatsoever on the way to Lakeville, except for the bad road. As soon as Napoleón appeared at the stagecoach door they headed out. He also went to San Francisco for his new job at Landsberger and Company.

Attila, Natalia, and their children had lunch with me. They headed back home at nine o'clock and. . . . I remained alone, alone, completely alone, since Salvador had gone to Sonoma very early that day. He returned at eleven o'clock, went to bed, got up while it was still dark, went back to his room, and I was left alone again, alone, completely alone.

It's still raining. I hope everyone is fine and having a good time together.

My leg is bad, the dampness is really hard on me. I need to distract myself in some way so as not to think so much.

---

18. C-B 441, box 1, folder 6, TBL.

I think that day after tomorrow I'll go down to be with all of you on New Year's Day. I think that Natalia (if Giovanari finishes her outfits) also will go down to the city.[19]

It's seven o'clock at night. I'm in my room alone, alone, completely alone. The sky is cloudy, the moon barely allows its opaque face to be seen. There is no breeze, no wind. The frogs are croaking scandalously. It's a gloomy night and I'm alone, alone, completely alone.

Don't forget to give Uladislao and Napoleón fifty pesos each.

Give my regards to Fannie (the elder) and to all the girls, as well as John, Jovita and her children, Arpad, and all the family.

Maybe I won't get sick and then I'll go there right away.

M. G. Vallejo

THE NEXT THREE LETTERS ARE ALL DATED MAY 1870, BUT THAT DATING cannot be correct since Francisca was in New York during that month. It would not have been possible for them to quote what they had written to one another a day or two previously, since those letters would have taken weeks to arrive. Mariano Guadalupe's letter of May 12 is in his handwriting, whereas Francisca's letters of May 10 and May 11 are copies made later. The copyist had access to Mariano Guadalupe's letter of May 12, and since that was dated 1870 the copyist decided that Francisca's letters had to be from the same year and therefore dated them 1870. Since Mariano Guadalupe's letter speaks of intense heat during the month of May, we have placed these letters in 1872, based upon newspaper accounts that reported abnormally high temperatures at the beginning of May 1872. The *Daily Alta California*, for instance, reported that the heat in San Francisco "late in the afternoon" during the May 1 festival was "disagreeable." Vallejo's letter also speaks of "suicides," and a widely publicized San Francisco suicide was reported in the *Sonoma Democrat* on the day before he wrote his letter.[20]

Mariano Guadalupe's dating of the letter may have been a simple mistake, since he wrote it in a very emotional state. But it also may have been by design, since Francisca complained in one of her letters that her husband had sent her the letter using her grandmother's name on the envelope rather than addressing the letter to Francisca Vallejo. Since Francisca was now the legal owner of Lachryma Montis,

---

19. This Giovanari is probably the wife of Pietro Giovanari, who had supervised Vallejo's Sonoma vineyards and then worked in the wine business with Arpad Haraszthy. Mrs. Giovanari was listed as a dressmaker in the 1877 California/Nevada business directory. McGinty, *Toast to Eclipse*, 36–39, 121; McKenney, *Business Directory*, 134.

20. *Sonoma Democrat*, May 11, 1872; *Petaluma Weekly Argus*, May 11, 1872; *Tuolumne Independent*, May 4, 1872; *Daily Alta California*, May 2, 1872.

her husband may have used her grandmother's maiden name as a way of trying to remind her that Lachryma Montis was, in his mind, still owned by him, not by her.

May 10, 1870 [prob. 1872][21]

Don Guadalupe,

   You say that my little letter of May 2 is very significant. I don't know which of the two letters might be more significant, yours or mine. What reason did you have for taking away the name I received when I married you? I accepted that name with all my heart, and with my entire body and soul. I received it from the hands of a minister of God, in the presence of men, women, and children, and in the presence of God Himself. You must remember that you and I swore that we would never separate. Do you have some cause or reason for taking away my last name? Have I dishonored it in some way? Oh no, no, no, no. Why are you taking it away from me? What does this say, what does this mean when a man takes away his <u>wife's</u> name? I'll be going home as soon as everything is arranged. John says it will be soon. After John leaves, I'll have to make room for all the things that are in my daughter Fannie's house. The house is going to be taken apart during the time they are on vacation. We will all go home together. Luisa and María would be very sad if they knew that I was leaving here.

Francisca Carrillo

Vallejo
May 11, 1870 [prob. 1872][22]

Don Guadalupe,

   I don't want to receive letters like the ones you wrote to me on April 28, May 2, and May 6, with that name you put on them. Do me the favor of not writing to me with that name, because it causes me great embarrassment in public. What are people going to say? That you have taken my name away from me because I am a <u>bad</u> woman? I'm not going to answer any more letters from you. Putting my name like that on the envelope of the letters is an insult, a scandal. I don't know what you are talking about in your letters to me. I don't understand any of it. It's frightening and it's shocking to read. Nothing you said in your letters has ever occurred to me. I have never thought about leaving my home. You are the only one who said you are a bastard. You claim that everything I said to you was insulting. You claim

21. C-B 441 FILM, reel 4, 194, TBL.
22. C-B 441 FILM, reel 4, 196, TBL.

that I said we should get a divorce. You were the one who said that, you brought it up first, you said that I was hindering your ability to conduct business. That is when I told you that it might be better for me to go some place where I would not be a bother to you. And I said that I was an old married woman and not some girl with whom you could do whatever you pleased. It is really hard for me to write, I can't continue. Don't write to me again using my grandmother's name. It breaks my heart to be called by that name.

Francisca Carrillo

Lachryma Montis
Sonoma Valley
May 12, 1870 [prob. 1872][23]

Francisca,

Never have I experienced such intense heat during the month of May since I have been in Sonoma. Its destructive effects can be seen everywhere in nature. I also think it has had an impact on the animals. In the newspapers the only things you read about are the destruction of plants, suicides, thousands of cases of insanity, people who cut off their heads and hands, people who throw themselves into the water to drown, and people who kill themselves for no other reason than because of the impact of the atmosphere.

Don't you think that you've gone insane? Those things you wrote in your two letters dated the 10th and the 11th which I have just received? What are you thinking, woman? Where did you get the idea that I took away your name? If I addressed the letters using your true family names, it's because you yourself have told me many times that you don't understand English. There have been times when you handed me the letters I had written to you because the address on the envelope said "Mrs. Gen. Vallejo," and you thought the letters were addressed to me. That is one reason. The other reason is that a few days ago you told me that you didn't like the letters I wrote to you to be addressed as "in care of anybody." But to make such a fuss about that? It's a bad, bad, bad misunderstanding or lack of understanding of what is happening. So, what is going on? Either I'm crazy or you are. You don't appreciate our children more than I do, nor do you love them more than I do. I want and wish for their well-being, their honor, and their reputation. Those who know me have seen it, and continue to see it. Why make them participate in our <u>misery</u> under the present circumstances? If you understand things one way and I another, we have very little time left to fight. Prudence and tranquility should be the rule to be an example for the family and for society, even if it's for appearances'

---

23. C-B 441, box 1, folder 6, TBL.

sake. Believe me, for God's sake, that when I have written my letters to you I have not intended in any way, shape, or form to take away your name, since every letter is written in the same fashion as always.

Believe me, what you wrote to me seems like a dream. Believe me when I say that I'm sincere when I speak to you. Believe me that it would pain me greatly if this craziness were to become public or be told to the family. It's about time that you do what you feel like doing, but not at the expense of the children and those with whom they are united.

You return the letters that I wrote to you because I <u>have taken away your name</u> in them. I have seen them, I read them, I reviewed them, and I read them again. Frankly, I can't find a better or different way to address you than how I always have, which is as "Francisca." I have <u>never</u> written a single letter that doesn't begin with that name. Why does that surprise you now? You are truly driving me crazy. I don't understand what you're saying nor do I understand what you mean. When we see one another I can explain this to you in one minute.

Always read my letters carefully and without misinterpreting them. I can't say anything more to you.

If you want, I'll go and get you and the girls. Here, the air, the home, the trees, the plants, the water, everything, everything will help you reconcile with the husband who, even though he is deficient, has known how to make something of the name given to his wife's children.[24]

The first advice I ever gave you in my life was "It's best to keep one's own counsel."[25] The world is the same now as it was back then. "He who goes outside his normal sphere is lost."[26]

Give my regards to Andrónico, Platón, Adela, and Lulú. Believe me when I say that your husband is without malice or insanity.

M. G. Vallejo

THE TWO YOUNGEST GIRLS, LUISA AND MARÍA, CONTINUED THEIR schooling. From Saint Catherine's Convent in Benicia they eventually moved on to the Convent of Notre Dame in San José. The mother superior of the convent, Sister María Teresa, was the eldest daughter of their father's older brother, José de Jesús. At Notre Dame the girls proved to be excellent students. They were deeply aware of their father's desire that all his children take their education very seriously. At

---

24. "Home" is written in English in this sentence.
25. *En boca cerrada no entran moscas.*
26. *El que se sale de su esfera normal se pierde.*

Convent of Notre Dame, San José, California.
Courtesy of the Library of Congress. No. 2002723880.

one point they believed the nuns were criticizing them for not applying themselves as conscientiously as they might. Fearful that such criticism might reach the ears of the father who expected so much of them, they decided to tell him that they thought such criticism was unjustified. As the girls undoubtedly expected, their father contacted the headmistress of the school, Sister Marie Cornelie. She wrote to Vallejo and assured him that Luisa in particular "may have taken to heart certain warnings or reprimands that were not meant for her, but rather for other students who do not excel in their studies." Sister Marie assured Vallejo, "Luisa and María are well behaved young ladies and they always apply themselves to their studies, something that the teachers find admirable." Indeed, Sister Marie continued, in the case of Luisa, "The award she received for her conscientious study habits is a testament to how well she is doing."[27]

At this time Vallejo was involved in legal proceedings to which he refers in the following letter and later, in July 2, 1874. The case involved a suit brought against him by San Francisco shipping merchant C. J. Jansen, who had allowed Plácido Vega to use one of his steamers to carry supplies to pro-Juárez forces. As compensation for this, Jansen received from Vallejo one of the promissory bonds on potential Mazatlán and Guaymas customs revenue that Vallejo had received from Vega. When the actual revenue did not materialize, Jansen sued Vallejo and received a judgment that Vallejo had to pay him almost $50,000.[28]

Vallejo
February 28, 1873[29]

Francisca,

Yesterday I arrived from Santa Cruz and came here to Vallejo to withdraw some money to pay for various things. First, to pay for fire insurance for the house; second, to give one hundred pesos to the Catholic Church; and third, to attend to Lulú's expenses while at Jovita's house. Lulú is doing very well. The singing teacher says Lulú has an excellent voice.

María is going with me tomorrow, Saturday. I'll also take her with me to Sonoma after she has a brief visit with the girls in San Francisco, and I'm released from court to return. Everyone here is fine. María is very well.

From San Francisco I'll send you sugar, candles, and other things for the house.

Give my regards to the boys and stay well. Take good care of yourself and accept the affection from the one who truly wishes you well.

M.G.V.

As John Frisbie's financial situation improved, he became a leading figure in Vallejo. When he brought his family back from New York, he purchased a large two-story house where he was able to entertain lavishly.[30] Francisca,

---

27. Sister Marie Cornelie to M.G.V., August 8, 1872, DLG-V 15, letter 1.

28. Miller, "Plácido Vega," 137–38; Emparán, *Vallejos*, 116; *San Francisco Chronicle*, September 16, 1873; *Daily Alta California*, July 17, 1874; Ramón de Zaldo to M.G.V., January 8 and January 20, 1874, DLG-V 61, letters 1 and 2.

29. C-B 441, box 1, folder 6, TBL.

30. Emparán, *Vallejos*, 270.

Home of John Frisbie and Fanny Vallejo Frisbie, Vallejo, California.
Courtesy of the Benicia Historical Museum. No. 2017.030.0074.

who maintained close contact with her daughters in Vallejo, became increasingly angry that Frisbie's obvious financial advantages were not being shared with her or her husband. She believed that her son-in-law's prosperity had been made possible by the generosity she and her husband had shown him for so many years.

As we have seen, she and other members of the family had been periodically grumbling about this for a decade. But Frisbie's now obvious prosperity intensified Francisca's negative views. In August she poured out her feelings in a long and emotional letter to Frisbie. In the end, her family convinced her not to send it.

August 26, 1873[31]
Sonoma

Señor Don Juan,

I pick up the pen, with pain in my heart and soul, but the great need I have to express myself is what has motivated me to write, even if my handwriting is poor.

---

31. BANC MSS 76/79c, box 1, folder 19, TBL.

This letter is on behalf of all my children, the poor dears. If I am unable to help them in some way or another, it is not my fault, and I don't want them to think that I am petty or miserable. Today, August 26, 1873, we don't have any meat or bread in this house, nor even one cent with which to buy anything. For meals I have had to make do with beef tripe, which Don Salvador Vallejo picked up somewhere. For many days we have been eating beef and lamb tripe, because we don't have any money to buy meat. Everything else is bought on credit at a store where we already owe about 350 pesos.

I am the cook. I am so hot. I suffer greatly. I have to wash the pots and the dishes two or three times a day. I don't have a cook. I have to wash all the clothes, and Lulú and María do the ironing, sweeping, and cleaning of the house. I don't even have a servant who can help me. I am everybody's servant. When a person is not used to that type of work, it becomes very burdensome. It is impossible for a woman my age to be strapped to a washboard for three or four days a week, and then, tired from that activity, go to the kitchen with hands that are sore and injured from doing the wash. And there, in the kitchen, her hands get cut or burned, and her feet get swollen from standing for so long. I am not going to mention every ache and pain or how much I am suffering because I would never finish.

I now must ask you, John, why is there so much penny-pinching for me and for my children? Why are you letting us die from hunger? If it were not for the fruits and vegetables, I don't know what would have become of us. Luisa, María, and I need shoes. Where will we obtain them? We need a number of things. How will we get them? From whom can we get them? The General is ill. Uladislao and Napoleón are so poor that the little they earn isn't enough for the two of them. The General gives me so little money that there isn't even enough to buy soap. Why, Señor Don Juan Frisbie, why am I asking you about this? Are you not the one to whom a very large amount of property was turned over? Didn't General Vallejo himself hand over some property to you without keeping a record of what you were doing, what you did, or what you are doing now? You do whatever you feel like doing when it comes to General Vallejo. Isn't it true that you are doing whatever you want to do to Guadalupe? Remember: Everybody knows that everything you have belongs to General Vallejo and his heirs, it doesn't belong to you. Isn't it true that you are still selling the lands and everything else, passing it all on to others, and hiding the property from the General and from me? I have seen with my own eyes, and I have heard with my own ears what the General said to me, which was that he was going to hand over everything to Captain Frisbie. He said that he wasn't familiar with American laws and that he couldn't manage his property. However, he thought that Captain Frisbie was a very good man and a man of honor, and he would know how to manage everything well. And, he was our daughter Fannie's husband. The General told me so many things that I, too, thought this would be a good idea. Don't you remember when you came to Sonoma as a huckster, and General Vallejo bought you a blue blanket and a number of other items, and he loaned you a room where you could put your things? Isn't it true that those were the only things you had in your possession? Do you remember?

Well, I certainly do remember. Do you remember when you started in Benicia? So many cattle, so many horses, so many people working. . . . You were the one in charge, you were the administrator, do you remember how much money you saved? Do you remember? I certainly do remember! Do you remember when you were going bankrupt and General Vallejo helped you out by giving you more property? I certainly do remember. And, I will remember for the rest of my life . . . what a warm welcome you have given my family, how well you treat Andrónico, the way in which you help Platón, how well employed Ula is because of you, what a great reputation you gave Napoleón. Instead of giving this to all of them, you took all of it away from them. You sold what Platón had . . . cattle, horses, a small house, some plots of land that his father had given him. You said that the other members of the family are good for nothing, they can't be trusted with anything, they are lazy, they don't know how to cope when they are given a job to do, they are passive, they sleep too much, they are very arrogant, they are always going for a stroll, they are indolent, they are spendthrifts, they are not worth anything, they barely have any talent, and they are of no use to anybody. The bad reports you were giving to the General about his children caused him to become angry with them. How many times have I had to defend them? How many times has the General wanted to throw them out of the house because you have said that my children are worthless? How many times have you found fault with my children and shared that with other people? When the General placed all the property in your hands, the children were very young. You were in a hurry to exchange the property the General gave you by selling it and buying something more to your liking. You really know how to grab what doesn't belong to you! Do you think that nobody is aware of this? Well, you're fooling yourself! We are all watching what you are doing. I can't put up with it any longer. I am suffering greatly from poverty and penny-pinching. I can never leave the house because I don't have one cent to my name. Nobody knows how much I am suffering or about the things I don't have. I feel worse for the General than I do for myself. He is always ill and doesn't know how to work. He is very frail. Why do you think we put up with you, and the General lets you do what you do? It is because you are married to our daughter Fannie, and because of her little children. Do you remember when you told me that you had planted a tree and that the tree was in bloom? Then you told me that the tree had fruit, and the business was going well, and as soon as the fruit ripened, we would have enough to live on? What happened to the tree? It probably froze. Ice probably fell on it. The fruit is probably frozen. But even though the fruit may be frozen, you should be more grateful. You should remember how generous Guadalupe was with you when you were poor. He gave you a lot of money and a lot of property, and he gave you my daughter Fannie. And how have you repaid him? By making Fannie believe you are taking care of us, giving us alms as an act of charity; that everything you give to the General, to me, and to my children is done out of goodness, charity, generosity, and is given freely. You are just putting on airs by making Fannie and everyone else believe you are providing for us. You might make Fannie believe that, but the rest of the world, no! no! no! Do you remember when Fannie said that I was the biggest squatter, as you have led her to believe? That you told her everything she has belongs to you? She thought I was going to take it all away from her. Whenever you have the opportunity to speak about us, you say very bad things in front of other people, in front of the servants, even in front of your little girls. When they set the table, they say that their Papá gave their Grandpapá the rugs, that if it were not for their Papá, Grandmamá's house would not have any rugs . . . and other such comments, which are irritating and tiresome. They say that their Papá paid for Lulú and María's schooling, and that their Papá had to support a very large family. Who has told those children so many lies? You and Fannie! Why haven't you told them the truth, which is just the opposite? You have taken control of our property, and that is why you have enough money to pay for the girls' schooling and your rugs, as well as the trips you are always taking to New York and around the world, traveling with family, and spending <u>enormous</u> amounts of money so that people will say you are very rich. And then you come and take away the small amount of rent that you had given to us, a paltry sum you would give to General Vallejo. How is it possible that you are so Jesuitical?

Enough talking on my part. General Vallejo is very ill these days. I am very tired and very old, and soon we both will die. That is what you want! But before that happens, <u>I</u> want to know how much property you have. I want it all laid out, everything, no <u>secrets</u> and nothing hidden! Then, when we know about everything, that is, when we are aware of everything we have, what is fair and what is ours . . . with nothing being hidden . . . what belongs to the General, to me, and to my children . . . when everything has been settled, then I want you to send me, on a monthly basis, an amount of money that is fair and that is mine by law. You do remember that this was General Vallejo's intention when he placed such a large amount of property in your hands. He didn't do that so you could keep it all for yourself. He turned the property over to you so that you could manage it well. That way we would have enough to live on and to educate my children without having to ask for favors. I don't want to wait any longer. If General Vallejo wants to continue to allow you to manage the property as you have done for more than twenty years, I want to know everything! The first thing that needs to be done is to eliminate all secrecy, nothing is to be hidden. General Vallejo's property shouldn't be hidden from anybody—not from me, not from the public, and not from my children. General Vallejo's property shouldn't be hidden from anybody, and least of all from those of us who are his heirs. General Vallejo hasn't stolen anything from anybody. He turned everything over to you, and even much more land, which had been given to him by the Mexican government. However, he refused to take more land for himself. He gave it to those who came to populate the area on this side of San Francisco Bay. Don't you remember that? We had so much property when you came. Everything you saw, managed, and still manage was not stolen. The government steals first and then men do. . . . one of those men was General Frémont . . . and then you. Do you remember when you didn't know where to keep the gold? Do you remember that you put the gold in one or two suitcases, then you took the suitcases full of gold to San Francisco? And then . . . you kept secret what you did with the money. And then you would say that you had gone bankrupt. No! no! no! It isn't possible to go bankrupt so many times, but you knew where you could get hold of more money. Even though you kept falling, you always had the means to pick yourself up again. The General would believe you and everything was done. I very much want to speak with you after you have received this letter.

I started writing this letter during the month of August, and as of today, October 8, I still haven't finished it. I write so poorly and so slowly that everyone who read this letter forgave me for that. In the end, I am happy that I said something. I know full well that nobody is going to listen to me. Everything written in this letter is the absolute truth.

Adela: I was writing this letter to John Frisbie, but your Papá didn't allow me to send it to him because he said that John would get mad, that he wasn't well, and that there are countless other considerations and issues [the General] has with him. However, he doesn't seem to have any issues with those of us who are suffering. I have a general awareness of what is going on and I am the one who has nothing. That is why I have mentioned everything that I remember and everything that I have witnessed. John is already rich and we are poor. He was given the property so that he could manage it well. Yes, he did manage it well, but he did it for himself and he left us poor . . . poor . . . poor . . . old, and sick. Yet, we still have the obligations of supporting and educating two daughters. And it's fine if he casts us, the old people, to one side, because we have benefited greatly from that "so and so" John.

Francisca María Felipa Benicia Carrillo de Vallejo

Sonoma
October 27, 1873

I finished writing this letter at 10 o'clock tonight, so that everyone can read it, but I have to obey your Papá. If I were an American woman, they wouldn't treat me like that, but I am a Spanish woman and that is why they do what they do.

As Francisca was composing the long letter to Frisbie, Platón realized that his mother was becoming very agitated. It is not clear whether Francisca shared parts of what she was writing with him, but at the beginning of October he wrote to her. He sought to urge her not to fixate upon the past and to focus upon the present and future:

Dear Mamá,[32]

I just received your letter, which pleased me greatly. I'm happy that you are well and that Papá has experienced some relief. It doesn't give me any satisfaction to write to you about the manner in which Papá lost or disposed of the property he had in the past. Perhaps he trusted others more than he should have. The truth of the matter is that now he has nothing left for anyone to steal. It doesn't matter if it is good or bad because everyone knows it to be true and it can't be denied. It's in the past.

Thank God that you have somewhere to live! Beware of anyone who comes around and wants to be your friend and makes false promises. Protect what you have left. Let's leave the past in the past, for there is nothing that can be done about it now. As Papá says, "If one isn't measured by the law of God, he is measured by the law of man." Papá had so much, and he was stripped of all of it.

Don't think that it's going to be easy to get back what you used to have. In the end, you have lost nothing more than land and insignificant things.

Dear Mamá, I ask you with all my heart not to think so much about the past, otherwise there will be no room in your mind to think about what is yet to come. Give Luisa, María, Ula, and Napoleón good advice. Be patient with Papá. Do it for me because I love him so much. God will help us.

Platón

Vallejo continued to address a series of family and financial issues.

---

32. Platón to F.B.C.V., October 6, 1873, C-B 441, box 6, folder 12, TBL.

I. Landsberger & Co. Arpad Haraszthy business card, 1871.
Courtesy of the California Historical Society,
California Business Ephemera Collection.

I. Landsberger & Co.
No. 429 Jackson Street
San Francisco
December 8, 1873[33]

Francisca,

It's noon. I just arrived from Vallejo, where I've been since I came back from Sonoma to look for a way to pay off old lady Boloff's bills, in addition to bills owed to other people, who bothered me so much every time they stared at me.[34] In the end, I paid all the bills owed in Vallejo, which amounted to close to $200. It wasn't done without a thousand <u>sacrifices</u>, but I have been able to rest.

Everyone in Vallejo is fine.

Now I'm going to go and see Jovita.

Give my regards to Lulú and Ula, Nap, etc.

M. G. Vallejo

---

33. C-B 441, box 1, folder 6, TBL.

34. Osip Volkov (ca. 1795–1866) was either a Russian deserter or a captive who arrived in California, where he became known as José Antonio Bolcoff. He married María Cándida Castro (ca. 1808–60) in 1822. Bolcoff served in a variety of political offices in the Santa Cruz region and corresponded with Vallejo. The family prospered during the Mexican era but lost money and land and incurred debts during the 1850s. The bill of $103 had apparently been owed to María Cándida but had never been paid, and a family member was now asking for the sum. Northrop, *Spanish-Mexican Families*, 2:49; Boloff to F.B.C.V., October 13, 1873, C-B 441, box 3, folder 7, TBL; Bancroft, *History of California*, 2:723; Gibson, *California through Russian Eyes*, 317.

Lachryma Montis
Sonoma
April 3, 1874[35]

Francisca,

At two o'clock on this Good Friday afternoon, I received your letter in which you tell me about Guadalupe's serious illness.[36] I barely had enough time to read it. I wrote a letter to Platón and sent it on the stagecoach from Napa. I also sent him your letter so that he would know everything.

I then sent him two telegrams indicating the seriousness of the illness. He responded by asking me to send him a letter explaining the illness. But that letter was already on its way. He should receive it this afternoon. I think he'll come, but it will be at the expense of his own patients in Vallejo. And it's going to cost him money, but what can be done?

I feel so very bad that my goddaughter is gravely ill. I've decided not to go because neither she nor Joaquín have had me come to their house. But if they need me for something, I'll go and help them. You know that I don't want anyone to think that I voluntarily get involved in other people's business, especially during critical moments such as this. I don't want to disrupt a family that looks upon foreigners such as myself with an evil eye, <u>thinking badly</u> about a person because they don't know or are unaware of the origin of things, or even how they managed to obtain the property.

I hope to God that Guadalupe gets better. I'm so sorry they waited so long before reaching out to Platón to cure her. They could have taken her to Vallejo for him to attend to her better. But what can be done?

Give her my regards. Tell her that her godfather blesses her, that he wishes for her to regain her good health, for her own benefit as well as that of her family. Also, give my regards to Joaquín.

Luisa, María, and Adela are fine. Give my regards to everyone.

M. G. Vallejo

San Francisco
July 2, 1874 (Wednesday)[37]

Francisca,

I couldn't leave court until late yesterday. Now we can leave here and go to

---

35. C-B 441, box 1, folder 6, TBL.

36. This was Guadalupe Cáceres. Born in 1831, she married Francisca's younger brother Joaquín in 1849. She bore eight children. By 1870, Joaquín was a hotel keeper in Sebastopol. Guadalupe died in May 1874. McGinty, "Carrillos of San Diego," 281–85; San Francisco de Asís Baptism 6525f; San Francisco Solano Marriage 357a; 1870 U.S. Census, Analy, Sonoma, California, Roll M593_91, 232B.

37. C-B 441, box 1, folder 6, TBL.

Henry Cerruti, ca. 1874. *Courtesy of The Bancroft Library, University of California, Berkeley.* POR: *Cerruti, Henry: 2.*

Sonoma. Today the girls are going to pay a few small bills. They are also going to see Jovita and go out together. Jovita's maid has been very sick.

It has made me very sad not to be at home, but that damn lawsuit in court has kept me busy. It's a very serious matter, but I think I'll come out fine.

It's possible that we will be in Sonoma day after tomorrow, Friday, or Saturday at the latest.

M. G. Vallejo

AT THE END OF MARCH 1874, ENRIQUE CERRUTI, A MEMBER OF HUBERT Howe Bancroft's staff, visited Vallejo at Lachryma Montis. For the next year and a half Vallejo worked with Cerruti, Bancroft, and other members of the Bancroft project as he composed his five-volume history of Alta California, which he titled "Recuerdos." He periodically sent money to Francisca in Sonoma and visited various family members and relatives as he traveled through northern Alta California with Cerruti, who was seeking documents and interviews from various people recommended to him by Vallejo.

Vallejo took the composition of his history very seriously. When Bancroft visited him and Cerruti in Monterey at the end of January 1875, he reported that Vallejo was more interested in accuracies than in speed. He said, "General Vallejo complained that Cerruti was constantly urging him on, that he was not satisfied unless

(left) Hubert Howe Bancroft. *Courtesy of The Bancroft Library,*
University of California, Berkeley. POR: *Bancroft, Hubert Howe: 22.*
(right) Hair comb worn by Francisca Benicia Carrillo on
her wedding day. Thomas Houseworth & Co. *Courtesy of the*
Autry Museum of the American West, Los Angeles. No. 2002.1.7.16.

they accomplished ten pages of manuscript a day, that they had done this for thirty days, but that he had plainly informed his tormenting secretary that he would not be hurried, but that made no difference."[38]

Vallejo found that members of his own family also wished to be involved in this project. Francisca, for example, wanted the tortoise shell comb she had worn at her wedding to be included in the parts of their manuscripts in which her husband or Bancroft might be discussing cultural issues. This comb had been purchased by her brother-in-law Henry Fitch in Cartagena, where it had been made. Francisca was convinced that it demonstrated that Californio society possessed a deep appreciation of cultural artifacts, and she insisted that the comb be handled with extreme care by the Bancroft staff. Cerruti stated, "I packed it up very carefully, for fear that it would break, and by keeping it constantly in my hands succeeded in delivering it in the same condition I had received it, to Mr. Oak, who ordered a copy to be taken by the photographers."[39] After he had successfully arranged for the comb to be photographed, he returned it to Francisca and recounted, "The comb after a delay of two weeks reached the house of the owner safely, who gladly

38. Bancroft, "Personal Observations," C-E 113:207, TBL.
39. Henry Oak was a senior member of Bancroft's staff.

replaced it in the same box in which she has kept it during the forty-two years it has been in her possession."⁴⁰

Vallejo also discovered that not all his children agreed with his assessments of California's past. Vallejo shared some of the pages of his history with Platón, who told him that he thought his father was at times being too harsh on the missionaries in particular, and on Catholicism in general. When he came to a passage in which Vallejo described "the scandalous conduct of the Mexican clergy," he told his father, "Papá, I think "Mexican clergy" should be specified or particularized, for not all of these people deserve to be classified or named even upon the same page. I would prefer to see the peccadillos of individuals rest buried from the exaggerated effects of modern spectacles and improved magnifying powers in the light of our advanced civilization." He continued, "I would counsel great prudence and care, less writing under a mistaken motive or from prejudice . . . you might cause a reflection against Our Holy Mother the Roman Catholic Church, who is without spot, or wrinkle, or any such thing."⁴¹

Family concerns continued to weigh on Vallejo. When he visited Mission San José in April he found that his brother José de Jesús was suffering from a very serious illness. Uladislao's persistent inability to find a stable and profitable career for himself bothered Vallejo. And he picked up some intelligence about marital difficulties Jovita was having with Arpad Haraszthy. A few years earlier Jovita had told her mother that she was trying to get Arpad "to rent me a house here in Vallejo." She said the reason was that "the rents are much cheaper than in San Francisco and it is healthier here. Our little Agostino and Carlos are not very strong."⁴² Incipient marital difficulties might have been another reason for her request.

[fragment, ca. 1875]⁴³

Guadalupe,

I received your last letter in which you ask me if I received the 30 pesos from the Italians. Yes, I did receive them, and I received 29 pesos from Doctor Van Geldern.⁴⁴ I then paid Corda 15 pesos and the butcher 30 pesos. I have 10 pesos left. I spent the rest. What you left me in the small trunk was no more than 5 pesos and a few reales from Mexico. It probably added up to 8 pesos and 11 reales. I don't spend one cent unless it is absolutely necessary. I don't have enough money to pay Allen or the stores. Every day I'm being charged for something.

---

40. Enrique Cerruti Research Notes, November 6, 1874. B-C 7, oversize box 11, folder 7, TBL.

41. Vallejo, *Recuerdos*, 2:941. Platón's comments were written in English.

42. Jovita to F.B.C.V., February 10, 1873, C-B 441, box 4, folder 28, TBL.

43. C-B 441, box 6, folder 5, TBL.

44. Charles Van Geldern, a native of Germany, was a physician in Sonoma. 1870 U.S. Census, Sonoma Township, Sonoma County, 19.

Monterey
January 19, 1875[45]

Francisca,

I arrived at this place last month on the 24th. Since it was Christmas Eve, I was invited to dine at the home of Señor Abrego.[46] After a lovely dinner, there was dancing "typical of this area" and more than one thousand cascarones were broken, which was a source of great delight for me.[47] I thought about you a lot. But I thought even more about Lulú and María, who have never seen that game, which the young people like so much. The cascarones were filled with pieces of tinsel and little colored papers. They also broke several of them on me. But I was able to get even with everyone, with the exception of a young girl who was walking close to me on the street. She said, "How are my little chicks? Peep, peep, peep." Since the eggs can be broken until the eve of Ash Wednesday, I'm hoping to get my revenge, but I don't know where she lives.

Ever since I arrived I've been very busy writing the history. General Cerruti is also very busy. He sends his regards to you and to all the girls.

Confidential! Ula wrote to me and he wants me to give him the rent from the barracks. I told him no. That rent is for you and the family. He also wants the small vineyard. I told him that I was going to work the land for the family and pay the "taxes," and that I would pay Napoleón to cultivate it.[48] He also wrote to me about some sort of business with stones or a stone quarry. I told him that, if he could set up the business, sell the stone for two reales a ton, and reserve the mineral rights, he should then have Wheaton draw up the papers.

It's very strange that after receiving one thousand pesos in silver Ula is incapable of starting up a business that will keep him busy and allow him to settle down. There is nothing about his behavior that pleases me.

I think I'll be finished soon and then I'll go to Sonoma.

Give my regards to Lulú and María, Napoleón, and Doña Carmelita. Don't get sick, don't get wet, and keep an eye on Demetrio's work.

Yours,
M. G. Vallejo

[In Cerruti's handwriting]:

My always lovingly remembered Señora: I send my sincerest wishes so that you will continue to enjoy very good health.

---

45. C-B 441, box 1, folder 7, TBL.
46. José Abrego was married to Josefa Estrada, the daughter of Mariano Guadalupe's older sister, María Josefa. Northrop, *Spanish-Mexican Families*, 2:1.
47. A *cascarón* is a hollowed-out chicken egg filled with confetti.
48. The word "taxes" is in English.

This photograph represents the room in which Mariano Guadalupe Vallejo worked with Henry Cerruti on the Bancroft project. Vallejo is standing in the center, with Cerruti seated at the left. Between them is José Abrego, whom Cerruti interviewed in Monterey in June 1874. To the right of Vallejo is Rosana Leese, daughter of Rosalía Vallejo. On the extreme right is Vicente P. Gómez, who conducted ten interviews with Californios for Bancroft. *Courtesy of The Bancroft Library, University of California, Berkeley.* BANC PIC *1987.025-PIC.*

The General is very happy. Since we arrived in Monterey we have been working very, very hard and the history is very much ahead of schedule. The girls here are very pretty and friendly. I already have a girlfriend.

A thousand greetings to Señoritas Lulú and María, and for you the sincere affection of your loyal servant and friend.

Enrique Cerruti

P.S. All the beautiful women in Monterey are anxiously awaiting the arrival of the beautiful Miss Lulú. Have her come quickly on the wings of a white dove.

Monterey
January 22, 1875[49]

Francisca,

I'm sending you one hundred pesos by way of the Express. The expenses here have been paid. I hope you received the rent from the barracks and also from the Italians. That money should be of use to you for any pressing needs up until February 1.

I'm now finishing the history of California. I'll return to Sonoma soon to reunite with my family.

I still haven't received any news from Doña Margarita. It seems to me that her latest promises, of having sent D. Félix Gibert to pay the bills she owes at Señor Guty's establishment in San Francisco, haven't been fulfilled either.[50] It's likely that Señor Gibert will come next month and we can clear up any doubts at that time.

It has rained so, so much here. Even though I've been laid up for a few days because of my pain, it hasn't been as sharp as when I had that attack at home. Each day I get better.

General Cerruti sends his cordial greetings to everyone, and I send my sincere affection to everyone, as well. If you can, send me a small box of sweet oranges with the leaves attached. Some are for eating and others are gifts for the señoritas (who only know about acorns). Your husband would be most grateful to you if you could do this.

M. G. Vallejo

Tell Luisa and María to write long and beautiful letters to me.

Monterey
March 15, 1875[51]

Francisca,

I finally will be leaving here next Monday, that is, on the 22nd. I'll arrive in San Francisco and probably arrive in Sonoma on Tuesday to see everyone.

Tell Jovita not to return to San Francisco until <u>we speak at great length</u> about . . . certain things. . . .

Tell Demetrio that I received his letters, but that I've been very busy and sick and that two steamships were lost last month while en route from New York to Liverpool.

49. C-B 441, box 1, folder 6, TBL.

50. Félix Gibert was a former *jefe político* of the territory of Baja California. He had been a close political ally of Margarita's father, Juan de Dios Angulo. Valadés, *Historia de Baja California*, 14. "Señor Guty" is most likely Alexander Guthrie, partner in the large San Francisco mercantile firm Balfour and Guthrie. Langley, *San Francisco Directory for the Year 1875*, 108.

51. C-B 441, box 1, folder 7, TBL.

City of Monterey, by Léon Trousset,
November 1, 1875. *Courtesy of the
Amon Carter Museum of American
Art. No. 1977.1.*

Tell Lulú and María that I'm going to see them again. As soon as the bridge over the Monterey River is repaired, we will spend some time at this place.

I already have written 1,300 pages of the history. My eyesight, mind, and body are tired; but I started this and it must be finished.

I haven't forgotten about Don Gibert's arrival. I have the bill ready and I'm sending you a copy of it.

I was told that Doña Carmelita had come to San Francisco, but if she hasn't give her a thousand greetings and my fondest regards.

Give my regards to Natalia, Nap, Ula, etc.

I'm waiting for <u>a bit of money</u> and then I'll leave. Give my regards to the Italians.

And you, dear wife (my bride), believe me when I say that I am your affectionate and sincere friend.

M. G. Vallejo

P.S. I was giving myself some time here hoping that the court case in Washington would be won. That way <u>I would be fairly rich when I arrived back in Sonoma</u>, with a fine coach, horse, etc., but it still hasn't been settled. Pray to God that it will turn out well soon, because you are the one who is going to win the lottery. Then we will have "fun."[52]

---

52. The word "fun" is in English in the original letter.

Mission San José
April 12, 1875[53]

Francisca,

The day I left Sonoma, I arrived here at this place where I found my brother, almost dead. You can only imagine how sad it was to see this. As he lay in his bed, surrounded by his entire family, he recognized me when I hugged him. Together we cried. His wife and all his daughters were also crying. My brother began to rally, and after half an hour he began to open his eyes. I held his hand and caressed it. That is how we spent most of the afternoon and well into the night. The next day he seemed a bit more alert. I stayed next to him the entire time.

Later a telegram was sent to Plutarco in Salt Lake (Utah) and another to Platón.[54] Both of them arrived yesterday and now my brother seems more animated. Platón offers <u>hope</u> and this energizes my brother, so much so that the family feels comforted. If he continues to improve over the next two days, perhaps they will let me leave. Platón will leave tomorrow. It seems as if I have been here to encourage my

53. C-B 441, box 1, folder 4, TBL.
54. Plutarco was José de Jesús Vallejo's son. See Kern, *Vallejos of Mission San José*, 51; Emparán, *Vallejos*, 128.

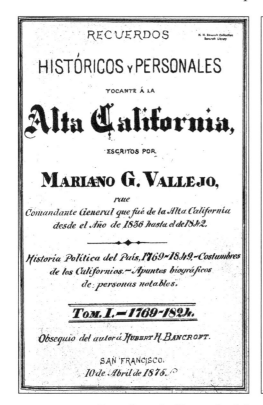 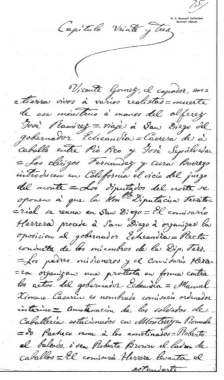

Pages from the "Recuerdos." *Courtesy of The Bancroft Library,*
University of California, Berkeley. C-D 17–21.

brother to live. That is why his wife and daughters are begging me not to leave so
soon.

Everyone sends their regards to you and to the girls. They want you to ask San
Antonio to cure their father. Take care of everyone and give them my regards.

Your husband,
M. G. Vallejo

Mission San José (Sunday)
April 18, 1875[55]

Francisca,
My brother has been improving somewhat over the past two days. He is speaking

55. C-B 441, box 1, folder 7, TBL.

Plutarco Vallejo.
Courtesy of California State Parks,
Sonoma Barracks. No. 243-x-2613.

clearly, his eyesight is better, and his chest is clear. He can move his hand and leg, up to a point, on the side of his body that seemed to have suffered paralysis from the stroke. Everything appears to indicate improvement, but he still can't walk. In order to get him out of bed each day, I have to lift him from the upper part of his body and Plutarco lifts his legs. We then put him on another bed. As soon as his bed has been changed, we put him back. The doctor is very hopeful that he will recover.

When they read Luisa's letter to him, he cried a lot. He wants me to thank everyone for having prayed to San Antonio for him. He believes that he's going to recover because of that. He has received all the sacraments.

If I abandon him, I think he will die, because if a short time goes by and he doesn't see me he starts looking for me everywhere. I think that if he continues to improve during this week I'll be able to return home. And if I <u>can</u>, I'll bring the girls back to stay here for a few days. He wants to get to know them, and it seems that if he can see them he'll improve. He likes it when my family visits him. He improved quite a bit when I arrived and even more so when Platón came. He cried when Platón left.

The train ride from here to Monterey is four hours. When Rosana, Luisa, and María arrive, I'll take them to Monterey and leave Rosana off there.[56] That way they will get to know their uncle and aunts. We'll return home soon, God willing.

My brother sends you thousands and thousands of greetings. Soledad sends so much love, as do Guadalupe, Encarnación, Carmelita, and Toñita, who is very weak and sick.[57]

---

56. Rosana is a daughter of Mariano Guadalupe's sister Rosalía.

57. Soledad Sánchez (1811–92) is José de Jesús Vallejo's wife. The others are their children. See Kern, *Vallejos of Mission San José,* 28, 30, 97.

Tell Luisa that I received her letter and to keep writing to me; tell María and Rosana the same thing.

When I passed through San Francisco, I found out that Napoleón was "Engue-chi" to an American girl from California, Miss Brown, and that it is serious.[58] I don't know if it's true or not, but that's what I was told.

Señor Gibert hasn't arrived yet. I've been told that Don Ramón de Zaldo is gravely ill.

Give my many regards to the girls.

Your,
M. G. Vallejo

Mission San José
Alameda County
April 19, 1875[59]

Francisca,

General Cerruti is taking the key to my trunk with him. That is where, among various papers of great importance, there is a yellow folder labeled "San Felipe Mines."[60] I need it urgently.

I just received a telegram from Monterey. It says that Rosalía is very ill and she is all alone. I think it would be good for Rosana to go [to Monterey]. Lulú and María can accompany her. That way they will get to know their uncle and aunts. Then I'll bring them back with me.

Among all my brothers, older sisters, and those who are ill, I seem to be the one with the "best liver." What can you do?

General Cerruti will serve as their escort.

M. G. Vallejo

ON APRIL 20, VALLEJO NOTIFIED FRANCISCA BY TELEGRAM THAT HIS brother was improving.

---

58. "Enguechi" is the way Vallejo heard the English word "engaged."

59. C-B 441, box 1, folder 7, TBL.

60. The words "San Felipe Mines" are written in English in the original letter. These were silver and lead mines in Inyo County whose ownership was being contested by various parties. Josephine de Zaldo to M.G.V., January 27, 1874, DLG-V 61, letter 4; Ramón de Zaldo to M.G.V., January 28 and January 30, 1874, DLG-V 61, letters 5 and 6; Chalfant, *Story of Inyo*, 248–56.

(above) *Mission San José, ca. 1870,
by Clyde Arbuckle. Courtesy of the
California Room, San José Public
Library, Clyde Arbuckle Collection:
csj_ARB-B082.*

(right) Telegram from Mariano
Guadalupe to Francisca Benicia.
*Courtesy of The Bancroft Library,
University of California, Berkeley. C-B
441, box 1, folder 7.*

Teresa de la Guerra, by Leonardo Barbieri,
1850s. Courtesy of The Bancroft Library,
University of California, Berkeley. POR:
Guerra de Hartnell, María Teresa de la:1.

Vallejo and Cerruti made a second trip to the Monterey area during the summer. During their stay in the city that had been the capital of Spanish and Mexican California, Vallejo had the great pleasure of introducing his two youngest children, María and Lulú, to the region in which he had been born and raised.

Abbot Home
Salinas City
July 28, 1875[61]

Francisca,

Late yesterday we arrived from San Francisco and immediately went to visit Teresa at her small ranch.[62] She was very happy to see the girls. Upon arriving at her house, I hid and let the girls go inside. The first thing Teresa said was, "These are Vallejo girls—Guadalupe's or Luz's daughters."[63] Since there was nothing else I could do, I went inside. We chatted for an hour and a half. She wanted us to stay and spend the night with her, but we didn't want to inconvenience her. So against her wishes, we came here to Salinas City. Tomorrow we leave for Monterey.

Luisa and María are well and happy. I was at Jovita's house in San Francisco. It's

---

61. C-B 441, box 1, folder 7, TBL.
62. Teresa de la Guerra, whom Vallejo and Cerruti had interviewed on March 21 at Rancho Alisal. See Beebe and Senkewicz, *Testimonios*, 55.
63. Francisca's sister Luz was married to Mariano Guadalupe's brother Salvador.

true that the house she moved to is a bit farther away, but it has everything a family needs. It's a block and a half away from the train and she has a servant. Jovita said nothing to me, not even a hint at any of her <u>suffering</u> and <u>difficulties</u>. Everything I had been told made me feel as if I had a <u>bitter pill</u> in my mouth, but I kept quiet.

In San Francisco we were invited to go to the theater, and we went.

Doña Paquita and Don Josef invited us to their home, and we spent many happy hours there.[64] They were very cordial. They served us a delicious dinner and we had a very "good time," as people say nowadays.

We also visited Frank Curtis's mother and she, as well as her children, have treated us very well. She is a very friendly woman and very generous.[65]

Here in Salinas, or rather Watsonville, we met up with "Carrigan," and he is as ornery as ever.[66] He barges into the house, upsets everything, and is opinionated and stubborn. He doesn't realize that he makes people mad. He wants to be waited on hand and foot because he is "so good looking" and he believes he deserves to be treated that way. He doesn't just pay you a visit, he wears you out for one, two, three, and four hours. This is tiring.

Goodbye. Give my regards to Natalia, Napoleón, and also Doña Carmelita. Don't forget Salvador and Uladislao. I send Lulú's and María's best wishes to you. And I send you mine most sincerely.

M. G. Vallejo

Monterey
August 23, 1875[67]

Francisca,

I'm sending you a "bill of exchange" for fifty pesos drawn against the Bank of Sonoma. Half of it is so you can pay the Chinese cook, Ha-Yen, and the other half is for expenses.

I hope Rafael has paid the rent on time.

This week I'll finish the history, and I think we'll leave here on Tuesday of next week. The girls are already preparing their clothing, that is to say, washing and ironing the dirty clothes and packing their trunks. There is so much damned dust here.

María bought stockings, petticoats, and camisoles here. She wants to spend a year at the convent in Benicia, which makes me happy. Both girls are fine and send

---

64. Possibly the hosts were Francisca and José Lázaro, who lived in San Francisco in 1870. He was a barber, and they were both born in Mexico in the early 1840s. 1870 U.S. Census San Francisco Ward 2, San Francisco, California, Roll M593_79, 183A.

65. Frank Curtis had been Lulú's boyfriend. Emparán, *Vallejos*, 432.

66. "Carrigan" is Nicolas Carriger, a native of Tennessee who had come to California in 1846 and farmed in the Sonoma region since 1850. See Emparán, *Vallejos*, 133, and Bancroft, *History of California*, 2:743.

67. C-B 441, box 1, folder 7, TBL.

Ledger entry for services rendered by Ha-Yen, the Vallejo's cook. Nine months' salary from January 1 to September 30, 1878, $25 a month, $225.00 total. *Courtesy of The Bancroft Library, University of California, Berkeley.* BANC MSS C-B 441, 9:1. *Vallejo,* MG *Accounts, 1829–1888.*

you their regards. They are sad because you are home alone, but I couldn't let them return by themselves. Very soon I will be in Sonoma.

M. G. Vallejo

❉ ❉ ❉

ON OCTOBER 20, 1875, NAPOLEÓN MARRIED MARTHA BROWN, DAUGHTER of an attorney for the Southern Pacific Railroad. She was a Protestant, not a Catholic, and the wedding was held at her family's home in Oakland and officiated by a Protestant clergyman. The couple honeymooned in Cloverdale before settling in Oakland. Francisca continued to spend time in Vallejo with her children. Salvador Vallejo, whose mental state had increasingly concerned his brother, began to become physically weaker and more fragile. He had difficulty walking, and since he could not retain an erect military posture he refused to allow himself to be photographed.[68]

---

68. McKittrick, "Salvador Vallejo," 328.

(left) Martha Brown. *Courtesy of California State Parks,*
Sonoma Barracks. No. 243–468–32.
(right) Napoleón Vallejo. *Courtesy of Santa Clara*
University Archives and Special Collections. POR-*Vallejo, 61–7-8.*

Sonoma Valley
October 16, 1875[69]

Dear Francisca,

 I'm sending you twenty pesos in gold notes.[70]

 Everything here is peaceful. Ula was here for quite a while. Three gentlemen from Petaluma came to visit me and chatted a lot about history. General Cerruti spoke at length with the "Editor of the Petaluma Argus."[71] He gave him a tour of the area, and they drank two bottles of wine. They already left.

 When all of you left, the Chinese man brought me my tea. I took a cup of tea and a piece of toast to Jovita and invited Doña Carmelita and Felicidad to accompany me. They happily joined me for breakfast in the dining room and ate all my toast. Later, for lunch, we had a small steak, carnitas with chili, and beans with cheese.

---

69. C-B 441, box 1, folder 7, TBL.

70. Vallejo writes "gold notes" in English in the original.

71. The quoted phrase is in English in the original. The September 3, 1875, issue of the *Petaluma Weekly Argus* contained this notice in the "Items of Local Interest" section: "General Vallejo and General Cerruti have nearly concluded their labors on the 'History of California.'"

Then Doña Carmelita and Felicidad left to sweep the rooms upstairs. In the meantime, I excused myself and went to put on a clean shirt before going to see Snyder, who they say is very ill. Ula said, "How much [money] will the widow be left with?"

Cerruti went to pick up the letters.

Give my regards to Señora Brown and Martha, and to the girls as well. And receive the affection of . . .

M. G. Vallejo

Doña Carmelita cleaned the bird cage and the birds.

Lachryma Montis
Sonoma
October 25, 1875[72]

Francisca,

Today I received a letter from Luisa in which she tells me in great detail about everything they have done—the wedding, her visit to the warship *Austriaco,* her visit with Jovita, and how happy she was to see them. The reason they all had to stay in Oakland was that Mrs. Cook insisted on it so much, they had to stay. You didn't tell me if you received the bit of money I sent you by means of the post office.[73] Nevertheless, I hope you received it. Jovita writes to me almost every day.

I always thought that no one from Vallejo would go to Napoleón's wedding. That's what I told them before I left. But he is already married and <u>happily married</u>, even though it may anger everyone from "A" to "Z." The archbishop, the priests, and all the others will issue their Church "interdictum" against him, as well as against everyone who attended the ceremony. But, "what's done, is done."[74] I'll need to have it out with everyone and fight until they all get over being angry. "They either stop resisting or they can hang themselves."[75]

Toñita seems to be much better. Yesterday she went with me in the phaeton to see Natalia. We visited with her for a while and then returned. Natalia is fine.

I bought, rather, I bought on credit, a piece of white linen.[76] Doña Carmelita is making me four undershirts and six undershorts. She is always singing. At night we have Salvador come and join us and we sing thousands of little songs until very late. That is how we spend the time.

I've been very busy constructing the well with Forsyth. He will be finished with the work tomorrow.

---

72. C-B 441, box 1, folder 7, TBL.
73. The words "post office" are in English in the original.
74. *A lo hecho, pecho.*
75. *O cabestrean o se ahorcan.*
76. The word "rather" is in English in the original.

The figs are already very dry.

Today I received a letter from Nap. He is in Cloverdale, very happy, and may return soon.

To Luisa: Your Uncle Salvador is always the same. He sends you his greetings. His room is beautiful, as always.

Yesterday Mrs. Fowler came to buy vegetables. Encarnación, Toñita's sister, says that they have been waiting for you at the mission with open arms.

My eyes are already hurting. Tell the girls to be good.

Come soon. I'm tired of being alone, and in spite of everything I need you.

Doña Carmelita is taking good care of your little birds and every morning she cleans their cage and brings them lettuce.

Goodbye, my eyes hurt.

Receive the sincere esteem and affection of your husband and good friend.

M. G. Vallejo

Lachryma Montis
Sonoma
November 16, 1875[77]

Francisca,

It has been raining almost continuously since the day after you left. The cold is beginning to be felt, and as a result the chimneys are being used to provide needed heat for <u>old people</u> and the infirm. Three days ago there was a very strong rain and wind storm. The trees were swaying so much from side to side that I thought they would break into pieces, but they have held up. The only bad thing that happened is that I'm going to have to do a lot of work with the <u>broom</u> picking up all the <u>green beans</u> and the leaves from both the locust tree in front and the fig tree. But, as the saying goes, "You can't get something for nothing."[78]

Salvador was very ill. The girls begged him to go to Napoleón's room so they could bathe him and put patches on him, that is, those things that stick to the places where one has pain. But he refused to do so under any circumstances. He is a bit better, however, thanks to a few <u>good swigs</u>. One day he was so very pale that I thought it was something serious.

I can't make any money from the grapes. The bank is a bank from . . . a bank that doesn't even have enough to pay for the water from the "Watter Works."[79] We are in a miserable state.

---

77. C-B 441, box 1, folder 7, TBL.
78. *El que quiere azul celeste, que le cueste.*
79. "Watter Works" is in the original letter.

Mariano Guadalupe Vallejo, 1875.
Courtesy of the Sonoma County Library.
Photograph Collection. cstr_pho 007334.

Toñita seems to be a little bit better, but the cold is bad for her. She is back to playing the piano and she gets exercise by walking around the living room.

Luisa and Doña Carmelita left yesterday to go and visit Natalia. They spent the entire day at her house. When they returned, Luisa told me that Natalia was sad because she couldn't go out. They promised her that they all would return and help her <u>sew her little curtains</u>.

I'm still terribly bothered by not being able to read, which for me is an unbearable problem. I can write, but it involves tremendous effort. If I can't read or write, I'll end up a good-for-nothing. My rheumatism is acting up again. It couldn't happen at a worse time because the months of January and February will be upon us. Sonoma is turning into a place full of old people who are suffering. Some are so fat that they are about to explode; others are just shriveling up and dying; others are drunks; and most of them are go-betweens and scoundrels. Holy Mother, give us a miracle. . . .

How is my sister-in-law? Josefina? And Anita? And Bailhache and Grant and all their little girls and boys?[80]

Give my regards to everyone and also regards from the girls. Tell José that he hasn't behaved well with his uncle with regard to the papers. Tell him that "Promising does not cause poverty, giving does."[81]

---

80. Francisca was apparently visiting her sister Josefa in Healdsburg. Josefa's daughter, Josefina, was married to John Bailhache, and another daughter, Anita, was married to John Grant. Northrop, *Spanish-Mexican Families,* 2:87–88.

81. José was probably Josefa Carrillo de Fitch's son, who lived in the town of Russian River, about thirty miles north of his mother's home. Vallejo and Enrique Cerruti were scheduled to visit Josefa toward the end of November, and

Grape arbor at Lachryma Montis, by Carleton E. Watkins.
Courtesy of The Bancroft Library, University of California, Berkeley.
BANC PIC 1974.019:066-ALB.

How was your trip on the stagecoach? How is your health? Be mindful of the dampness and the cold. It seems to me that you are happy with your people and aren't even thinking about us. It doesn't seem like you are trying to come back here any time soon. That's fine. Enjoy it as much as you can. The affection from one's own people is very sweet when there is complete trust, but it isn't always like that. Do you remember the way Molera was received? There is no love in that house.

Receive the esteem of your good friend and husband.

M. G. Vallejo

Vallejo had probably asked José to collect some family documents in preparation for the visit. 1870 U.S. Census, Russian River Township, Sonoma County, 18; Beebe and Senkewicz, *Testimonios*, 69.

Salvador died in February 1876 at Lachryma Montis. Soon after his death, Lulú wrote to her brother Platón: "We <u>all</u>, Papá in particular, think of dear Uncle every day, and have as many laughable anecdotes. . . . Uncle Salvador's room has been cleaned out and the doors left open for airing, and every time any of us look in that direction, we imagine and almost believe he is there." She continued, "Poor Uncle, we have missed him beyond expression, and then, what a consolation to know he acted his part nobly towards the last. He has left this world of trials and disappointments to one of uninterrupted and ineffable happiness."[82] The death of his brother was probably responsible for the more reflective tone Vallejo struck as he discussed his children in a letter to Francisca in April:

Lachryma Montis
April 14, 1876[83]

Francisca,

I imagine that you are surrounded by the whole family, <u>young</u> and <u>old</u>, much like a mother hen who is trying to cover all her many chicks with her wings. That is one of life's joys, and it is proof of having fulfilled the mission that nature intended for humanity, as well as the Divine commandment from the Supreme Creator to "grow and multiply." Fannie is beautiful and she is a good mother to her lovely offspring. Adela is also a beautiful woman, full of life, but without a large family. If she were in better health she could have at least a dozen more, which would keep her occupied.

Andrónico is a good man who knows no other way of being than to be honest. But today honesty is not enough, especially if a person wants to be able to rest a bit and live comfortably in old age. <u>It is necessary</u> "to do what everyone else does" or else look like a good-for-nothing. As the proverb says, "You are known by the company you keep."[84] But poor Andrónico is not a trickster.

Platón is a fine, young doctor with firm principles, a good Catholic, almost ascetic. I believe his profession provides him with enough to support his family. I think he's happy with his position. So, all things considered, the family brings honor to us. I believe you should be proud to be surrounded by them. Isn't that true? Well, "Enjoy them because you deserve them."

Ever since you left I've been taking care of the kittens that were born . . . Foni, Furino, Flora, and Chato. Each one bites me a lot.

Molina continues to milk the cows, and the Chinese man is doing what you told him to do with the milk.

---

82. Lulú to Platón, March 3, 1876, C-B 441, box 12, folder 13, TBL (written in English); *Daily Alta California*, February 19 and 20, 1876.
83. C-B 441 FILM, reel 2, 8–9, TBL.
84. *Quien con lobos anda a ahullar se enseña.*

Doña Pachita wrote me a very long letter and sent another one for you.[85] She wants <u>to come</u> with her family and spend some time here. She also wants to know how much it would cost per week. I told her that you were away from home, but she could come, and that you would arrange everything. Even though the house is small, there should be no problem accommodating her.

I was thinking that Doña Carmelita's room could be for the servant and the children, along with Carmelita.

The boy is still cleaning. Everything will shine like a mirror.

Lulú wrote to me, asking for a few pesos, and I sent them to her. She, Jovita, and María are fine. They might be in Vallejo today. But if they aren't, Lulú says they will be there tomorrow, Saturday.

Go to confession and repent for all your mischief. And don't come back with a sour look on your face. I authorize you to go to confession on my behalf.

Tell Adela that her oranges were not sent by Express or to South Vallejo either. The box was sent to "Vallejo Crossing" instead and it should be there.

<u>Kiss all of our descendants</u> and believe that I am your

M. G. Vallejo

THE NEXT TWO LETTERS DEAL WITH A PLAN VALLEJO HAD FORMULATED for obtaining and selling some land in Baja California. The situation that sparked this project stretched back to the 1850s. During that decade, Baja California, a territory of the Mexican Republic, was invaded by a small American filibuster force led by William Walker. The force took La Paz in November 1853, and Walker declared Baja California an independent entity. But he quickly had to abandon that location and move north to Ensenada, from which Mexican forces forced him to retreat back to the United States within a few months. For the rest of the decade, the political situation in northern Baja California remained chaotic, as various factions took advantage of the confusion created by the Walker incursion. By the end of the decade, the population of the northern frontier was very scant. Historian Pablo Martínez speculated that there may not have been more than a dozen families in the area.[86]

To deal with this situation, the territorial government of Baja California, aided

---

85. "Pachita" is Vallejo's spelling of the name Paquita.

86. Private American mercenaries who invaded parts of Latin America in the mid-nineteenth century were called "filibusters," after the Spanish term *filibustero*, which meant "freebooter" or "buccaneer." The subtitle of Rosengarten's book is *The Life and Death of William Walker, the Most Notorious Filibuster of the Nineteenth Century*. Rosengarten, *Freebooters Must Die*, 37–56; Woodward, *Republic of Lower California*; Taylor, "Historical Summary of Lower California," 67; Martínez, *Historia de Baja California*, 405.

intermittently by the Juárez national government, encouraged various colonization efforts to increase the population of the northern part of the territory. Bibiano Dávalos, a military official in the region, proposed that Mexican families living in Alta California be encouraged to settle in Baja California. Other colonization efforts undertaken by both the territorial and central governments also tried to ensure that a good proportion of potential colonists would be Mexicans.[87]

Vallejo was able to keep up with these events through contacts with some of Francisca's relatives in Baja California. Some of her Carrillo relatives married members of the Montaño family, and additional marriages brought the Angulo family, which had settled at Rancho Santa Catarina, into the relationship as well. One member of this extended family network was Asunción Montaño de Angulo, Margarita's mother. As we have seen in the letter of February 24, 1870, Vallejo was in regular contact with both of Margarita's parents. Indeed, his hospitality to Margarita may well have stemmed in part from his desire to strengthen his relationship with her parents—for Vallejo, always on the lookout for schemes that might help him recover from the financial reversals he was experiencing, was beginning to think that it might be profitable to purchase some of the Santa Catarina lands and then sell them to Mexicans in Alta California who would find a move to Baja California attractive.[88]

However, the discovery of precious metals in the Baja California peninsula, gold in the north and silver in the south, led some Anglo-Americans to enter Baja California as potential miners in the 1860s. The aggressive behavior of these Americans and their encroachment upon traditional tribal lands eventually led to tensions between them and Baja California's Indigenous populations. These tensions became acute in the mid-1870s. In 1876 a group of Indigenous people near Tecate complained to the local authorities that "the Americans here intended to murder them all." The Indigenous people fought back. A few months later a rancher in the region reported that "the Indians are still stealing his stock. These depredations can scarcely be checked as affairs now stand." Because of such tensions, Vallejo had to abandon his Baja California project.[89]

87. Valadés, *Historia de la Baja California*, 186; Taylor, "Mining Boom," 472, 475.

88. Martínez, *Guía familiar*, 14, 20, 35, 152, 582, 890.

89. *San Diego Union*, June 4 and July 26, 1876; Bancroft, *North Mexican States*, 2:775; see also *Daily Alta California*, March 19, August 16, and December 13, 1875; *Sacramento Daily Union*, August 5, 1876.

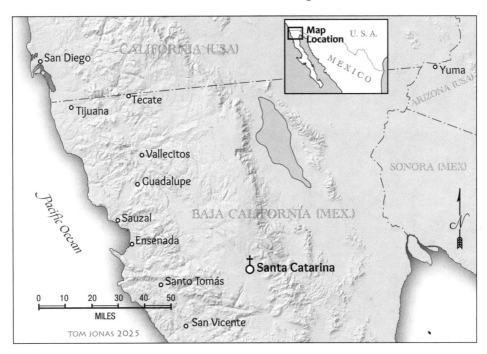

Northern Baja California and the location of Santa Catarina.
Drawn by Tom Jonas.

Commercial Hotel
Montgomery Avenue and Kearny St.
San Francisco
August 21, 1876[90]

Francisca,

There is a proverb that says, "After swimming so hard, to end up drowning on the shore."[91] That's what happened to me with the sale of the land at Santa Catarina on the Baja California frontier. The sale was already well under way.

What happened is that when I and those who wanted to buy the land were about ready to head for San Diego to look at the land, news arrived of an Indian uprising at the Colorado River involving the Indians of that area and those from San Diego and Temécula. The Indians murdered rancheros in that area. The families have returned to San Diego. Even the commissioner from Mexico, who had come to arrange the land titles, also took refuge in San Diego. So the people who were going to purchase my land in Santa Catarina have changed their mind about buying it, at least for now, saying that they can't take possession of it, which makes sense.

90. C-B 441, box 1, folder 7, TBL.
91. *Después de tanto nadar, venirse a ahogar en la orilla*, which basically means "so much effort for nothing."

St. Mary's Hospital, South Beach, San Francisco, 1866.
Courtesy of the Library of Congress. Lawrence & Houseworth Collection.
LOT 3544–37, *no. 383.*

The Mexican consul told me that neither he nor the government can take measures to pacify the Indians due to a lack of money. And he doesn't know how or when everything will settle down, which means I've wasted my time and lost the little bit of money I had. It's all bad news at this end. It seems to me that <u>everything about Baja California</u> is cursed.... [This letter is incomplete in the file]

Commercial Hotel
San Francisco
February 21, 1877[92]

Francisca,

After I arrived in this city on Saturday, I went to see Jovita and Lulú. They are fine, as are Agustina and Carlos. From there, I took the carriage and headed to Santa María hospital to visit Don Germán.[93] I found him to be very weary because of his illness, but he was quite capable of carrying on a conversation. He asked about you and the whole family. He also remembered Doña Carmelita. He sends his greetings to everyone.

The doctor arrived shortly after. He had only been there but a moment when Don Germán told him that he wanted him to perform the operation to remove the fluid from his belly. Soon everything was set up and I myself assisted the doctor. He inserted the small cannula and the patient had no adverse reaction. About four gallons of fluid was released and he felt great relief. It seems that he continues to improve up to a certain point. Today, Monday, I wasn't able to go and see him, but they say he isn't worse. I hope the poor man gets better because he has suffered greatly. Anita and Pomposa are also helping him as much as possible, even though the hospital provides all the assistance one could hope for.

Yesterday, Sunday, Jovita sang in the French church.[94] She sang well.

I haven't been able to conduct any business regarding the land in Baja California. Everyone is asking me to give them peaceful possession of the land, but I can't because that area is engaged in an open revolution. Nothing is safe there, not even one's life. That is the kind of luck that always pursues us.

I saw Mrs. Chipman yesterday on the Oakland steamer.[95] She sends you her

92. C-B 441, box 1, folder 8, TBL.

93. Probably José Germán Piña, son of Lázaro Piña, one of Vallejo's most important soldiers in Sonoma. José Germán had been granted Rancho Tzabaco, a 15,000-acre tract in Sonoma County in 1843. Bancroft, *History of California*, 4:780; Hoffman, *Reports of Land Cases, Appendix*, 41. The hospital mentioned is St. Mary's Hospital in San Francisco.

94. This was the Église Notre Dame des Victoires, founded in 1856 to serve the French Catholic immigrants during the gold rush. Jovita's singing talents were well known. A newspaper article describing her 1879 funeral service noted that she "was particularly admired for her superior musical accomplishments. Her voice was fine and well cultivated, and those who knew her were frequently enchanted by her power of expression." *Daily Alta California*, July 17, 1879.

95. Caroline Elizabeth McLean (1835–1912) was married to W. W. Chipman, a founder of Alameda.

regards. She is always the same. If I see her again, I'm going to <u>tease her about the</u> <u>guitar</u>, the one with the broken strings that is always in a corner.

I saw my sister, Mrs. Cooper, at the hospital. She is fine and seemed very robust to me and in good health, "so far."[96]

Some of the Mexican men have gone to visit Niagara, others are still here waiting to see what happens with the politics in Mexico.

Give my regards to everyone.

M. G. Vallejo

I'm planning on returning to Sonoma on Thursday or Saturday.

San Francisco
February 23, 1877[97]

Francisca,

I wrote you a letter yesterday but I don't know if I sent it, or if I left it behind at Jovita's house. I'm sending this one to you very early today, to let you know that tomorrow, Saturday, I'll be in Sonoma with Luisa and Señor Prieto. He promised me that he will accompany us and stay at the house for a day or two. It's necessary to prepare a fine dinner.

We are all fine. Give my regards to everyone.

M. G. Vallejo

THE JOVITA-ARPAD MARRIAGE WAS PROVING TO BE PROBLEMATIC. IN March 1877, Vallejo learned from Arpad that Jovita had requested a divorce. Fearing that Jovita had been influenced by the people she met in San Francisco, Vallejo spent some time at their home. Even though Jovita told her father about Arpad's behavior toward her, Vallejo feared that the resulting scandal would damage the entire family.

---

96. The words "so far" are in English in the original letter.
97. Melville Schweitzer Collection, MS Vault 55, box 1, folder 2, California Historical Society, San Francisco.

Arpad Haraszthy. *Courtesy of California State Parks, Sonoma Barracks, No. 243-x-3215.*

1126 Pine St.
San Francisco
March 13, 1877[98]

Francisca,

The moment I arrived at the pier I ran into Arpad, and later at his office he explained to me "the how and the why" (from his perspective) about the divorce between himself and Jovita. Then I went to see Jovita. She also explained her reasons. The story behind it is that Arpad wrote Jovita a letter telling her to ask him for a divorce. Since she wanted a divorce she immediately went to see Mr. Brooks, who took on the case. I then went to see Brooks and spoke with him for a long time. Mr. Brooks does not like divorces at all, but he has to do what Jovita has requested if a scandal can't be avoided. He would like for Jovita to go and live with us for one year as a trial separation, but Jovita doesn't want to do that because she says she'll lose the rights to the furniture, her money, etc. And she is certain that after one year has passed she'll be in the same position she is in now. Arpad has to give her half of the property they have acquired together, in addition to child support. So I don't know what to think or what to do. Arpad says for me to manage the case, because I will look out for Jovita's honor and her interests as well as those of their children and the Haraszthy family.

With all my heart I would like to avoid a scandal and placate Jovita somewhat, but she has her mind made up. Tomorrow I'll see what I can do and tonight I'll chat with them a bit more.

---

98. C-B 441, box 1, folder 8, TBL.

Jovita Vallejo Haraszthy.
Courtesy of California State Parks,
Sonoma Barracks. No. 243-x-3240.

I'm writing to you in a hurry. My eyesight is bothering me and every so often my head suffers from vertigo. I, who have so much work to do and needed some peace of mind, have come here to find that I have to deal with this business, which is so bad for my own situation.

Give my regards to the girls, Doña Carmelita, and Eduardo.

M. G. Vallejo

Commercial Hotel
San Francisco
March 22, 1877[99]

Francisca,

After countless chats and long conversations with Jovita, as a friend, an adviser, and also a father, I haven't been able to make my advice prevail with regard to the divorce, no matter how I framed the subject. Despite my largess ("so far") with regard to such matters, I'm surprised to find Jovita being so obstinate.[100] She told me that she has no other option than suicide, an insane asylum, or a divorce. She didn't consult with me at the beginning, because she knew I would tell her to stay with her husband. "Papá," she told me, "only he who carries the bier knows how much the dead person weighs."[101] Arpad has written various letters to her asking

---

99. C-B 441, box 1, folder 8, TBL.
100. In the original letter "so far" is in English.
101. *Sólo el que carga las andas sabe lo que pesa el muerto.*

for her forgiveness. And now that I've seen that a reconciliation is impossible, divorce is inevitable. This will result in a horrible scandal, "whatever is meant to be will happen."[102] To prove before the courts why a divorce should be granted, a huge scandal and lots of money are necessary, especially if one of the parties resists and defends their case. Besides, it's such a long process.

Adela probably has told you how determined Jovita is. It is known that she is surrounded by people who view marriage as a plaything; but if "holy liberty" proclaims it, you will see that social dissolution, which is based on the family, will arrive very soon.

It is true that men (machos) are generally guilty, because nine out of ten men are bad. And I believe that nine out of ten women are good.

Now you see how I view the situation, but the family is the only thing that keeps society together. Frankly, I can't find a solution. Civilization pushes us to the brink. I hope the exalted hand of the Almighty or the breath of His infinite divinity will intervene for the good of all beings.

What an example for young people! Give my regards to the girls, Luz, and Carmelita.

M. G. Vallejo

I accidentally wrote on paper from the "Commercial Hotel." I'm staying at Jovita's house.

ON MARCH 26, ARPAD WROTE A LONG LETTER TO JOVITA:

San Francisco
March 26, 1877[103]

Jovita,

With feelings of kindness I address you these lines and ask of you once again to forget the past and return to me as my wife. I am not only willing, but even anxious to acknowledge to you, all those errors that I have committed, as I have already acknowledged them to your Father, to General Frisbie, and to Mrs. Hancock.[104] And I hope, Jovita, that you will pardon these.

I must own that my nature is hasty and impetuous—that I get angry easy, and suffer long; but I have never done you a deliberate injury, or said an unkind word

---

102. *Lo que fuese sonará.*
103. C-B 441, box 4, folder 27, TBL (written in English).
104. Ida Hancock, Arpad's sister.

to you, unless at the time, I was suffering bitterly from some cause or another. And if you know how I have suffered, too, you would be quick to return to me.

Remember Jovita, that all my griefs have heretofore, whether fancied or real, been ever zealously locked in my own bosom—for I had no confidant, nor would I have where you were concerned.

By the painful experience of the last few days, I have found that the slightest wrong, though even fancied, when locked in your own bosom wrings your heart with a torture untold greater than if confided to another. And when the crises does come, it comes with fearful force.

We have misunderstood each other for years, and the incidents which have lately transpired have proven a painful lesson, which I never shall forget. And I do earnestly assure you that this misunderstanding is the sole cause of our troubles. Why not then come together once again, since we know this cause and with the example of the past before us, endeavor to lead a new life, and wring from the future many happy days—more than we have ever had in the past. If you consent, I assure you that I will do everything in my power to secure our mutual happiness. There is always plenty of time to appeal to the courts; but, when our case gets so far, there is no receding, it must go on [to] the bitter end. Jovita, I beg of you in the name of everything that you have ever held sacred, think of the things that would have to be said by yourself, and the things that would have to be said of others. NO, no, in this your cooler moment you cannot consent to urge the matter to that point, and in justice to yourself, Jovita, I must say, that you will!

I do not beg of you to return from fear of injury to parties you suppose guilty, for I do most solemnly deny the grave charges that you have so often made to your father. I deny each and every one of them. I am innocent of them all, and do constantly desire you to verify what I have asserted. My motive for wishing you to return is a nobler, a holier one—the reputation of our two families, the welfare of our two beautiful children, and a sincere affection for yourself.

There are many things, Jovita, that I desire to say to you, but it would take too long to commit them to paper, I therefore beg you to give me a personal interview, where we can be alone and uninterrupted, that I may tell you, once and forever, things which I think you ought to know concerning my conduct. You can now accord me this favor, for we have both had ample time to cool our angry passions, and settle our minds down to serious reflection.

In conclusion, Jovita, let me recall to your memory the times that you have come to me and asked my forgiveness! That forgiveness, when ever asked, was always given <u>immediately</u>. I am now before you and ask [for] yours!

Will you be less generous than I?

Your husband,
Arpad Haraszthy

✳ ✳ ✳

JOVITA CONSENTED TO ARPAD'S REQUEST, AND THEY MET THAT EVENING at her house. Vallejo was in another room and did not hear the conversation, but he was able to report to Francisca the results of the meeting:

1126 Pine St.
San Francisco
March 26, 1877[105]

Francisca,

It's nine o'clock at night and I'm writing to tell you about the sad and unfortunate situation between Jovita and Arpad. After many conversations, advice given to one and to the other; listening to the complaints and grave accusations, some serious and some apparent; consulting with various members of both families such as Adela, Frisbie, and also Ida H. de Hancock, all who in some form or another have tried to persuade Jovita to agree to a reconciliation; nothing has been achieved, despite Arpad's many letters asking her to forgive him, repenting a thousand times over, like Mary Magdalene, for having sinned and provoked the divorce. Right now (after I have been in this house, day and night, for eighteen days) Arpad has asked that Jovita give him an explanation face-to-face, since they had not spoken with one another. And now they are talking in the living room. I'm in Jovita's room waiting for the result. This won't be the end of it, but it should lead to a good understanding and will help them avoid more of the mortifying sorrow of the last few weeks, which have been truly dreadful. Jovita isn't going to yield so easily. I'm sure that her position is advantageous with regard to the legitimacy of the facts. But the scandal is going to be huge and shocking! Arpad "provoked the bull but couldn't handle the goring."[106] Arpad underestimated the woman with whom he was speaking. This was not the Jovita he thought he knew. He is repentant and doesn't know what else he can do to reunite with his wife. He is promising and swearing to live happily and content. Can this be true? Who knows: The "<u>disturbances of the heart</u>" are (often) very damaging and very plausible.[107] Sometimes it is necessary to protect oneself from them. Don't you think so? <u>We who know</u> our own weaknesses, <u>know about</u> all these things from experience.

But the scandal, the families, the children, etc. We still have two single daughters at home who are witnessing these things happen to their very own sister. Even

---

105. C-B 441, box 1, folder 8, TBL.

106. *Llamó al toro y no aguantó la cornada.*

107. The parenthetical "often" is in English in the original letter.

though she is in the right, this is bad, very bad, extremely bad. For Jovita, this is a hellish sacrifice, but what about the children?

Eleven o'clock at night

The meeting has ended. Jovita is giving in (not because she wants to) because of the children. It <u>seems</u> that she is yielding, but she has all day tomorrow to respond.

Tuesday, 27

I copied Arpad's letter, even though I felt a very sharp pain in my eyes. I'm including it here for you to read.

Carmelita arrived yesterday. She gave Jovita your message and she left for "Berclay" by way of Oakland to see her brother.[108]

This week I'm planning on bringing this <u>mess</u> to an end. I'll go home to get away from so much gossip. Then I'll tell you everything.

Today Arpad wanted to take Jovita to the theater but she refused; also to the park, and she refused. He has promised so much to all of us that it is starting to scare us.

This letter is for you; don't let it out of the house.

<u>Confidential</u>: Attila wrote to Arpad and told him that Lulú and María are very much against him. That is what Arpad told me. Even though he appears to be repentant, he is a very bad man. He has an evil heart.

God willing that he behaves well from now on. If not, Jovita will leave the house. Give my regards to everyone.

M. G. Vallejo

I have Arpad's first letters, the originals. You will see them soon.

IN THE MEANTIME, THE SILVER MINING BUBBLE IN WHICH FRISBIE'S Vallejo bank had invested burst and the bank failed. Vallejo's first reaction was to ask Epifania if her family needed any help. He wrote her:

Doña Carmelita Domínguez has just informed me on your behalf that you are financially ruined and you don't have any money at all. If that is the case, my entire home is at your disposal, without hesitation.

I don't know anything. John hasn't said a word to me about it, so that is why I think this may be somewhat of an exaggeration. Neither can I believe (in case there might be a grain of truth to this) that all of my property that is in Frisbie's hands (a <u>trust</u>) from which I

Attila Haraszthy.
Private Collection.
*Courtesy of Brian D.
McGinty.*

receive $250 a month from the interest on $30,000, in addition to the interest on the land, lots, etc., would have suffered in the bankruptcy or seizure of assets.[109]

Nevertheless, you all have a home here. I would be happy to welcome you under my roof and be together again.[110]

But he shared his own sentiments about Frisbie's failure with Platón. He told him, "This last stroke of luck has left me feeling older than a centenarian."[111] Vallejo suddenly found himself without money. He realized that he was in a very similar situation to many of the old Californios who were "so broke or poor."

Commercial Hotel
San Francisco
April 4, 1877[112]

Francisca,

It seems that the furious storm that was unleashed regarding the situation with Jovita has been followed by a period of calm. The sea that had been so filled with turbulence has now calmed down and continues to be serene and peaceful. May it please the Heavens to keep it that way, and that never again will we have to hear

---

109. The underscored word "trust" is in English in the original letter.
110. M.G.V. to Epifania, September 25, 1876, C-B 441, box 1, folder 7, TBL.
111. M.G.V. to Platón, October 26, 1876, C-B 441 FILM, reel 3, 50, TBL.
112. C-B 441, box 1, folder 8, TBL.

or see such disagreeable things happening to our loved ones. Fortunately, we didn't have anything to be embarrassed about on our side, this time.

I've been trying to obtain a little bit of money from my old friends (when I had money, I did all kinds of favors for them) to put my business affairs in good order. However, no one has wanted to loan me one single peso. They are a bunch of thankless ingrates, among them are Mr. Brooks and Madden, whom everyone says are quite rich. So I'm very troubled. Who knows what I'm going to do? If I can't find any money in two or three days, I'll have to abandon my business affairs for now, in their present state, even though everything has been very well prepared and the prospects are excellent.

We shouldn't expect to receive anything from our people. They are all poor, very poor. Yesterday, our friend Pickett loaned me <u>one peso</u>! I was grateful to him for the manner in which he did this, because it was a gesture of goodwill, even though I didn't need it. I had about five pesos in my pocket. I invited him to have dinner with me and I spent four reales on the food for both of us![113]

Give my regards to Luisa, María, and Natalia.

M. G. Vallejo

Commercial Hotel
San Francisco
April 6, 1877[114]

Francisca,

Late today, at nine p.m., I received a telegram from Lulú. She told me the following: "Don't come home. Mamá will meet you in Vallejo tonight."

Since I haven't told anyone that I was going to Vallejo, nor have I even thought about going there, I was surprised by the telegram. I couldn't come up with a reason why Lulú would send me such a telegram. Tomorrow I'm supposed to leave for Sonoma. I don't want to go because it means that I will leave pending the business you know about. But I have to return because of a tremendous lack of money, money needed to continue arranging things, as I told you in my last letter. In addition, I don't want to incur any more debt at this hotel where I've been staying since the situation with Jovita was resolved.

So I'm writing this letter to you to tell you not to come. If you were to come, I would be even more stressed than I am now, because I wouldn't have any hope of obtaining even one real to pay the hotel bill for both of us. I, who had been "building

---

113. As we have seen, Vallejo often used the word "peso" for dollar. Eight reales constituted one peso, so four reales was fifty cents.
114. C-B 441, box 1, folder 8, TBL.

castles in the air" thinking about so many good things, haven't lost hope yet.[115] There is another proverb that says, "With patience one can attain everything."[116] What is bad is that I'm so old and easily deceived. As more time passes, I'll have less physical strength to go out and make a living, not for me, but rather for the family.

Jovita and María are fine. I go and see them every day at the house, after managing my way through countless labyrinths and shenanigans by my land procurers.

I'm already tired from pounding the pavement. Besides, <u>our people</u>, almost all of them, are so broke or poor. It's hard to believe that most of the time they have nothing to eat. There is so much poverty. I'm bored.

Luisa is at Fannie's house in Vallejo. That was a good suggestion. I hope she will be fine there for a period of time.

Give my regards to Doña Carmelita and tell her that I haven't had time to visit her sister Doña Paquita, even though her husband has invited me on various occasions. But I do know that she is well.

The smallpox outbreak continues, but now it isn't as strong, even though people do die every day of the week.

Ula is fine, so are Napoleón and his wife.

This week I'll go to Sonoma for a few days to rest, until I get word from the men who want me to go to Guaymas to inspect the mines they want to buy in that part of Mexico.

In the meantime, receive the sincere respect of your husband.

M. G. Vallejo

Give my regards to Natalia, Attila, and children.

---

115. *Haciendo castillos en el aire.*
116. *La paciencia todo lo alcanza.*

Our Lady of Guadalupe Church.
Courtesy of DeGolyer Library, Southern Methodist University. Ag1997.1990.

CHAPTER 5

Patriarch and Matriarch
1877–1891

After the collapse of his bank, John Frisbie immediately began to seek out other ventures. His experience with the California Pacific Railroad encouraged him to look for other railroading opportunities. But this time his focus was on Mexico, where various Americans were already engaged in seeking rail construction contracts. Hoping the presence of a former officer in the Mexican army might help his efforts, Frisbie convinced Vallejo to join him. Vallejo traveled by train to Chicago. From there he and Frisbie went to New Orleans, where they boarded a ship for Veracruz. Then they took the train to Mexico City and checked into the Hotel Iturbide, located in the central section of the city, five blocks from the Zócalo, the city's central plaza.

Vallejo's initial reactions to Mexico City were ambivalent. In a letter to Platón, he expressed how impressed he was by the architecture of the cathedral in the Zócalo as well as the grandeur of the Shrine of Our Lady of Guadalupe. He wrote, "The cathedral and sanctuary are stupendous and grandiose. The Colegiata de Nuestra Señora de Guadalupe, two miles away from the cathedral, is perhaps the most beautiful building in the world in terms of its architecture and decoration. That is where the Guadalupana is located. I went up to the sanctuary, knelt down, kissed the feet of the Virgin, and touched her with my hands. The heavy frame and the immense rays of light are made of solid gold."

He added, "I made a point of sitting in the archbishop's chair. The Father who was my guide told me that Archbishop Alemany also sat there, and with reason. In the center of the paved area is the vault of Viceroy Bucareli, who contributed so much

Viaduct that Mariano Guadalupe Vallejo would have crossed when traveling by train
from Veracruz to Mexico City. *Courtesy of DeGolyer Library,
Southern Methodist University. Ag1982.0027.*

to the founding of Alta California."[1] But at the same time that he was enthralled by
these architectural qualities, he was repelled by the bad air and what he considered
the destitute condition of the large number of Indigenous people in the capital city.

In an interview with a Mexican newspaper, he took the tone that Frisbie hoped
would gain him an audience among the city's elite: "I was born a Mexican; my ancestors
were Mexican, and I have always maintained with my sword the honor of Mexico. . . .
The day Mexico has a railroad, which devouring distance unites it with California,
commerce and industry will flourish."[2] Frisbie and Vallejo eventually obtained an
audience with the country's finance minister and with President Porfirio Díaz.

Frisbie received enough encouragement from his conversations with Mexican
officials that, by the end of July, Vallejo was hopeful that some sort of deal might
be struck in the next few weeks.

---

1. M.G.V. to Platón, June 18, 1877, C-B 441 FILM, reel 3, 61, TBL.
2. *Daily Alta California*, August 3, 1877, quoting the Mexico City *Monitor Republicano* of June 27, 1877.

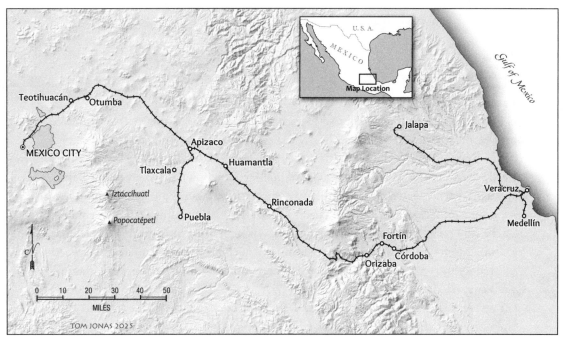

Railroad line from Veracruz to Mexico City.
Drawn by Tom Jonas.

Hotel Iturbide, No. 75
May 28, 1877[3]

Francisca,

Last night, Sunday, I arrived in this city, tired and quite battered about after traveling on land and water for eighteen days, but I am well and healthy. The crossing from New Orleans to Veracruz was seven days and the heat was excessive. Veracruz is a very beautiful city, but it was extremely hot, which caused me to suffer greatly. Yesterday we left for Mexico City and traveled by train for three hundred miles through the most picturesque mountains in the world.

The train from Veracruz to Mexico City is truly stupendous because of its construction and the route it follows. It is truly something miraculous. I have to write quickly because the mail is leaving very soon. Give my many regards to Lulú, María, Doña Carmelita, and Natalia. I will write a longer letter next time.

M. G. Vallejo

3. C-B 441, box 1, folder 8, TBL.

Hotel Iturbide
June 7, 1877[4]

Francisca,

I am finally in the capital of the Mexican Republic, our former native land. We arrived on May 27, so I have been here for eleven days.

The first impression I had of this place made me feel that this was a bad omen. It produced a sadness in me, and a sense of melancholy took hold of my whole being. It wasn't until today that I was able to conquer it by a supreme effort and <u>necessary</u> determination, since the situation doesn't lend itself to any other alternative.

The general aspect of the city, having been within it, seems sad to me. Add to that its inhabitants on the streets and it seems sinister. There is no similarity between our habits and customs in California. The contrast is greater than one can imagine. I am surprised and it pains me.

I was very sick during the first six days. Besides the difficulties of the trip and all of the noise, one can't breathe the air here. It chokes you. The polluted air is truly unbearable. In addition, the sight of thousands upon thousands of Indian men and women carrying their children on their backs in a state of decrepitude, in rags and tatters, thousands upon thousands of donkeys carrying grasses and clay pots that get in one's way on the streets, and others carrying coal, is such a miserable sight.

On the other hand, the cathedral and the sanctuary are truly stupendous and grandiose works of architecture. The ornate decor inside is astonishing. On the outside the construction is sumptuous and imposing. Both the inside and the outside are testaments to the men who founded them. However, it makes one feel pity, sadness, and a sense of compassion to see so many people scattered about on the glazed floor tiles amidst the immense naves, massive columns, and opulent altars. Seeing people seated on the floor here and there as they listen to Mass <u>contrasts</u> with the glorious music, so stupendous that it enraptures and is an ecstasy worthy of another civilization.

There is so much good here, but also so many bad things that I can't describe now.

Tell Carmelita that I have looked everywhere for her husband, and I can't find a trace of him, but I will continue doing everything possible.

I think a lot about you, Lulú, and María. When I think about Jovita I feel a deep sadness in my heart. Poor thing, whenever I have dreams about her, I dream that she is unhappy.

Today I am going to visit the president.

My eyesight is bad, and I can't write any more.

---

4. C-B 441, box 1, folder 8, TBL.

(*above*) Cargadores, 1880. Mexican street scene by William Henry Jackson.
Courtesy of the Library of Congress. LC-D418–8559.
(*below*) Cathedral of Mexico City, 1880, by William Henry Jackson.
Courtesy of the Library of Congress. LOT 3160.

Patio of the Hotel Iturbide, Mexico City. *Vistas Mexicanas, 175.*
Courtesy of DeGolyer Library, Southern Methodist University. Ag1985.0372.

Goodbye, Francisca. Give my best to our children, to Doña Carmelita and Ricardo, and also to the Italians.[5]

Your husband,
M. G. Vallejo

Everything here seems warlike. There are troops everywhere; thousands of armed men inundate the streets and plazas.

Hotel Iturbide, No. 75
Mexico
July 30, 1877[6]

Francisca,

The steamer *City of Mexico* arrived at Veracruz yesterday. We are planning to leave on it today if the men from the government resolve the business we have

---

5. Ricardo is Carmelita's son. 1870 U.S. Census, San Francisco, Ward 8, 137.
6. C-B 441, box 1, folder 8, TBL.

pending before the ministries regarding the railroads. If the decision is favorable, it is probable that we will stay here another twenty days to get it all settled properly. But if it is not favorable, we will leave on this steamer and head straight to Washington, and from there to California. I pray to God that it will be resolved soon, for a thousand reasons. The first is that I can't have peace of mind being away from the family. And the second is because in this land one can't live with any sense of security. The entire country is in an uproar. It is a diabolical labyrinth, a frightful "pandemonium" with no hope of salvation. The society is horribly corrupt down to its very foundations. What a pitiful country, yet so rich and so beautiful!

The population of Mexico City is 300,000 inhabitants, but <u>250,000 are full-blooded Indians</u> and they wander around the streets as if they were on their rancherías. Some are naked and others are half dressed. Think of them as if they were the likenesses of Isidora and Bill, and Vicente and Jesusa.[7]

It is eight o'clock in the morning and General Vega is coming into my room with another general by the name of Ballesteros, along with General Palomares. This situation will keep me from writing at greater length. General Vega is fine and sends affectionate greetings to the whole family.

I have asked him frequently about Domínguez, Carmelita's husband, and he tells me that it has been many years since he has heard anything about him, despite the fact that he has tried to find out something. He believes he was killed in a battle near Guadalajara.

Give many, many greetings to the whole family, to Carmelita and Ricardo, and also to the Italians.

Doña Carolina is sending some little Mexican souvenirs to you. I am bringing them. She is sending a rebozo to Jovita.[8]

Frisbie already knows how to speak Spanish, even though it is a bit jumbled.

Goodbye. I send to you and the girls the affection of your husband.

M. G. Vallejo

AS IT TURNED OUT, THE SHIP ON WHICH VALLEJO AND FRISBIE WERE planning to leave Mexico sank before it arrived in Veracruz. So they had to remain longer in Mexico City than planned. But the longer Vallejo stayed in Mexico City, the more negative his opinions became, especially about the Indigenous population of Mexico's capital. In a letter to Adela at the end of August, he wrote:

---

7. Indigenous servants at Lachryma Montis.
8. A *rebozo* is a shawl or wrap.

The population of the city is 300,000 inhabitants (300,000!). Forty thousand of these people are white and they are found in the center of the city and on one main street. There are so few that they are like one in a million. The rest of the population consists of Indians, unrefined Indians, who almost always run around without clothes, all of them barefoot, basically naked. How shocking for a foreigner to see such a spectacle! It is a horrible thing. I'm not exaggerating. On the contrary, I can't express in this letter, with any sense of decency, the reality of what one sees on the streets of Mexico. The Indians carry everything everywhere. They carry coal, straw, firewood, barrels, wicker baskets, little children, and anything else that an Indian can carry. And the Indian women do the same, but they are half dressed. They wear a type of skirt wrapped around their buttocks, with one child strapped to their back and another at their breast. It isn't rare to see them taking care of <u>their needs</u> in public, on the streets, in the open air.[9]

He elaborated on these themes in a letter to Francisca at the end of August:

Hotel Iturbide
August 30, 1877[10]

Francisca,

The steamer on which we were supposed to leave for the United States at the end of July sank before arriving at Veracruz, so we have had to wait another twenty days. There was no other way to leave Mexico. This city really is one in which you "get out if you can." This country is so very backward in terms of its roads or its means of communication with the world.

It makes me sad, and I am very embarrassed to tell everyone that this entire country is ripe for conquest. The few white people who are here are subject to the control of the immense multitude of Indians, as well as to <u>others</u> who are half black and are at the head of public affairs. They mistrust all white foreigners who come here because they think that when the white race becomes the majority they will no longer have a place in society. As soon as they hear the word "emigration" they start to tremble, as if they had been electrified by fear or anger. But they will not be able to stop the hand of fate. It is necessary for other people to come and conquer them.

Mexico City has 300,000 inhabitants and of that number 260,000 are Indians who infest the streets, half naked. Some are completely naked, and others wear ragged clothing and no shoes. They are loaded down with coal, mats, and pots. The Indian women sell tortillas and all types of food, leading one child by the hand while holding another child who is nursing. There are many good things in this city just waiting for another type of people to come and give it new life. It is necessary for at least five million white families to emigrate to this country.

---

9. M.G.V. to Adela, August 8, 1877, C-B 441 FILM, reel 4, 30–32, TBL.
10. C-B 441, box 1, folder 8, TBL.

Man carrying baskets. *Courtesy of the DeGolyer Library, Southern Methodist University. Ag1997.1190.12.*

This country has many elements of prosperity and wealth, but they can't be exploited today. Even though the lands are very fertile, agriculture is in its infancy and the Mexicans don't have the means to export products to other countries of the world. The mines are very rich, more so than those in California. Even though some of the mines are being worked, their exploitation is held back due to the instability caused by continuous revolutions.

When I go out on the street, I become acutely aware of the stench caused by so much filth, misery, and so many Indians. I have so many things to tell you when I return, God willing. I think you will be shocked when you hear what I have to say. I don't want to tell you about it in a letter.

I have only seen one sewing machine in the dressmakers' shops. The seamstresses sew by hand, seated on very low benches, and so do the men in the tailor shops. Some of them are more bent over than "Don Pepe."

I have thought about Carmelita a lot when I have seen the poor women sewing without machines. I asked them why, and they told me that "machines are not allowed because they would take work away from the poor people." They don't use, and I haven't seen, <u>one single broom</u> with a handle to use for sweeping. And they give the same reason: it is because the Indians would stop earning money from the sale of their straw and cane brushes. Everything here was made or built by the old Spaniards. There is nothing from <u>our</u> contemporaries.

Adela and Jovita have written to me, and it pleases me to see their letters. Fani has not written to me, nor has Andrónico. Fani must think that, because she is now a grandmother, this releases her from her duties as a daughter, but it doesn't. She hasn't written to her husband either. There have been times when John has felt very sad. Even though she may act this way out of pride, she is no better than her father (by a long shot) nor her husband, who has always treated her well.[11] Jovita is suffering, but the world is an evil place and it is necessary to suffer in order to be reborn. She deserves to be happy and she should be happy. Arpad wrote me a very flattering letter. I haven't answered him yet. I can't forget how he treated Jovita.

In Veracruz the yellow fever is destroying the population. Thirty to forty people die every day; therefore, I am afraid of that disease.

The mail is about to leave, and I don't have any time to write more. This letter is going on an English boat. The train is already leaving and I am taking my letter to the American minister.

General Vega just came into my room. He sends greetings to you and to the whole family.

Give my regards to everyone.

Your,

M. G. Vallejo

ONCE FRISBIE DECIDED THAT HE HAD DONE ALL HE COULD IN MEXICO on this trip, he told Vallejo that they could depart. But yellow fever in Veracruz made Vallejo reluctant to leave Mexico by the same route by which he had entered. So they were in the capital on September 16 for the celebration of Mexican independence. Vallejo wrote to Lulú the next day and said, "Yesterday, September 16, was a very, very, very solemn day: 14,000 men, soldiers, many generals, etc."[12]

As September wore on, Frisbie became more desirous of leaving to do some business in Washington, D.C., on his way to visit relatives in Syracuse. Vallejo, however, refused. On September 26 he told Frisbie, "On October 3, two friends of ours are leaving for Acapulco. One of them is Don Félix Gibert. I want to go with them. I will take the steamer that stops at Acapulco on the 15th. That way I will be able to get to know this interesting part of the country. Then I will go to

---

11. The parenthetical "by a long shot" is in English in the original letter.
12. M.G.V. to Lulú, September 17, 1877, C-B 441 FILM, reel 4, 33–35, TBL. The word "yesterday" is in English in the original letter.

La Paz, Baja California, where I will probably be able to acquire some land, which very soon will be worth thousands of pesos. From there I will continue on to San Francisco."[13] But the tremendous heat he encountered shortly after beginning his overland trek to Acapulco made him abandon that plan after only twenty miles. So Vallejo reluctantly decided that going through Veracruz, as Frisbie had already done, was the only option. He decided to wait in Mexico City until it appeared that the yellow fever in Veracruz was abating.

Mexico
September 26, 1877[14]

Francisca,

The attached letter will inform you about the situation in the city and port of Veracruz. We were supposed to leave for California from this port. The outbreak of yellow fever is devastating the population, and even the passengers who are <u>only</u> transferring from the boat to the train are dying. Frisbie wants to leave, but I have refused. Now that the disease is worse than ever, he has told me that we must leave. That is why I wrote him the attached letter. I would rather go by land to Acapulco and from there travel to La Paz to see if I can settle <u>something</u> regarding the issue related to Margarita, not with her, but rather with her parents.

Give my regards to Lulú, María, Natalia, and Attila and family.

Believe me that I am always your

M. G. Vallejo

Don't forget to give my regards to Doña Carmelita.

Consulate General of the United States of America
Mexico City
October 17, 1877[15]

Francisca,

I will leave for California via Syracuse on the first steamer that arrives in Veracruz. There no longer is any yellow fever. Frisbie went on ahead, "risking his neck," but he arrived safely, thank God. He was determined and very much needed to be in Washington during these days. That is why he left.

13. M.G.V. to Frisbie, September 26, 1877, C-B 441, box 1, folder 9, TBL.
14. C-B 441, box 1, folder 9, TBL.
15. C-B 441, box 1, folder 8, TBL.

Give my many regards to everyone, Lulú, María, Carmelita, Natalia and family, and Attila. Send them also to Fannie and family, Platón and family, Andrónico, Jovita and children, Ula, and Napoleón and his wife.

When I left Vallejo, I weighed 231 pounds. I weighed myself four days ago in Cuernavaca and I weighed 191 pounds. 231–191 = 40.

I have shrunk from not eating, or rather from eating poorly. I am so skinny I can barely walk, but I am handling it because it would be crazy to die among these people.

Your husband,
M. G. Vallejo

A FEW DAYS AFTER SENDING FRANCISCA THE ABOVE LETTER, VALLEJO wrote to his daughter Lulú. He told her: "Today, the steamer *City of Mexico* arrived from New York in very bad condition, so bad that it had to stop in Havana for repairs, and it has to return to New York. That voyage will take 12 to 15 days. I don't feel up to taking such a long trip, so I will wait for a steamer to arrive from Liverpool, which can navigate to New Orleans from here in five days. It should arrive at the beginning of November and I will board that ship and reunite with Frisbie in Syracuse. Then I will head for California."[16]

Vallejo finally left Mexico City on November 14 and traveled to Veracruz. From there he took a boat to New Orleans. He told Lulú with relief, "A hurricane from the north was expected at any moment but it didn't appear while we were crossing the Gulf of Mexico." From New Orleans he took a train to Syracuse.[17]

St. Charles Hotel
New Orleans
November 19, 1877[18]

Francisca,

Today I arrived in this city. I left the capital of Mexico on the 14th and traveled through Veracruz, where 15 or 20 people die from yellow fever every day. Some,

---

16. M.G.V. to Lulú, October 22, 1877, Mariano Guadalupe Vallejo miscellany, MS 2204, California Historical Society, San Francisco.

17. M.G.V. to Lulú, November 27, 1877, C-B 441 FILM, reel 4, 44–47, TBL.

18. C-B 441, box 1, folder 8, TBL.

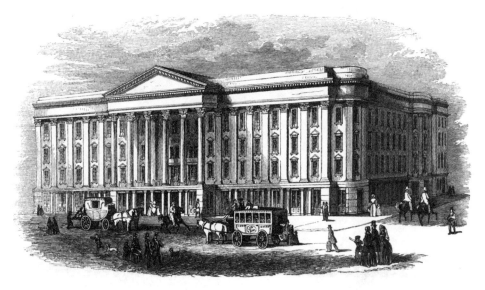

St. Charles Hotel, New Orleans.
Courtesy of the Library of Congress. LC-622673647.

who had been there for just a few hours, died. Others died simply because the wind of the city blew on them. Damned China![19]

Tomorrow I'm leaving for Syracuse to reunite with John and Adela. Then I'll head for California. In the meantime, give my regards to Lulú, María, Natalia and her children, Attila, etc., and don't forget Doña Carmelita.

M. G. Vallejo

VALLEJO ARRIVED IN SYRACUSE ON NOVEMBER 23. A MONTH EARLIER, Adela and Levi Frisbie's daughter Adelita (Lily), who had previously spent a few years at school in Syracuse, had married Dennis McCarthy, a Frisbie family friend.[20] Vallejo had been in Syracuse on his first trip to the East Coast in 1865. On his current visit he was very impressed by the coldness of the weather. He told Lulú, "It's snowing and cold. The homes, streets, trees, and everything under the sun are covered by snow, so white that it resembles the dress of a virgin bride who covers herself with a veil of innocence. It's lovely to watch the snow fall, yet very

---

19. Vallejo was reflecting a common racist belief of the time that yellow fever came from China, the land of the so-called yellow peril.

20. Emparán, *Vallejos*, 298, 300.

Salina Street, Syracuse, New York.
Dennis McCarthy worked at a wholesale dry goods store on this street.
Syracuse City Directory, 1876–1877, 220.
Courtesy of the New York Public Library. NYPG91-F 154:016.

uncomfortable for people like me who can't tolerate such extreme cold." He also noticed the bustle of commercial activity and how Syracuse had grown since his last visit. He reported, "Syracuse is a beautiful city of more than 60,000 people with wide tree-lined streets. Every twenty minutes immense passenger trains crisscross the city. And thousands upon thousands of vessels come down from the lakes of New York along the canals. The vessels then go back up by means of locks. I saw this city eleven years ago and it had 10,000 inhabitants!"[21]

21. M.G.V. to Lulú, December 10, 1877, C-B 441 FILM, reel 4, 50–53, TBL.

Adelita "Lily" Frisbie. *Courtesy of the Autry Museum of the American West, Los Angeles. No. 2002.1.4.54.*

Syracuse
November 24, 1877[22]

Francisca,

Yesterday I arrived in this city, and I got together with Adela, which gave me immense pleasure. I also saw Adelita, who is married to a young man named Mr. Carly.[23] He seems like a very nice fellow. According to what everybody says, he has a very good character and fine manners. May God bless them, and may they be happy.

Today marks nine days since I left Mexico City, traveling on the ocean and on the continent by way of New Orleans, day and night, without resting for a single moment. But I am here now, and I am just waiting for John to return from Washington so that I can then return to California as soon as possible.

I am beginning to regain my health. In Mexico I lost forty-one pounds and I was very sick the entire time, but I never wanted to tell you. Thank God that I left that country! It kept me physically and morally ill. My tongue is tired from so much talking and at times scolding many people whose opinions are so different than mine.

I am writing from the house of Adelita's husband. Adela is also writing to the doctor at this very moment. All three of us send you and the girls our greetings.

Goodbye until next week or a bit later. Give my regards to Natalia, Attila, and family.

M. G. Vallejo

Give my regards to Carmelita and Ricardo.

---

22. C-B 441, box 1, folder 8, TBL.
23. This is apparently how Vallejo heard the name McCarthy.

Syracuse
December 8, 1877[24]

Francisca,

Today, Saturday, we were supposed to have left for California, but John has not yet returned from Washington. Lynch told me last night that he would be coming tomorrow, Sunday. Therefore, we won't be leaving until next week—that is, if there is no obstacle to get in the way of our trip.

It is freezing cold here. Everything is covered with snow, but the house where I am a guest belongs to Adela's son-in-law, Adelita's husband, and he as much as the others (of course) take excellent and loving care of me.[25] Of course, the heaters that are used in the winter keep the house at a good temperature from top to bottom.

Adela has just told me that she received, at this very moment, a letter from Lulú in which she tells her, among other things, that everyone at home is fine.

It is possible that we will travel together to California, but I can't say so for sure since Adela is waiting for letters from the doctor.

I have so much to say about things in Mexico that the ideas don't all fit in my head. It feels like my brain is melting or my skull is exploding from thinking so much about that unfortunate country. So many illusions dispelled! And to think that none of this can be remedied by the Mexicans themselves is a great loss. It is necessary for a new civilization to pull them along or make them disappear.

Goodbye. Give my regards to everyone.

M.G.V.

WHEN VALLEJO RETURNED TO CALIFORNIA IN DECEMBER AFTER A seven-month absence, he was immediately confronted by a variety of issues. He discovered that his daughter María had become romantically involved with American James Harry Cutter. He made some inquiries about Cutter and was pleased by the reports he received on him and his family. Cutter's father had been a gold rush pioneer, an organizer of one of the first volunteer fire companies in San Francisco, and the city's harbor master. Vallejo also was forced to testify in legal proceedings about a land dispute in Sonoma between two Americans, Martin Nathanson and

24. C-B 441, box 1, folder 9, TBL.
25. The parenthetical "of course" in this sentence is in English in the original letter.

Jacob Snyder. Since he had sold the land in question to the Nathanson family in 1853, the Nathansons appreciated his testimony.[26]

Also, Vallejo was encouraged that his trip to Mexico with Frisbie had given him a reputation in some circles as a railroad promoter. He hoped to get some money from potential railroad investors who wished to have him make contacts for them in Mexico, but nothing developed from this project.

Palace Hotel
San Francisco
January 27, 1878[27]

Francisca,

From the moment I arrived here from Sonoma, I've been constantly busy dealing with different infinitesimal things. As soon as I arrived, I began to inquire about the family of the young man who wants to marry María. So far everything seems favorable. If it doesn't rain tomorrow I'll go to Oakland to get information from Señor Brown.[28] I'm told that he knows the Cutter family.

I was in Vallejo for five days until Frisbie left with some of the family. Based on an arrangement that has been made, I believe I'll receive 100 pesos each month, which is a help, under the present circumstances. If you add that to the small rent from the Italians and the amount from the sale of water, it totals $150 a month.

It has rained heavily here [   ][29] and not to get wet. . . . Jovita is much improved. She gets up but doesn't leave her room because of the bad weather.

I asked the black woman to loan me some money and she responded in a letter that I'm including here for you. But I do have a bit of hope that she'll loan me the money. I hope she keeps the promise she made.

My brother José de Jesús is very ill, according to what Guadalupe wrote me from Mission San José.[30] Maybe he'll get better if the weather improves. But there is no cure for old age, and my brother is already 80 years old, an age that makes a person start looking at the bier that will take him to his tomb.[31]

I pay one peso per day at the "Palace Hotel," which is very inexpensive, but I don't know how I'm going to be able to get by. I'll return home very soon.

26. M.G.V. and F.B.C.V., "Deed of part of Lot 25 in Sonoma to Dorothea Nathanson, 1853," C-B 13, doc. 275, TBL.
27. C-B 441, box 1, folder 9, TBL.
28. "Señor Brown" is Harvey S. Brown, the father of Napoleón's wife Martha. Emparán, *Vallejos*, 384–85.
29. Part of this section from the original letter was removed (cut out with scissors).
30. Guadalupe is José de Jesús Vallejo's daughter.
31. Vallejo visited his brother periodically over the next few years and reported on his condition to members of his family: M.G.V. to Platón, August 16, 1879, C-B 441 FILM, reel 3, 79, TBL. See Kern, *Vallejos of Mission San Jose*, vii.

Give my regards to everyone and tell María that I never forget about her. I wish I had a lot of money in order to [   ]³² for when she leaves the house.

Palace Hotel
San Francisco
February 5, 1878³³

Francisca,

I was ready to go to Sonoma last Saturday but the business with Nathanson has detained me. Tomorrow I have to be in court to give my testimony. Soon we'll see the result.

Regarding the loan I requested from my sister (Mrs. Cooper), nothing has happened yet, in spite of her promise, but I do have some hope. That is why I'm here against my will, so that my sister doesn't lose sight of me. But it seems that if someone is able to live at the "Palace Hotel," he should have a lot of money. The truth is that it is the least expensive hotel in the city—$1.00 a day.

It seems that Jovita is better, but I think she is suffering in her soul. She is unhappy with her husband and I feel sorry for her. It is such a pity! Arpad is a barbaric man, with no heart or conscience. But what can be done? That little bolero verse says it well, "Before you fall in love, look first upon where you set your sights so that you won't cry later."³⁴ The odd thing is that Jovita is six months pregnant. What bad luck! Poor woman.

Lulú is fine.

Give my regards to María and Carmelita and receive the affection of your husband,

M. G. Vallejo

It has rained torrentially and I'm afraid to go outside.

Palace Hotel
San Francisco
February 7, 1878³⁵

Francisca,

Much to my regret, and against my will, I'm staying here with hopes of piecing together a plan that will open up a path for me. Some Americans from New York want to establish or build a railroad line from Acapulco to Mexico City. And they

---

32. Section cut out from the letter.

33. MS Vault 55, box 1, folder 2, California Historical Society, San Francisco.

34. *Antes que te apasiones, mira primero donde pones los ojos, no llores luego.*

35. C-B 441, box 1, folder 9, TBL.

José de Jesús Vallejo.
Courtesy of California
State Parks, Sonoma
Barracks. No. 243-x-3506.

want me to go with them to obtain a permit from the Mexican government so they can build it. Naturally, I accepted the proposition. But before leaving, they have to give me $8,000 in gold, whether I obtain the permission or not. They are mulling over my decision.

You see, even though I detest going to Mexico for a variety of reasons, and more so because of the danger on the Gulf and Veracruz, I need to find some way to make a living without so much anguish.

I can do a lot with $8,000. For example, I can leave you $2,000 for all the expenses, $1,000 for María, $1,000 for a life insurance policy valued at $40,000, $1,000 for the round trip, and $3,000 to spend in Mexico on food and clothing. That way, if I drown or they kill me, you are left with $40,000. And if nothing happens to me, nothing is lost. But I don't like this trip. Nevertheless, "beggars can't be choosers."[36] If I make this deal, I'll need to take a servant with me. I need help because I tire easily.

I'm moving forward with the matter regarding the bit of land from the San Francisco presidio. I pray to God that I can establish my claim.

They say that Mrs. Chipman has already arrived with her new husband.[37] And we will also move forward with that business.

My sister still hasn't said anything to me. I'm still waiting.

Doña Gabriela Soberanes told me today that Anita wanted to see me and speak with me. Since it was raining I didn't go, but I'll go tomorrow.[38]

---

36. *La necesidad tiene cara de hereje.*
37. After Chipman's death in 1873, Caroline McLean Chipman married John W. Dwinelle, who died in 1881. Guinn, *History*, 2:468.
38. Gabriela was the widow of Henri Cambuston, a Frenchman from Mexico who became a teacher at Monterey. He died around 1860. She became a language teacher in San Francisco. Langley, *San Francisco Directory, 1882*, 254. In 1877 she was recorded as living with an "A. Cambuston." This might well indicate that the Anita mentioned by Vallejo was her daughter. Langley, *San Francisco Directory, 1877*, 188; Bancroft, *History of California*, 2:740.

Today I finished giving my testimony in court regarding the Snyder and Nathanson lawsuit. We shall see what comes of it. Mrs. Nathanson was pleased by my testimony.

According to one proverb, "If you try all options, one of them is bound to work." "You can't succeed if you don't try."[39]

We'll soon find out what ensues from so many little business dealings.

They still haven't sent me the $100 from Vallejo. I'm waiting every day for that money.

I haven't gone to see the girls in two days because I've been in court and it's raining so much. Money is very scarce.

Give my regards to María and Carmelita.

Your,

M. G. Vallejo

In his search for funds to support his family, Vallejo resurrected an older assertion of his—that in 1834, Governor Figueroa had given him some land in what was now the U.S. Army Presidio in San Francisco. María helped him translate some documents he thought buttressed that assertion. In addition, even though Jovita and Arpad were still together, the relationship remained strained, even after Jovita became pregnant. The situation became so difficult that Jovita asked her brother Uladislao to stay in the house with her.

Palace Hotel
San Francisco
February 15, 1878[40]

Francisca,

Last night I received your letter and I'm answering it (without wearing my spectacles because I don't know where I left them) by telling you that in my last letter I alluded to the small rent to be received from Caminata and Van Geldern in order to apprise you of what we could have each month.[41] I didn't say this because

---

39. *Quien con todas va, con alguna encuentra. Perro que no anda, no encuentra hueso.*

40. C-B 441, box 1, folder 9, TBL.

41. John Caminata (or Camanada) was a vineyard worker who rented land from Mariano Guadalupe. Emparán, *Vallejos,* 119, 231.

Palace Hotel, San Francisco, 1875, by Carleton E. Watkins.
Courtesy of the California Room, California State Library,
Sacramento, California. No. 2018–0786.

I thought we hadn't economized, for I'm very much aware of that. In that same vein, I mentioned this so you would realize that my being here means that I need <u>something</u> to pay for my room and board. I also need to pay to have the papers certified, so that I can present them in court for my claims against the presidio. Up until now everything has been going well. If I abandon this, we'll get behind and all will be lost.

The black woman still hasn't said anything to me regarding her promise. Anita sent for me and (<u>because she considered me to be in a state of need</u>) she gave me $100. I obviously refused to take the money. This is more of an insult than anything else. They just don't know any better.

If I can, I'll leave on Saturday, because I have no other alternative. I have to pay room and board here every day.

Give my regards to everyone.

Your,
M. G. Vallejo

It's eight o'clock at night and Cutter, the fiancé, has just left my room.

San Francisco
February 18, 1878[42]

Francisca,

I'm so busy with the matter regarding the presidio that I've barely had a chance to eat. So far, it all appears to be going in a positive direction, and I have hopes that I'll win the lawsuit, primarily because everybody wants me to win. Your cousin Bautista is here helping me.[43] The men from the government archives already gave me certified copies of my claim.[44] Even though I have to pay for the papers, I want to have my rights to that place well documented. May Heaven grant that it works in our favor.

In one of the "closets" in my room there is an elastic stocking that I used to put on my leg.[45] If it isn't in the closets, it's probably in the black trunk. Send it to me via Express.

Jovita is better, but very pregnant. If Attila buys the lots down from Jovita's, he himself can draw up the deed. You can sign it and then send it to me. The number of lots is on a small map in the closet in my room.

Give my regards to everyone.

M. G. Vallejo

※ ※ ※

WITH HER HUSBAND SPENDING SO MUCH TIME IN SAN FRANCISCO, Francisca continued to do what she had been doing for so many years, managing affairs at Lachryma Montis and maintaining contact with her children. A glimpse into how she managed to do this can be seen in a letter she wrote to Platón on March 8, 1878.[46]

Dear Platón,

After sending my greetings to you, Lili and your children, Andrónico, Fani, Adela, and all of my grandchildren and great-grandchildren, tell them that I am sending them this small gift. For Lili—a string of chili peppers, two dozen oranges,

42. C-B 441, box 1, folder 9, TBL.

43. Juan Bautista Alvarado was Vallejo's nephew. Even though he lived in San Pablo in the East Bay, Alvarado spent much time in the 1870s in San Francisco. Miller, *Juan Bautista Alvarado*, xii, 157–58.

44. The word "claim" is in English in the original letter.

45. Vallejo uses the English word "closets" in the original letter.

46. F.B.C.V. to Platón, C-B 441 FILM, reel 3, 62.

a jar of jelly. For Fani—three dozen oranges and a jar of jelly. For Fanita Sequeira—a dozen oranges.[47] For Adela—a string of chili peppers, two dozen oranges, and a small blue jar of jelly. For Andrónico—a dozen oranges, a small blue jar of jelly, and half a string of chili peppers. Everything is packed in a box. I'm sending two dozen oranges. Ask Padre Luis if he would like some. They are the last of the season. Don't laugh at the way I write. Give everyone my best wishes.

Your Mamá,
Benicia de Vallejo

Everything is being sent on the stage coach from Napa. It is all packed in a big box and there is also a sack of chili peppers. The stage coach driver is in charge of the delivery. I hope nothing gets lost. Goodbye, your Mamá.

VALLEJO REMAINED IN SAN FRANCISCO, TRANSLATED DOCUMENTS WITH María and, as always, was on the lookout for any project that might bring him and his family some money.

Palace Hotel
March 13, 1878[48]

Francisca,

Lulú and María went to Vallejo this morning with Sequeira. The poor man begged them so much that they couldn't say no.

Adela gave María a very beautiful silk outfit that she no longer uses, and María sent it out to be altered here in San Francisco.

I asked Lulú to see if she could get Platón to come up with $100, or however much he could loan me. Who knows if poor Platón will be able to do that, but I need some money to pay for the hotel, the witnesses, and the notaries. The matter regarding my claim to the presidio property appears to be very good. I've wanted to handle it myself so that the lawyers don't rob me. Your cousin Bautista does a good job helping me.

Tomorrow the girls will come from Vallejo, and I'll see if they've brought me any money. If not, I don't know what to do.

If you write me in time, I'll leave on the steamer *Donahue* tomorrow afternoon.

---

47. Antonio de Sequeira, an employee of Frisbie's bank, married Epifania and Frisbie's daughter Fanita in 1875. Emparán, *Vallejos*, 274.

48. C-B 441, box 1, folder 9, TBL.

Steamship *James M. Donahue* moored at Donahue Landing,
Sonoma County, California, 1878. *Courtesy of the Sonoma County
Library Photograph Collection. cstr_pho 043262.*

I asked Frisbie for $20, which he very gladly gave me.

As soon as you receive this letter, send me a telegram so that I'll know if you're staying in Vallejo. I can't go by that route because <u>it costs double</u> and I only have enough for my passage to Sonoma.

Pickett loaned me $1.00 voluntarily, and I told him I was grateful.

<u>Confidential</u>: I think it is very probable that I'll be going to Mexico very soon with Frisbie, that is, if our plans receive a favorable response, for it is necessary to look for some way to make a living. I don't know when I'll leave, but I think within ten days, that's if the situation in Washington is settled. Frisbie will leave for Washington on Monday with the utmost <u>urgency</u>. "There is always someone ready to take advantage of a chaotic situation."[49]

Give my regards to everyone.

M. G. Vallejo

Palace Hotel
San Francisco
March 15, 1878[50]

Francisca,

I saw Adela at Jovita's house today. Among the things she told me was that Fannie had given you her sewing machine. If that's true, there will now be two sewing

---

49. *A río revuelto ganancia de pescadores.*
50. MS 2204, folder 1, California Historical Society, San Francisco.

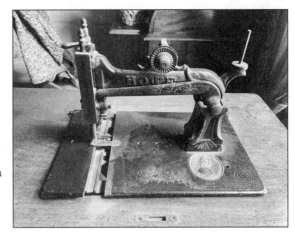

Howe sewing machine at Lachryma Montis. Photo by Ronnie Cline. *Courtesy of California State Parks, Sonoma Barracks.*

machines in the house. Since "necessity knows no bounds,"[51] necessity has made me think it would be good to sell Carmelita the machine that is in her room before she buys another one, which would result in three sewing machines. . . .

I'm not able to obtain one single peso from anywhere, and I'm hard pressed to pay the notaries and the hotel. I've been here for two months and it's not possible to stop eating. Now I'm paying double because María has to eat and she has her own room. If you want me to sell the sewing machine, send me a telegram telling me to sell it, or if not, tell me DON'T SELL.

Your,
M. G. Vallejo

Palace Hotel
San Francisco
March 18, 1878[52]

Francisca,

I'm constantly busy with the business you already know about. Each day I make a bit of progress, but since "I don't have wings to fly,"[53] I can't go up very high. Each step I take comes with a sigh and a dizzy spell. And I can't do what I know has to be done.

I have a lot of writing to do, first in Spanish, and then between María and myself

---

51. *La necesidad tiene cara de hereje.*
52. C-B 441, box 1, folder 9, TBL.
53. *Me faltan las plumas para volar.*

we translate everything to English. This saves me from having to pay translators 25 or 30 pesos per page.

I wrote to my sister again about the loan, but I still haven't had any response.

I asked Mr. Brooks for a loan of about $200 and he told me that "he didn't have any money to pay his own expenses." I wrote a very ingratiating letter to Bancroft and he hasn't paid any attention to it. So you can imagine how upset I am. I have to finish up this business and also deal with the hotel expenses, especially now that María is here, even though it's against her will, because she would like to go to Sonoma.

Fannie will come from Vallejo day after tomorrow, Wednesday, and then leave from Oakland to go back east, and from there perhaps to Mexico. Everything, everything happens at the same time. María also has me in suspense and mortified with regard to her wedding. Young Harry, her fiancé, is here every single day. He does nothing but "kill time," as the saying goes. It makes me feel sad and anxious not being able to proceed with the wedding with some sense of decorum and elegance. I can't get the wedding cards printed, which is something people do nowadays. The fiancé can't do anything either. I don't know what to think.

Jovita is so-so. She says that Arpad is behaving well. Luisa says the same thing, but I sense that something is not right with what is going on there. Ula lives at Arpad's house because Jovita wants him to. This proves that she's somewhat afraid. Adela should be coming this week to stay with Jovita, then Lulú will go home, and María will as well. I would like to do the same.

Goodbye.

Your,

M. G. Vallejo

Palace Hotel
San Francisco
March 19, 1878[54]

Francisca,

Your letter (with your little request) dated yesterday, arrived today, Tuesday, at six o'clock in the evening. I gave María the little note you sent her. Carmelita came so she could go with María to the stores, and I obviously read to her what you said about the sewing machine. Tomorrow we'll see how much that type of machine costs at the stores where they are sold. I'll sell Carmelita the sewing machine we have in Sonoma. Believe me, I'm only doing this because of the pressing circumstances in which I find myself. And also because you already have another good

---

54. C-B 441, box 1, folder 9, TBL.

Adela Vallejo Frisbie.
Courtesy of the Autry Museum
of the American West, Los
Angeles. No. 2002.1.5.76.

sewing machine in Vallejo, like the one Fannie gave you. I think that everyone will go home this week. If Adela keeps her promise to Jovita about coming to stay with her, then Lulú, María, and Carmelita will go together. Ula is fine, and everybody sends you their regards.

Your,
M. G. Vallejo

UPON HIS RETURN TO CALIFORNIA, JOHN FRISBIE, ENCOURAGED BY THE contacts he had made in Mexico, began making preparations to move himself and his family there. At the end of January he and most of his children departed for Chicago, where he finalized arrangements about his trip.

At the end of March 1878, Epifania and her daughter Fanita left the Bay Area to join John Frisbie and the rest of their family in Chicago. They were accompanied by Fanita's husband, Antonio Sequeira. When these last three family members arrived in Chicago, the entire family then traveled to Mexico to start their new life there. Closer to home, Vallejo was learning more about his daughter María. Four years earlier Kate Bancroft had described María as "very gay and lively."[55] Vallejo was discovering that the courtship rituals in which this daughter engaged right in front of him were not at all to his liking.

---

55. Kate Bancroft, "Journal: My Trip to Sonoma," 71/18c, vol. 3, 8, TBL.

Thursday
Palace Hotel
San Francisco
March 21, 1878[56]

Francisca,

Fannie and her daughter little Fannie left this morning to meet up with Frisbie in Chicago and from there to leave for New Orleans on their way to Mexico. We were together in their rooms last night until one o'clock in the morning, and many relatives from both sides, as well as many friends and acquaintances, came to say goodbye to them.

When the moment came for Fannie to leave, she could not control herself, and she threw herself into my arms, screaming and crying, thinking of nothing else but her mother and her father. She was screaming like a woman in despair: "Papá, Papá, I will never see you again, nor mother either. Ay! Papacito, I am going to Mexico. . . . I will never see both of you again!!!" She was out of control, crying and screaming, so much so that it was necessary to close the doors of the rooms.

In the midst of her expressions of sorrow, she asked me to give you her regards and commend her to God. In the end, it was a very tender scene in the presence of the entire family and other people who also were crying.

This morning, we all went to accompany them to Oakland where, as the train was pulling away, the scene from last night was repeated. They finally left and we lost sight of them.

Today, at eight o'clock in the evening, I received a telegram from the summit of the Sierra Nevada, and Sequeira tells me that they are fine and they send their greetings to everyone.

I think María and Lulú will leave here on Saturday, and it is possible that Doña Carmelita will also leave.

It is good that you have received the "check" for $100.[57] Don't forget that I want to be able to at least pay the hotel bill. María's stay here has doubled the amount of our expenses and, believe me, I can't find a solution to this.

I received the $40 you sent me, and I still have the money in my pocket to pay the hotel.

Jovita continues to be about the same. She seems very depressed. I find this to be very sad because she will be giving birth soon, and she says that Arpad is behaving himself, even though it causes her embarrassment to say so.

---

56. C-B 441, box 1, folder 9, TBL.
57. The word "check" is in English in the original letter.

(left) James H. Cutter. *Courtesy of California State Parks,*
Sonoma Barracks. No. 243-x-3219.
(right) María Vallejo Cutter. *Courtesy of California State Parks,*
Sonoma Barracks. No. 243-x-2974.

María and the young man Cutter have angered me. They are silly and imprudent and believe they <u>already</u> can do whatever they want to do in my presence. I truly do not think the same way they do. <u>Others have already gone out to hunt and they have not gotten married</u>. "There is many a slip between the cup and the lip."[58]
Goodbye.

Your,
M. G. Vallejo

Palace Hotel
San Francisco
March 29, 1878[59]

Francisca,
  I received the $50 you sent me by Express.

---

58. *De la copa a los labios hay gran distancia.*
59. C-B 441, box 1, folder 9, TBL.

Don Ramón de Zaldo died at nine o'clock last night. I received the news today from San José.

I think Carmelita is leaving tomorrow, Saturday, on the *Sonoma*. That is what Mrs. Romo, a friend of hers, told me late today. I haven't seen Carmelita for many days. I was also thinking of leaving, but the lawyer went to Sacramento and I don't want to leave without seeing him about <u>my issue</u>. I arrived yesterday from "Half Moon Bay," where I went to look for Vicente Miramontes so he could act as a witness.[60] I got really tired and very wet. I rode in his "wagoncito" without a top.[61] I was only covered by an umbrella, and it was very windy.

Last night Ula was helping me translate some documents for my lawsuit.

Tell the girls that I miss them. I become bored and tired here, alone in my room. If it were not for Bautista, who comes to my room every once in a while, I would have given up.

Jovita is fine, up to a certain point, she's <u>just waiting</u>. I feel sorry for her and I feel compassion for her. Poor woman!

It rains a lot here. I always feel like my heart is in my mouth,[62] just waiting for the pain in my side to come back. But God has spared me from that for now.

If I don't leave tomorrow afternoon on the *Donahue*, I'm planning on leaving on Tuesday. In the meantime, pray for your

Companion

WHEN IT BECAME CRYSTAL CLEAR THAT MARÍA AND CUTTER WISHED to marry, since he was an Episcopalian Vallejo asked Archbishop Alemany to speak with him and explain how a Catholic-Protestant wedding might be possible. Alemany did so and reported to Vallejo that he found Cutter to be "a young man with very fine manners." But, the archbishop continued, "We were unable to come to an understanding, for he was unable to persuade me to his way of thinking and I was unable to persuade him to mine." Cutter most likely refused to promise the archbishop that he would allow any children from that marriage to be baptized as Catholics. However, a few days later, Alemany wrote Vallejo, "I am very glad that the tractable and intelligent young man J. Cutter has happily consented to what I asked of him, so I include the necessary dispensation."[63]

---

60. "Half Moon Bay" is in English in the original letter.
61. "Wagoncito" is in the original letter.
62. *Jesús en la boca.*
63. Joseph Alemany to Vallejo, April 24, 1878, DLG-V 2, letter 8; Alemany to Vallejo, April 30, 1878, Vallejo Family Papers, California State Parks, Sonoma.

Telegram from Arpad Haraszthy to
Dr. Platón Vallejo, San Francisco, May 6,
1878. "Jovita died yesterday, an attack of
apoplexy, deliver immediately. Arpad
Haraszthy." *Courtesy of The Bancroft
Library, University of California, Berkeley.
Vallejo Family Papers, C-B 441* FILM, *reel
3, 64.*

At the beginning of May 1878, after a difficult pregnancy, Jovita gave birth to a
baby girl, but the baby did not survive and Jovita herself died a few days later. Jovita
and Arpad, along with Natalia and Attila, had not been married in a Catholic
Church, but rather at Lachryma Montis. However, the wedding had been conducted by a Catholic priest, Father Peter Deyaert. At the time of the wedding
he was headquartered in Napa, but he traveled throughout Napa, Sonoma, and
Solano Counties administering liturgies and sacraments to various groups and
congregations. His formal records were accordingly scattered throughout the area
and not kept at one particular parish church. And Deyaert, who died in 1876, was
not available to vouch for the Catholicity of the wedding service. Since there was no
easily accessible record of Jovita's Catholic marriage, Church authorities originally
refused permission for her funeral to take place at the St. Mary's Cathedral in San
Francisco or for her to be buried at Calvary Cemetery at Lone Mountain in the
city. Her coffin was simply being stored at the cemetery.[64]

Vallejo and Francisca were furious. Although Vallejo had certainly never been a
terribly fervent Catholic and his "Recuerdos" had downplayed the role of missionaries in the formation of California, he had contributed financially to the Church.

64. "Our History," *St. Helena Catholic Church,* https://sthelenacatholic.com/our-parish; *Sacramento Daily Union,*
    January 5, 1876.

His Grace Joseph Sadoc Alemany, csd, *Arch Bishop of San Francisco*, 1879. Britton & Rey, lithographer; Henry Steinegger, artist. *Courtesy of the Library of Congress.* loc No. 2012645529.

Cerruti noted in 1874 that Vallejo "contributes greatly to the support of the Sonoma chapel."[65] And, shortly before Jovita's death, Vallejo had prevailed upon his daughter María's fiancé James Cutter to satisfy the Church's conditions so that María could be married in a Catholic ceremony. In addition, Francisca had volunteered for various church activities. In 1874, Archbishop Alemany had appointed her president of the Altar Society of the Church of San Francisco Solano in Sonoma. He wrote of her, "She wishes to obtain donations to be used to decorate the church altar. We commend her zeal in seeking the assistance of the faithful in such a pious goal."[66] Given that background, Vallejo and Francisca could not understand why the archbishop or other Church authorities had never asked them if Jovita had been married in a Catholic ceremony. Vallejo wrote a bitter letter to Platón:

> Today I returned from San Francisco with a heart filled with sadness, shame, and humiliation because of the conduct of the Catholic priests with regard to the funereal honors or semi-honors on behalf of my daughter Jovita. The family and I have resented this very, very much. Relatives and friends have been scandalized by the conduct of those who call themselves pastors of the Christians. I know that I don't deserve such rude and cruel treatment, and my family even less so. You can believe me when I say that none of this is going to end well. It's true that a misunderstanding or ignorance on the part of the clergy has nothing to do with the religion, but it does open the doors to scandal. And it causes a <u>cooling</u> off of one's <u>internal</u> worship and a detesting of <u>external</u> worship.
>
> The archbishop came to this "vale of tears" to bless the home of the <u>rich</u> owner, Colonel

---

65. Cerruti, *Ramblings*, 92; on contributions to the Church, see, for example, Vallejo's letter to Francisca on February 28, 1873, in chap. 4 of this volume.
66. Alemany to F.B.C.V., May 16, 1874, C-B 441 film, reel 4, 62, tbl.

Hooper.[67] He passed close by the <u>poor</u> home of General Vallejo. But Su Señoría <u>didn't even have the decency</u> to stop and "console those who were grieving," which is considered an act of compassion.[68] And he knew that your mother was very, very ill.

"Tempora mutantur, nos et mutamur in illis."[69]

Everyone here is suffering.[70]

The next day, Vallejo wrote directly to Archbishop Alemany:

> So as to prevent more difficulties and gossip regarding the funeral of my deceased daughter Doña Jovita de Haraszthy, whose body can be found deposited in the pantheon of Calvary Cemetery, on behalf of her husband Señor Arpad Haraszthy, whom I have represented and continue to represent with regard to this funeral, I am contacting you directly, Su Ilustrísimo, to see if you would be so kind as to give me written permission so that my daughter's funeral service can be held in the cathedral, with the solemn pomp that corresponds to her status as a Catholic and her social position, with her body lying in state.[71] Those are her husband's wishes as well as those of my entire family who mourn her death, thus silencing the gossip that resulted from the proceedings of the day that her body was deposited in the Pantheon.[72]

Even though Platón was able to use his Catholic Church contacts to find the marriage records and Jovita did eventually receive a Catholic burial, this did not occur until July 15, 1879, fourteen months after her death. And the funeral service was held not at St. Mary's Cathedral but in the chapel of Calvary Cemetery at Lone Mountain, where Jovita's remains had continued to be located for those fourteen months. Vallejo's and Francisca's bitterness toward Alemany continued to be strong.[73] Years later Vallejo wrote to Alemany and expressed feelings that were still close to his heart. He told the archbishop that his actions had been "unjustifiable":

> That unjustifiable action seemed even more unjustifiable to me because my family has served and been devoted to the Holy Church for generations. That is why a small gesture of goodwill, or at the very least a less rigorous stance, would have been appreciated by us during a time of extreme sadness.
>
> I have no idea what you were told that would make you believe that you were obligated to submit us to such a display of public humiliation, which was more like an insult reserved only for criminals.
>
> My daughter Doña Jovita's marriage was celebrated by a Catholic priest. Therefore, your being told the contrary was vile and cruel slander that did not merit being heard. If you had had the courtesy to ask me about it, I would have told you the truth and then you would not have pronounced your sentence without listening to the defense. It is for that very reason

---

67. George F. Hooper, a well-to-do San Francisco banker, had moved to Sonoma in 1876. He had a vineyard and house near Lachryma Montis. See Munro-Fraser, *Sonoma County,* 667.
68. *Su Señoría* is, literally, "Your [or his] Lordship," a term of respect.
69. Latin for "The times change, and we change with them."
70. M.G.V. to Platón, May 9, 1878, C-B 441 FILM, reel 3, 63–64, TBL.
71. *Su Ilustrísimo* is, literally, "Your Most Illustrious."
72. M.G.V. to Joseph Alemany, May 10, 1878, Archives of the Archdiocese of San Francisco.
73. Joseph Alemany to Platón Vallejo, May 20, 1878, 76/79c, box 2, folder 11, TBL; McGinty, *Toast to Eclipse,* 76.

that I believe Jovita's right to be defended is now even more sacred, since death has sealed the lips of this innocent person who was falsely accused.

With regard to whether she had fulfilled her Paschal duty or not, your informant may have also been casting aspersions on her. Who was that person who had such intimate knowledge about Jovita's life? And why were that person's accusations believed without giving us the opportunity to put up a defense?

In your letter you say, "A judge, whether ecclesiastical or civil, must make decisions based on the testimony that is presented to him." My response to that is, yes, Señor, but if a civil or ecclesiastical judge is basing his decision on testimony, he should hear from both parties. Otherwise, how would he know he is carrying out justice?

If Jovita had been a hardened criminal, her mortal remains would not have been treated any more harshly by the Church. Is there any greater or more cruel insult that could have been heaped upon me? What have I done to deserve such contempt? The dagger pierced my heart, and blood will continue to pour from my heart until I, too, am lowered into my grave. In the meantime, Señor Arzobispo, if you believe you have fulfilled your duty, I have nothing to say with regard to your conscience. You are your own witness and God, the eternal judge who will judge <u>both of us</u>, will apply the sentence we both deserve.

I wish you many years of life and much happiness. I remain your attentive servant.[74]

Arpad continued his wine and champagne business and eventually became president of the state board of viticulture. Napoleón continued working for Arpad's company. María and James Cutter had planned to be married on May 8, but because of the deaths of Jovita and the infant they postponed the wedding for a week. Their first child, whom they named Leo, was born the following February. His parents gave him the nickname "Tweedie," a variant of "Sweetie," and his grandfather often referred to him as "Don Tweedie." Francisca spent a good amount of time in San Francisco helping her daughter take care of him and his sister, Alma, who was born in 1881.

Vallejo wrote a series of letters to Francisca describing happenings at Lachryma Montis and in Sonoma. The only immediate family member who remained close by was Natalia. She and her husband, Attila Haraszthy, lived first at the Buena Vista property and then in a house they built closer to Lachryma Montis. Attila planted a vineyard on his property there, but it was soon afflicted by phylloxera.[75]

While Vallejo was alone at Lachryma Montis, he spent a decent amount of time delivering water from the spring there to various establishments in Sonoma. But that left him with plenty of time to think about his family, and especially about the education he had provided for all of his children. His dispute with Alemany and the fact that Platón's Church contacts had helped arrange Jovita's Catholic

74. M.G.V. to Joseph Alemany, December 15, 1884, C-B 441 film, reel 4, 171–73.
75. Emparán, *Vallejos*, 311; McGinty, *Toast to Eclipse*, 156; McGinty, *Strong Wine*, 468.

Arpad Haraszthy's exhibit at the Mechanics' Institute Fair,
1895, showing the "Eclipse Champagne." By Isaiah W. Taber.
*Courtesy of the California Room, California State Library,
Sacramento, California. F869 S3 T22 1895.*

burial service seem to have put religion more at the forefront of his mind. Religion
had been prominent in his own traditional education in Monterey decades earlier,
and one of the main texts had been a catechism written by Jesuit Gerónimo de
Ripalda. His memories of that catechism were not pleasant. In his "Recuerdos" he
had written, "Father Ripalda's catechism! Who among the old Californios does
not know Father Ripalda? Is there anyone with even the slightest ability to reason
and the freedom of conscience who does not detest that monstrous and fanatical
code? This code is similar to a venomous serpent that wraps itself around the heart
of young people in order to slowly devour it."[76]

But Platón's help put him in somewhat of a different frame of mind. Perhaps as
a way of thanking his more religious son, in a letter he wrote to him a few months
after Jovita's burial, he said,

---

76. Vallejo, *Recuerdos*, 2:999.

"What is the obligation of parents with regard to their children?" (This is stated in the Christian Doctrine of Father Ripalda.) "Raise them, educate them, and provide them with a place in society that is not against their will." In fulfillment of that holy doctrine it is necessary to "earn one's daily bread" and also money, in order to educate them and give them some status in the world, based on their disposition and talents. In that way, when children reach adulthood they will think for themselves, and all that will be left for their parents to do is to give them advice. I know this from experience.[77]

That aspect of his experience surfaced in his correspondence to Francisca.

San Francisco
December 14, 1878[78]

Francisca,

First of all, I saw María as soon as I arrived. She is fine and has very good accommodations on Sutter Street.

I don't think I can leave today. The gentleman who contacted me arrived early today, and I'm going to begin conferring with him this afternoon. He wants to discuss business in Mexico. I told him that if I'm successful in these efforts he can count on me to go to the capital, even though I might die en route.

Dr. Frisbie is in Vallejo. I don't think he has gone to Mexico. This morning I sent a telegram to Platón and he answered me.

Tell Carmelita that I went to the establishment where Ricardo works to see what I could find out. Señor Prescott told me that Ricardo is doing well in all respects; that he is a hard worker; and that he is very pleased with him. He added that Ricardo would soon be promoted to a better position.

Give my regards to everyone at home.

Yours,
M. G. Vallejo

I haven't seen any of the old women who were accusing me before I left Sonoma.

Lachryma Montis
October 29, 1879[79]

Francisca,

The Chinese man continues to be very sick. Last night I made him some tea, but

---

77. M.G.V. to Platón, August 28, 1879, C-B 441 FILM, reel 3, 81, TBL.
78. No. 243–396–2, California State Parks, Sonoma.
79. C-B 441, box 1, folder 9, TBL.

he didn't get any better. This morning he was worse, and I personally made him two pieces of toast with butter and a coffee pot filled with tea. Later I prepared my very delicious beans with green chili and onion. Between Jacobino and myself, we ate all of it for lunch, right from the very pan in which it was made. After we finished, I washed the dishes, closed up the kitchen, and . . . until the evening. At 11 a.m. the Chinese man asked me for one peso to buy medicine. When he left for Sonoma he was very sick.

I hope that you all arrived safely and that you found Mrs. D. as happy and flattering as always, with her heart in her hand, and a smile on her lips.[80] (Give her a kiss from me) and give my regards to my beautiful daughters.

Goodbye, until Sunday [perhaps],[81]

M. G. Vallejo

Lachryma Montis
[no date, probably 1880][82]

Francisca,

I received your two letters and I took care of what you requested. Today, the small box of oranges was sent by Express, and I also sent Harry a demijohn of fresh water from Lachryma Montis.

I'm very busy working with the carpenter Grisimo. I'm not telling you the type of work so that you will be surprised when you see it.

Natalia has been suffering from an extremely bad headache for two days. Yesterday she didn't get out of bed, but she is better today. Attila, as usual, comes to the dining room to get the latest "news" and then we go and have "lonche." In the afternoon, as he is heading back to his vineyard, he stops again to find out the latest "news."

Give my regards to Harry and to "Don Tweedie."

M. G. Vallejo

I already know that you bought yourself a hat and a cape. Lulú says that you are very nicely "packaged" as you wander about. Give "Don Tweedie" a kiss.

---

80. "Mrs. D" is Oriana Day, an artist who created a series of paintings of the missions, presidios, and other historical buildings. She and her husband lived in Vallejo and were introduced to Mariano Guadalupe by Platón. She had visited Lachryma Montis in June 1879. See Emparán, *Vallejos*, 335–37.

81. The brackets are Vallejo's.

82. C-B 441, box 2, folder 3, TBL.

Lachryma Montis
March 24, 1880[83]

Francisca,

No sooner had the locomotive's whistle announced the departure of the train when bursts of black smoke started to flow from the smokestack, forming a serpent in the air. Then Jacobino appeared before me with a small tin pitcher to use to take some milk.[84] He greeted me and said,

"Patrón, Sir, what the hell are the Patrona, Miss Lulú, and Carmelita doing in San Francisco?[85] Every day they go out, and then go out again . . . and walk and walk and spend money and lots more money. I don't like it that Miss Lulú is always going to <u>Fansancisco</u>[86] . . . one month . . . another month . . . and months and what the hell does that mean? And now the Patrón and Carmelita, too . . . and the Patrón is all alone without any money to buy anything, like a bit of meat and tobacco to smoke. What the hell! That isn't right!"

"But young man," I replied, "they are just going for a walk. The Patrona goes to see Miss María and the little baby. Don't you understand that she goes to see her daughter?"

He responded, "Who the hell cares about a daughter, or a baby, or anything else! What the hell! They should be here taking care of the Patrón. If the Patrona wants to look at little babies she should make one herself and then take care of it. What the hell!"

"But the Patrona can't have <u>bébes</u>. She is old."

"Yes she can," said Jacobino. "What the hell! It isn't hard. Look Patrón, my Mother is also old and as fat as the devil and she makes babies."

"Yes," I told him, "But the Patrón can't."

"No? What do you mean no? And why is it that my Father can?"

"Because your Father is Italian and the Italians are possessed."

"How are babies made, Patrón?"

"With a little machine, like the one Adam and Eve had, that you know how to pronounce from the <u>blue book</u>."[87]

"And the little screwdriver and the shrimps, half of each one?"

"Yes, with that little machine," I told him.

"Holy shit! Hey, Patrón, I want you to buy me one of those little machines.

---

83. C-B 441, box 1, folder 9, TBL.
84. Jacobino was the seven-year-old son of field worker Anton Cominiti. 1880 U.S. Census, Sonoma County, Enumeration District 120, 12; Emparán, *Vallejos*, 231.
85. *Patrón* means "boss" and *patrona* is "female boss" or "wife of the boss."
86. Vallejo spelled "San Francisco" the way the boy pronounced it. The first time Vallejo reported in the letter that the boy had referred to San Francisco, he abbreviated it the way it was often done as "San Franc°." But as he reported that the boy was becoming more agitated, Vallejo wanted to let Francisca know the way the boy was actually pronouncing the name of the city, so he spelled it out as "Fansancisco."
87. The "blue book" was possibly a catechism or devotional book for children.

Francisca Benicia Carrillo de Vallejo. This photograph was taken on August 24, 1880, the day after her sixty-fifth birthday. She is wearing the hat and cape mentioned in Vallejo's letter to her. *Courtesy of California State Parks, Sonoma Barracks. No. 243–40–22.*

Would Mr. Shocken have one? Of course he must have one but they say it doesn't work, that it is necessary for the doctor to fix it. Listen, Patron! It's already late. I'm on my way to school and my Mother is waiting for me. I'll come back again in the afternoon. Bye."

The poor boy left and I remained alone, alone, alone, thinking about you crossing the bay in good weather. Give my regards to María, to "Don Tweedie," and to Harry. Don't forget, pay a visit to Mrs. Pool if you can.[88]

M. G. Vallejo

Vallejo
Friday
November 12, 1880[89]

Francisca,

Ever since I had the meeting with Pomposa at María's house and with Mrs. Cooper in the park, nobody has had any idea where I am. I came to Vallejo to see Platón regarding the matter with Molera, etc., and I went with Adela from there to Platón's house to "see the chichos."[90] And from there I went to "Mrs. Day's Studios." I spent the entire day there making corrections on the paintings. And from there I went to Platón's house.

88. Anna Eugenia Wiley Poole was the older sister of Platón's wife, Lily. Emparán, *Vallejos*, 322.
89. C-B 441, box 1, folder 9, TBL.
90. The word *chichos* is Vallejo's way of expressing the diminutive *muchachitos* ("little children").

Encarnación Vallejo de Cooper.
*Courtesy of the Autry Museum of
the American West, Los Angeles.*
No. 2002.1.4.58.

Tomorrow, Saturday, I will travel to Napa and then end up at the depot at the Sonoma Plaza.

M. G. Vallejo

Lachryma Montis
March 19, 1881[91]

Francisca,

Rosina came yesterday to buy a recently calved cow. Tell me if you want to sell it and how much we should ask for it. He'll pay cash. Let me know right away. That way, if I can make a deal, I'll be able to send you the money to buy a . . . cape.

The Italians are having a dispute. I think that Perazo and his family are separating from the Compañía and "who knows" how we'll get along with the others. Grisimo went to work as a carpenter somewhere else. He still hasn't made last month's payment.

Today, Saturday, I'm planting olive trees where I told you I would plant them, that is, where the orange trees that dried up had been.

Mr. Minik wandered over here. He fixed the back staircase banister and the window in Lulú's room.

I hope María gets better soon. Give her my regards. Kiss "Don Tweedie" and don't forget Harry.

---

91. C-B 441, box 1, folder 9, TBL.

Alma and Leo "Don Tweedie" Cutter. *Courtesy of the Autry Museum of the American West, Los Angeles. No. 2002.1.3.59.*

Natalia, Attila, and the family are fine.
The trees in the plaza are beginning to look beautiful.
Goodbye.

M. G. Vallejo

Lachryma Montis
May 30, 1881[92]

Francisca,

A few minutes after you left here, Adela went to Natalia's house, leaving me "alone with my soul." As you can imagine, I was in great pain because of a toothache. Half my face was swollen. In addition, I had a sharp pain in my left eye. Since I was alone and there was no one around who would make fun of me or label me a coward, I started to moan and groan and bellow like a wounded bear. I suffered so much for four hours! But at the end of that time, I found a way to help relieve the pain: I started gargling with whisky, which produced an abundance of saliva and caused a burning sensation down to my soul. The pain appears to be easing. I hope this is God's will.

I hope you had a pleasant trip, with no seasickness, and that you all are happy. Give my regards to everyone.

The Solitary Man

---

92. C-B 441, box 1, folder 9, TBL.

June 23, 1881[93]

Francisca,

Everyone is fine. Doctor Van Geldern died at one o'clock this morning. His illness was an inflammation of the intestines.

Give my greetings to Adela and the doctor.

M. G. Vallejo

Lachryma Montis
July 14, 1881[94]

Francisca,

La Tuca gave birth to four little puppies yesterday. Two died because no one was there to assist her. But two lived because Doña Carmelita was there to break the water sack that envelops all creatures when they are born. The first puppies drowned. They were males. One was like the father and the other one like the mother. The puppies that lived are the same color as Toni, and the little female is dark.

I'm sending you the letter Ula wrote to Lulú so that you will know about Ramona, Juanita, and their families. Send Ula's letter back to me so I can return it to Lulú.

Ula is asking for photographs of the whole family, from his Papá down to his <u>youngest sister</u>, without thinking about how difficult it is to put together such a collection, when <u>one</u> doesn't even have fifty or sixty pesos <u>to spare</u>. However, poor Ula wants to please his nice cousins. They truly are very good, very pretty, and generosity personified.

Give my many regards to Harry, and kiss "Señor Don Tweedie" on my behalf. Lulú and Carmelita join me in sending our sincere affection.

Yours, as always,
M. G. Vallejo

93. C-B 441, box 1, folder 9, TBL.
94. C-B 441, box 1, folder 9, TBL.

Lachryma Montis
July 19, 1881[95]

Francisca,

You have really fallen in love with San Francisco. María improves when you are with her and that surely must make you very happy. Well, nothing could be more natural. Take care of her and stay with her for as long as you . . . like. Everyone here is fine, but I'm very tired because of the business with the water. I have to get up at five o'clock in the morning to go into Sonoma to distribute the water. Then at seven o'clock in the evening, I have to turn the machines back on. And for what? Just to "earn the daily bread" with much effort and fatigue. If I weren't so old and could bend down a bit, things would be different, because everyone has to work in order to live. But I shouldn't have these types of needs at this age. It is the power and the will of God.

The sale of the church was finalized. It seems that they are going to construct a new one on the site that is at the entrance of the white gate, where it leads out to the grove. There will be a convent and a house for the priest.

The plumbing that brings water from the "springs" of "Juan Viejo" for Attila's new house has already been finished, and it is well done.[96] Attila and Natalia are extremely happy. The house looks very nice and it is close to being finished. The water goes up to the roof.

A plague of little birds has arrived and they are eating the fruit. Before they eat everything up, I'm sending a small box of fruit to María so that she will remember that her Papá doesn't hold a grudge, but rather knows how to forgive. For if she sincerely asks for his forgiveness, repentance produces contrition, contrition brings on the tears, and tears soothe the soul. I don't understand the hierarchy between a father and a daughter in any other way. Under every circumstance a child should always be humble, respectful, and reverent (any how)[97] toward their father. Defiance and an irate tone with him . . . are serious offenses against Nature, and even more so against a father who has been vigilant and attentive to the child's education and has provided for her well-being (so far).

Well, give my regards to María, Harry, and kiss Don Tweedie.

M. G. Vallejo

---

95. C-B 441, box 1, folder 9, TBL.
96. Vallejo uses the English word "springs" in the original letter.
97. The parentheticals "any how" and then "so far" are in English in the original letter.

Lachryma Montis
August 24, 1881[98]

    Those who have signed this letter have the pleasure of sending their good wishes to Señora Doña Benicia Carrillo de Vallejo on her birthday, wishing her many more years of life, peace, tranquility in her soul, and prosperity in this world.

    In the manner in which we remember her, with pleasure and sincere affection, may she also keep us in her good graces and believe us wholeheartedly when we say, as always, that we are her dear friends.

M. G. Vallejo
Lulú and Carmen

By the early 1880s, Mission San Francisco Solano was in very dire shape. A priest had not been regularly assigned to the church for years, which meant that services were conducted a few times a month by a priest who would come to the mission from St. Vincent Parish in Petaluma. Archbishop Alemany decided that the growth of Sonoma County, which was home to more than 25,000 people according to the 1880 census, necessitated the construction of a more permanent parish in Sonoma. So, to finance the construction of a new church, he sold the mission property to Solomon Schocken, who had previously purchased the old barracks just across the street. Schocken made a down payment in May and the sale was completed by July. While the new church was being constructed, services continued to be held in the old mission chapel. The first service in the incomplete new church was held on Christmas 1881, and the finished structure was formally dedicated by Archbishop Alemany in June 1882.[99] Mariano Guadalupe had mixed feelings about having to abandon the mission that had meant so much to him and his family for half a century. Francisca, whose mother and brother were buried in the mission cemetery, was bitter about the sale, and her bitterness toward the archbishop boiled over in a letter to her husband.

---

98. BANC MSS 76/79c, box 1, folder 28, TBL.
99. Smilie, *Sonoma Mission*, 115.

Lachryma Montis
December 25, 1881[100]
Merry Christmas

Francisca,

Christmas Eve finally arrived and the first Mass in the new church was celebrated at midnight. Luisa and her pupils sang quite well. In spite of a lot of mud, and the fact that it was so dark that night, many people attended. The church was full.

Natalia and Lulú worked very hard arranging things and setting up the altar with paintings and more.

The old church was left abandoned. Forty-five years after it was constructed and having served as a temple for the Catholics, the <u>Catholic archbishop sold it to the Jewish people</u>. Do you remember that I built that church for my soldiers and fourteen of our children were baptized there? Do you remember that Mass was celebrated in this temple every Sunday and that the troops of the garrison would come to church in their uniforms, line up in formation, and then set out on their marches? Do you remember that at the time the chalice and the host would be raised, the Divine Sacrament would be honored? And finally, do you remember that your mother and one of your brothers are buried there?

It is better not to remember those things because, in addition to causing sadness, one can see that his work and his money have been wasted. Instead, the payment is a blow across the nape of my neck and a public insult, just like what happened to us with Jovita when the Church scorned us because we wanted to bury her there. Remember? And this is the same person who caused that scandal and who sold the Catholic church to a Jewish person! And the church is <u>currently</u> serving as a Jewish temple! Such a desecration! And the people who commit that desecration call themselves Christians! So many absurdities are committed by those very people who are entrusted with keeping the true religion thriving! The Protestants are right to ridicule the abuses of the Catholics and to call us fanatics. God only wants to be worshiped "in spirit and in truth."

It is eight o'clock at night. Tweedie is happily chatting with me in my room. Luisa is in the dining room with Minnie (the long-legged one) warming themselves by the fire. I am writing this little letter to you so that you will give my regards to María, Harry, and the little girl, wishing them some relief and hoping that they regain their health.

Goodbye.

M. G. Vallejo

---

100. C-B 441, box 1, folder 9, TBL.

San Francisco
December 29, 1881[101]

Guadalupe,

I received your little letter dated the 25th, in which you bring up such important and sad memories, which have no remedy. This broke my <u>heart</u> and I started to cry, but then I started thinking that "if there is no remedy to be had, then it is better to just forget," even if one doesn't want to, because if we don't forget, we will die of sheer sadness. Nobody knows the things that have happened like you and I do. Our children don't even know, nor do I know what happened to you in the past.

If my Mamá and my brother Juan were here, I wouldn't feel so sad. But this business of having to move the dead is terrible. May God give us strength and courage to do it. My poor Mamá, she was such a good Catholic. Do you remember that she always went to sweep the church, and that she herself begged Father Quijas to bury her next to the Holy Water? And now we have to remove her from there. It is a disgrace, it is fate. It seems that the priests are intentionally doing this. They are always looking for ways to hurt you, and it is all because we are poor. They no longer have any interest in you. These priests have no feelings, they have no heart. Even though you did favors for them when you were rich, now that you are poor they don't know who you are. And, besides, they are taking away what you have. They are scoundrels. For them, the church is a store, a butcher shop, and a bakery. Yet, even that is better, because if things aren't being run properly, the police will handle it.

These priests do whatever they want, and they do it with hypocrisy, sanctity, and lies. There are no police here who watch over things. There are so many things I want to say against the priests! But what do I gain by doing so? <u>Nothing. A person could inform the bishop. What a bishop!! He is worse than all the priests put together. He has a withered-up heart that is dry, dry.</u> No! no! no! That man doesn't know anything about a mother's love. He knows nothing. The woman who gave birth to him was one of those women who take water to the priest's house, and she gave birth to him there. In the darkness of the night, the baby was then taken to a convent. When they arrived at the convent, an old priest opened the door. He received the baby, took him to a small, dark room, and left him there until the next day. At nine or ten o'clock the next morning the extremely old priest remembered that he had left the boy there. He saw that the baby was alive, and he rushed out of the room. He picked up a rag and part of an old coat and soaked them in dirty water. He formed the cloth into the shape of a nipple and placed it in the baby's mouth. That is how they fed him. The old priest gave him the name José Alemany. When he was older, he used to play with skulls and other parts of the dead. They raised him and educated him within the confines of the convent, where he would

---

101. C-B 441, box 6, folder 5, TBL.

play at saying short Masses and giving short sermons. He never had a relationship with a woman. He did, however, love an extremely old Irish woman. If some woman had fallen in love with him, she probably was some disgraced nun who was going through life like the wandering Jew. I imagine him as ugly, indecent, and probably old, stuck in the middle of a poisonous tarantula's nest. Don't you imagine him as some sort of clever animal: a panther or a hyena, a hawk or a cat? I can't compare him to a bear or a lion because they aren't that mean. I can only compare him to another priest, but there is nobody as evil as he is.

Yes, he has a withered heart. He has no soul, and he does not possess that all-encompassing, pure, holy, and selfless love. Only a father of a family and a mother like me can appreciate the love of our children and the love of our parents in that way. There are no words to describe this! Only God can.

You will help me rebury my dear Mamá and all our children who died. When they are all together, I will be happy. Goodbye.

Benicia de Vallejo

AT THE BEGINNING OF 1882, VALLEJO'S OLDER BROTHER JOSÉ DE JESÚS died. He had been in ill health for quite a while. A few years earlier, in 1879, Vallejo had told his son Platón this about his brother: "Ever since he suffered the attack of paralysis a number of years ago, he has been very weak, more sickly, and delicate. In addition to that, he is already in his eighties. I was sad to come home, leaving him in that condition, but what can be done?"[102]

In August 1882 the last girl at home, Luisa, married Ricardo de Emparán, whom she had met on one of her visits to San Francisco.[103] He was currently the Mexican consul at San Diego, and the couple moved there shortly after the wedding. However, Luisa returned to Lachryma Montis so that she could give birth to her first child, Anita, there. She and Ricardo then spent some time in Mexico City, where they visited Epifania and her family. Luisa returned to Lachryma Montis for the birth of her second child, Carlos, as well. She stayed there while Ricardo went back to Mexico on business. A third child, Raoul, was born in 1885. Luisa made her home at Lachryma Montis while Ricardo made several business trips back and forth to Mexico.

During the last half of the 1880s both Guadalupe and Francisca found their activities more limited by the age-related conditions they were experiencing. He

---

102. M.G.V. to Platón, August 16, 1879, C-B 441 FILM, reel 3, 79, TBL.

103. Vallejo received a congratulatory letter about the wedding from Ramón Corona, a member of the American embassy staff in Madrid. Corona to M.G.V., December 7, 1882, DLG-V 16, letter 1.

Luisa Vallejo Emparán's children,
December 5, 1888. (*left to right*)
Carlos, Anita, and Richard.
*Courtesy of The Bancroft Library,
University of California, Berkeley.*
BANC PIC 1978.195:10-PIC.

periodically went to San Francisco, constantly in search of any kind of project that might promise additional funding, none of which materialized. He then had to write to Frisbie for money, since his son-in-law was doing better in Mexico than he had done in California. Indeed, connections rather than business ventures were responsible for Frisbie's success there. His association with Leland Stanford, currently a U.S. senator from California, and with Stanford associate Henry Huntington resulted in his being given the position of lobbyist for the Southern Pacific Railroad in Mexico. He also escorted Porfirio Díaz on his 1883 trip to the United States. Frisbie eventually gained possession of a ranch outside of Mexico City. In 1884, Vallejo told him that he needed "$7000 or $8000 pesos to replace the wooden pipes [that carried water from the spring on their property] with iron ones." He also confessed to Frisbie, "We don't have any money to pay the taxes."[104] The next year he said that the city of Sonoma was forcing him to remove some of the pipes from the streets and the plaza. He told Frisbie, "It will cost $2000 pesos to do the removal. I have $500 pesos. I most urgently need for you to send me the rest of the money."[105]

Mariano Guadalupe and Francisca's more infrequent letters generally spoke of domestic matters, although there is little mention in their surviving correspondence of Uladislao's difficulties obtaining the regular employment his parents desired. In 1878 he sought unsuccessfully to obtain a position with the Bancroft Company. When that failed, he tried to borrow money from Bancroft to finance a trip to Mexico. He said that his service in the Mexican army in the struggle against the

---

104. M.G.V. to Frisbie, August 17, 1884, C-B 441, box 2, folder 1, TBL.

105. Hart, *Empire and Revolution*, 124, 212; Schell, *Integral Outsiders*, 2–5; M.G.V. to Frisbie, April 23, 1885, C-B 441, box 2, folder 2, TBL.

French would enable him to lobby successfully for the position of Mexican consul in San Francisco. When that trip did not materialize, he asked Frisbie, now living in Mexico, to try to get him appointed as a customs official in Baja California. Frisbie wrote a pro forma request to Porfirio Díaz, but nothing came of it. Uladislao finally obtained a position as a tax collector in Sonoma. But in 1887 he absconded with a good amount of the Sonoma tax levy for that year in his possession. He went first to Mexico and then to Guatemala. He never returned.[106]

Lachryma Montis
December 28, 1882[107]

Francisca,

Today I received the attached letter from Emparán, in which he complains that I don't write to him. Yes, he does have reason to complain, but I don't have time to write. He doesn't take into account that I'm always so distressed, many times my eyesight is poor, and I'm busy with so many things, trivial, if you will, but <u>diabolically necessary</u>. I'll write to him tomorrow. In the meantime, send him the letter I wrote to you telling you about our Christmas Eve. Sending him that letter will be good for both of you. That will keep both of you entertained for a good while. Don't forget.

Today I received a letter from Frisbie and one hundred pesos. I'm very grateful to him for that, because the money helped me pay the taxes.[108] I asked for the rest of the money in the form of a loan.

Tomorrow, or day after, the Italians are leaving. May God look after them.

The little house where we keep the firewood is full. That should last us a couple of months. Everyone at home is fine.

Give my regards to everyone and kiss María, Leo, and Alma.

M. G. Vallejo

Palace Hotel
September 22, 1883[109]

Francisca,

Yesterday I received your simple yet wise little letter. I appreciate the good wishes you send me, which I will not forget. However, in addition to the experience I've

106. Uladislao to Hubert Howe Bancroft, August 20, 1878, B-C 7, box 11, folder 12, TBL; Emparán, *Vallejos*, 372–74.
107. C-B 441, box 1, folder 10, TBL.
108. Vallejo writes the word "taxes" in English in the original letter.
109. C-B 441, box 2, folder 1, TBL.

Receipt from the Palace Hotel, November 1, 1883.
Courtesy of The Bancroft Library, University of California, Berkeley.
C-B 441, box 9, folder 12.

acquired in every type of business during my long life, I'm convinced that it's time for me to take care of "NUMBER ONE" first. Number one is you and me. We've already fulfilled our mission in society. We had a large and extensive family; we raised them, educated them, and gave them standing which was not against their will, based on what is demanded by religion and society. So we should derive some satisfaction from this, without vanity, but yes with pride to think that we have lived long enough to see fulfilled the obligation we entered into in our marriage more than fifty years ago. Thank God that He granted us such a long life so we could see our children's children and die in peace, blessing all of them. Amen.

I'm working and hope to obtain a decent amount of money, that is to say, enough money for you to be happy so that the house can be remodeled and plumbing installed to bring water from the spring at Lachryma Montis. This will give us, or rather will produce, enough for us to live comfortably. And if there is any extra, it will be of use to us for the rest of our lives, however much time we have left. We will be able to rest without so many trials and tribulations.

The rights requested in Mexico have been obtained. When they arrive and I have control of them, I think I will obtain several thousand pesos for me and for those who have helped me obtain the rights.

Today or tomorrow I think I'll be able to settle some other <u>very important</u> business that will produce (based on how it is prepared) some thirty or forty thousand pesos, or maybe more. I'm delighted by the prospect that this might actually happen within a few months.

You need to realize that I'm not here for the pleasure of being here. No, I've remained in the city because I've been forced to do so by the circumstances that surround me. Here is where business is conducted, here is where the people reside. People lie all the time. Everyone wants to ensnare those who approach them. The wealthy people are the big fish who always want to swallow the small ones. I have an appointment at 10 o'clock in the morning and another at 2 o'clock in the afternoon. Then I have two or three more appointments on another day. Some people come prepared with money, but they want to cheat the one who is left behind, etc., etc., etc.

One cannot break away from anyone. It's an endless chain of talking and, when it seems that the matter has finally been brought to a close, nothing really has been accomplished, and the whole thing starts all over again. I'm tired and bored.

I've forced myself to go to the theater three times since I've been here. Each time I've left angry and my eyes were hurting. You know I don't like frivolous theatrics. There is too much of that going on in <u>real life</u> and we all have a role in it.

I don't visit anyone else's home except for Ramona's. I spend some time with her chatting and eating watermelon. You know that she's ill and feeble and unable to go outside. I say my farewells and return again another day, if I have time. Ramoncita and the rest of the small family seem to care for me quite a bit. They always remember you and send you their greetings.[110]

Once I went to visit María and took Lulú with me. Emparán served us a very fine lunch.[111] She was very happy. Leo screamed when he saw me, and Alma went to greet me at the door of the house. They send you many greetings. Harry came to my room very early three days ago to tell me that his business had gone <u>bankrupt</u> and he didn't have ten cents to his name. I was shocked, but I told him that he could consider our home to be a refuge and I gave him ten pesos I had in my pocket. When we see one another I'll give you some more details since I don't want to waste paper. Harry returned today telling me that a commercial establishment (Mr. Cotin) had proposed to him that he establish a branch office in Portland, Oregon, and that Harry would be a partner. Harry and another partner would divide the earnings between the two of them. In return for managing the business in Portland, Harry would receive a salary of $150. Of course, María would go with him. We'll see how she reacts.

---

110. Francisca's sister Ramona was living with her daughter, whom Mariano Guadalupe calls "Ramoncita," on Mission Street. The daughter was married to ship captain Frederick Hilliard. *San Francisco City Directory, 1883,* 553, 1079, accessed through Ancestry.com.

111. The word "lunch" is in English in the original letter.

María Vallejo Cutter
and Luisa Vallejo
Emparán. *Courtesy of
California State Parks,
Sonoma Barracks. No.
243-x-2958.*

My eyes are hurting a lot. I can't write any longer.
Give my regards to everyone.

M. G. Vallejo

IN THE LAST-HALF DECADE OF HIS LIFE, IN SPITE OF HIS CONTINUING
financial difficulties, Vallejo became something of a celebrity, a walking symbol
of an increasingly romanticized version of pre-U.S. California. In 1886 he spoke at
the Fruit Growers Convention in Sacramento and planted a tree on Yerba Buena
Island during California's first Arbor Day celebration. In 1887 a New Jersey merchant wrote to a business acquaintance in San Francisco about a real estate project
in Mexico in which Vallejo might become involved: "The General's name helps it,
for we here know of him well. His name belongs to the whole people of the U.S."
And in 1888 he was inducted into the Chico chapter of the Native Sons of the
Golden West.[112]

---

112. Beebe and Senkewicz, *Mariano Guadalupe Vallejo*, 194–95; James Lindsley to Manuel Brockelbank, June 1, 1887,
    C-B 441, box 5, folder 5, TBL; *Langley's San Francisco Directory for the Year 1887*, 134.

State of California Office of State Board of Horticulture
San Francisco
Monterey
September 12, 1887[113]

Francisca,

First, if it can't be done any other way, then ask Ula for the five pesos to pay the Chinese cook for his eight days of work. When I came, I paid him up through last Tuesday.

Second, I'm happy that you received the barrel of sugar that my sister (Mrs. Cooper) sent you from San Francisco. She told me that the sugar was very good for making sweets. When I arrived in San Francisco I went to see her and she already had the barrel ready, but she didn't know how to send it to Sonoma. I immediately put the address on the barrel and sent it on the steamer.

Lulú wrote to me. In her letter she told me everything that was happening at home and that everyone is fine "so far."[114] I was very happy to hear that.

I've enjoyed walking with Ricardo and showing him all of Monterey. I think he likes the landscape, the bay, "Pacific Grove," Big Meadow, Cypress Point, Fisherman's Wharf, the Pines, Mount Parnassus, the Del Monte Hotel, etc. When we return, which will be very soon, he'll tell you all about our trip. Yesterday the weather was quite beautiful and we were invited to have lunch at noon at Abimael's house. At four o'clock Doña Clementina Heintz invited us over for dinner and we ate at six o'clock. We've been well fed.

My sister Rosa[lía] is very ill with infirmities of old age. She is seventy-five years old. It makes me sad to see her. She is very worn out and very poor.

Tomorrow, Wednesday, we'll leave here. Soon we'll see one another. Carolina is much better. It seems that the climate in Monterey agrees with her. She sends you a thousand expressions of affection.

Kiss Lulú, Anita, Carlos, and Raoul. And you, try to stay well. It's possible that one of these days we'll get out from under the present circumstances.

Goodbye. Until Saturday.

Yours sincerely,
M. G. Vallejo

---

113. C-B 441, box 2, folder 2, TBL.

114. The words "so far" are in English in the original letter. Written on letterhead of the State of California Office of State Board of Horticulture. No. 30 Post St., Corner Kearny. San Francisco, Cal.

Mariano Guadalupe Vallejo at Lachryma Montis, 1888.
Courtesy of California State Parks, Sonoma Barracks. No. 243-x-778.

Lachryma Montis
August 28, 1888[115]

Francisca,

I'm feeling a bit better and that is why I'm writing to you in my own hand, even though with some difficulty. For in addition to feeling weak because of my last illness (diarrhea),[116] you know how much I suffer with regard to my eyes when I write. But I do this with pleasure to tell you that I'm sending you in the mail the small bottle of medicine that did you so much good when you were here. Keep taking it: <u>ten drops in each lump of sugar at bedtime.</u>

Tell Adela that I received her last two letters and I'm grateful to her. Also, have her tell my beautiful little friend who lives in front, Miss Mae, that I received her little letter. As soon as I feel better, I'll answer her.

---

115. C-B 441, box 2, folder 2, TBL.
116. The parenthetical "diarrhea" is in English in the original letter.

Mariano Guadalupe Vallejo, January 1, 1889.
Courtesy of California State Parks,
Sonoma Barracks. No. 243–1-1424.

Everyone here is fine. They send their greetings to everyone. And you, take good care of yourself and don't worry, because "he who worries, is just killing himself."[117] I'll do as much as I can around here. Lulú takes care of me like a good daughter.

Goodbye, says your

M. G. Vallejo

VALLEJO'S LAST LETTER TO FRANCISCA THAT WE HAVE WAS WRITTEN from the Union Hotel in San Francisco in November 1888. In that letter he expressed the hope that "we will be able to walk together in peace and harmony in the little bit of life that we have left."

Union Hotel
San Francisco
November 20, 1888[118]

Francisca,

I arrived at this place today, at four o'clock in the morning, after traveling all night seated on the train. I'm a bit tired, or better said, sleep deprived, but not sick. It's a very dreary day, it's raining, and the streets are muddy. I'll try not to get my feet wet, as you reminded me. You can see that I'm writing to you so that you won't be worried about me, nor will Lulú and the rest of the family be worried. I hope, (<u>at</u>

---

117. *El que se apura se mata.*
118. C-B 441, box 2, folder 3, TBL.

least) from here on out, that we'll be able to walk together in peace and harmony in the little bit of life that we have left. As elderly people we should at least maintain tranquility at home for our families and relatives on both sides. If some member on either side of the family does something wrong, we should correct them, and with dignity and prudence advise them to do good and to avoid scandal. "He who is without sin, let him cast the first stone,"[119] as Jesus said when the woman was being judged. We are no better than Jesus. Remember that we have sons and daughters.

Give my regards to everyone, from Ricardo down to Raoul. I'm fine.

M. G. Vallejo

In April 1889, Epifania and John Frisbie, along with two of their younger daughters, visited Lachryma Montis. Two months later Vallejo drew up his will. It stated, "I give and bequeath to my beloved wife Benicia F. Vallejo all my estate, real, personal, or mixed and of every kind and description, that I may own at the time of my death, for her sole use and benefit." The will explicitly added, "I do not bequeath anything to my sons Andrónico, Platón, Uladislao, Napoleón, or to either of them, nor to any of my daughters, Epifania, wife of Gen. Frisbie, Adela, wife of Dr. Frisbie, Natalia, widow of A. F. Haraszthy, deceased, Luisa, wife of R. Emparán, María, wife of Mr. Cutter, or to either of them, for the reason that I have already given to my said children, and to each of them, what I consider their full share of inheritance."[120] His use of the phrase "all my estate, real, personal, or mixed" indicates that he realized he was not the legal owner of Lachryma Montis.

In January 1890, Lulú sent a telegram to Epifania in Mexico saying that their father was failing. Epifania was able to arrive in Sonoma a few days before her father died on January 18, 1890, surrounded by many of his children and grandchildren. Epifania telegraphed her husband in Mexico, who immediately responded, "Our tears mingle with yours. Do all possible for dear Grandmother. Pay all funeral expenses."[121]

Francisca suffered a stroke about a month after her husband's death. She recovered somewhat but was only able to speak and walk with difficulty after that. Her widowed daughter Natalia, who lived in a house near Lachryma Montis to which she had moved with Attila after the phylloxera infestation at Buena Vista, looked after her constantly. Benicia had drawn up her own will a few months after her husband's death. In that document she had bequeathed to her two youngest daughters, Luisa and María, "the old family homestead known as 'Lachryma Montis,'

119. *El que no tenga culpa, tire la piedra.*

120. M.G.V., Final Will and Testament, C-B 441, box 10, folder 5, TBL.

121. Epifania Frisbie telegram to John Frisbie, January 18, 1890, C-B 441, box 4, folder 12, TBL; Emparán, *Vallejos,* 279–82.

(*left*) Telegram to Genl. J. B. Frisbie from Epifania Frisbie, Calle Nueva No. 6, City of Mexico. January 18, 1890. "Father died at one thirty this morning. Fannie." *Courtesy of The Bancroft Library, University of California Berkeley. C-B 441, box 4, folder 12.* (*right*) Telegram to Dr. Levi Frisbie from Adela Vallejo de Frisbie, January 18, 1890. "Father died at one thirty this morning. Funeral Tuesday morning. Notify Pioneers and publish Vallejo paper and Native Sons. Adela V. de Frisbie." *Courtesy of The Bancroft Library, University of California, Berkeley. C-B 441, box 4, folder 8.*

being all the lands included in a declaration of homestead made and filed by myself and my late husband M. G. Vallejo, and of record in the Recorder's Office of the County of Sonoma in the State of California, and all the lands joining or forming a part of the set homestead, whether described in said declaration of homestead or not together with the appurtenances thereunto belonging."[122]

Natalia, whose husband had lost much of his money attempting to revive his wine business before his death in 1886, tried to convince her mother to divide the property more equally among all of the children. She told her brother Platón that her mother agreed with this, but at the end of November Francisca was struck by paralysis and was unable to have the will changed.

122. F.B.C.V., Last Will and Testament, C-B 441, box 10, folder 5 (written in English).

Form No. 1.

THE WESTERN UNION TELEGRAPH COMPANY.

This Company TRANSMITS and DELIVERS messages only on conditions limiting its liability, which have been assented to by the sender of the following message.
Errors can be guarded against only by repeating a message back to the sending station for comparison, and the company will not hold itself liable for errors or delays in transmission or delivery of Unrepeated Messages, beyond the amount of tolls paid thereon, nor in any case where the claim is not presented in writing within sixty days after sending the message.
This is an UNREPEATED MESSAGE, and is delivered by request of the sender, under the conditions named above.

THOS. T. ECKERT, General Manager.   NORVIN GREEN, President.

NUMBER	SENT BY	REC'D BY		CHECK
2n	A	18 Paid	via Galveston	

Received at *Sonoma 4.45 PM.*   Jan 30th 1891

Dated *Mejico*

To *Mrs. Natalia Haraszthy*

Sonoma

We mourn with you the death of our beloved mother funeral expenses provided as here to fore advised.

John and Fannie [Frisbie]

(*above*) Telegram from John and Fannie Frisbie to Mrs. Natalia Haraszthy, January 30, 1891, Sonoma. "We mourn with you the death of our beloved mother, funeral expenses provided as here to fore advised. John and Fannie." *Courtesy of The Bancroft Library, University of California, Berkeley. C-B 441, box 4, folder 13.*

(*left*) Natalia Vallejo Haraszthy and her two daughters. (*Left and center*) Natalia (Tala) and Eleanora (Lolita), ca. 1885. *Courtesy of The Bancroft Library, University of California, Berkeley.* BANC PIC 1978.195:14-PIC.

On January 28, 1891, Natalia telegraphed Platón with the message, "Come immediately, mother dying. Tell Andrónico." Francisca Benicia passed away on January 30, 1891. Once again, Frisbie paid the funeral expenses. Francisca was buried beside her husband at Mountain Cemetery, not far from Lachryma Montis.[123]

---

123. Natalia Haraszthy to Platón Vallejo, June 19 and November 22, 1890, January 7, 1891, BANC MSS 76/79c, box 1, folder 15; Natalia Haraszthy telegram to Platón Vallejo, January 28, 1891, C-B 441, box 1, folder 7; John and Fannie Frisbie telegram to Natalia Haraszthy, January 30, 1891, C-B 441, box 4, folder 13, all in TBL.

Conclusion

*I*n 1887, on one of her final trips from Mexico to visit her parents, Epifania Vallejo Frisbie brought her daughter Fanita and Fanita's daughter Juanita with her. She convinced her mother Francisca to go to San Francisco with the three of them, and the four of them sat for a photograph at the Montgomery Street studio of renowned San Francisco photographer I. W. Taber. The result was the famous "Four Generations" photo.

The photograph highlights the diversity of backgrounds that constituted the multigenerational Vallejo family, for each of the four women had been born in a different location. In addition, each woman's father had also been born in one of four different locations. Specifically, the father of the oldest person in the picture, Francisca Benicia, had been born in Baja California, and she herself had been born in San Diego. The father of the next person in line, Epifania, had been born in Monterey, and she had been born in the priest quarters of secularized Mission San Francisco Solano. The father of Epifania's daughter Fanita had been born in New York, and Fanita in Vallejo. Finally, the father of the youngest person, Juanita, had been born in Portugal, and she had been born in Mexico.

The same kind of diversity of origin was present among the pallbearers at Vallejo's funeral in January 1890. Three of them, Andrónico, Platón, and Napoleón, were sons of Mariano Guadalupe and Francisca Benicia. Two others, Agoston and Mariano Haraszthy, were sons of their daughter Natalia and her husband, Attila, who had been born in Hungary. Two others were sons of Epifania and John Frisbie. One son, Platón, had been born in Philadelphia, and the other son, Leo, had been born in Vallejo. Two additional pallbearers were Arpad Haraszthy, who, like his brother, was Hungarian born, and James Harry Cutter, who was a native of San Francisco.[1]

---

1. *Sacramento Record-Union*, January 22, 1890.

Four generations portrait, 1888, by
Isaiah W. Taber: Epifania Vallejo
de Frisbie (*left*), granddaughter
Fannie Frisbie Sequeira (*above*),
Francisca Benicia Carrillo de Vallejo
(*right*), and great-granddaughter
Juanita Sequeira (*below*). *Courtesy
of The Bancroft Library, University
of California, Berkeley.* POR: *Vallejo,
Mariano Guadalupe, Mrs.:8.*

These diversities of origin point to the tremendous diversities of ethnic identity
the extended Vallejo family exhibited. Mariano Guadalupe and Francisca Benicia's ancestry was rooted in northern New Spain, yet none of their girls married a
person with a similar ancestry. Each of them contracted an interethnic marriage,
and these marriages occurred after California became part of the United States.
As a result, the partner in the marriage who was born in California was in many
ways the immigrant newcomer, seeking to assimilate into a culture that seemed
to be much more hospitable to their husbands. The girls who married the Frisbie
brothers married partners who had been trained in two of the most prestigious
occupations in nineteenth-century America, law and medicine. The girls who married the Haraszthy brothers married men whose father had already spent almost
a decade in the American Midwest and had quickly been able to fill a variety of
political offices, such as marshal and sheriff in San Diego, when he first arrived
in California.[2]

The boys who married did not do so until all four of their sisters had already been
wed, but they also experienced a sense of not entirely belonging to the land in which
they lived. The Vallejo son who had been trained in medicine at Columbia and had
served in the Union forces during the Civil War discovered that he needed John
Frisbie's assistance to obtain a position with the Pacific Mail Steamship Company.
When the son who graduated from Santa Clara College was looking for a position,
he also had to rely upon Frisbie to obtain a position with a local railroad. And all

2. McGinty, *Strong Wine*, 177–241.

of this was occurring while the new government under which the family lived was taking away money and land from their mother and father.

In these circumstances the Vallejo children experienced a mix of what Jessica M. Vásquez, in her study of twentieth-century immigrant Mexican American families, has termed the "spectrum of thinned attachment and cultural maintenance."[3] At times their attachment to their own ethnic background seemed to be weak, as they learned English, studied in American schools, wrote letters to their mother in a language she did not understand and, especially, adopted greater initiative than their Mexican parents thought appropriate in matters such as a marriage partner. In this they were ironically living out the consequences of their father's insistence that they assimilate as fully as they could to this new culture. At other times they appeared to have a greater awareness that they were going further than their parents had intended, sometimes not maintaining the cultural traditions that were so dear to their father and mother. When Adela wrote her father begging him to come to her wedding, the tears she shed as she realized how much her decision was hurting him were apparent in her words: "Dear Papá, if you love your child, you must come. It is my only wish, and I pray you will not be angry with me." At such times they could appreciate the sense of loss and isolation their parents sometimes experienced. Very often they found themselves living in an indeterminate middle ground between these two poles, such as when María would please her father by helping him translate Spanish documents and annoy him by exhibiting what he considered to be inappropriate behavior with her American boyfriend.

This family had to negotiate what was for them a very strange landscape. In many ways they were like so many immigrant families in nineteenth, twentieth, and twenty-first century America. But there was one crucial difference. The Vallejo family had not planned to come to America. Rather, America had suddenly and unexpectedly come to them.

As we have seen, the arrival of this foreign culture created a host of issues for this family and for the larger Mexican community of which they were a part. In this particular family the women, especially Francisca, tended to assess matters in a more consistently direct and pragmatic fashion than their male counterparts. The resolve and fortitude with which she confronted John Frémont and Archibald Gillespie during the 1846 Bear Flag rebellion continued to make itself apparent in the way she approached other men over the next forty years. She often reproached her husband for being too concerned with his own business affairs, for neglecting his family, and for not appreciating the efforts she consistently put forward to keep her children fed, clothed, and educated. Even though she never sent her son-in-law John Frisbie the 1873 letter denouncing what she took to be his lack of gratitude for what she and her husband had done for him, she made those feelings known in no

---

3. Vásquez, *Mexican Americans across Generations*, xi, 33–90.

Mariano Guadalupe Vallejo and family members at Sonoma, mid-1880s.
Courtesy of the California Historical Society. FN-30504.

uncertain terms to her daughter and other family members. And her denunciation of Church authorities, especially Archbishop Alemany, for what she regarded as their lack of appropriate concern in the case of her daughter Jovita's death sparked her husband to not let the archbishop forget what the family regarded as his inattention to his pastoral responsibilities. She consistently understood the issues that she, her husband, and their extended family had to confront in this new situation in which they found themselves. She tended to be much more skeptical than her husband as to whether they would ever restore themselves to the social position they had occupied before the American takeover.

On his better days, her husband realized that what she said was true. Toward the end of their lives, he began his September 22, 1883, letter to her by reflecting on what they had been able to accomplish with their children. We believe that, by focusing on their children, he was telling her that he realized and appreciated that the major portion of what he was describing had actually been performed by her.

Mariano Guadalupe Vallejo and Francisca Benicia Carrillo de Vallejo.
Courtesy of California State Parks, Sonoma Barracks. Nos. 243–1-1421 and 243–1-1394.

We think this is an appropriate way to end this consideration of the successes and failures, triumphs and tribulations, joys and sorrows of this remarkable family:

Yesterday I received your simple yet wise little letter. I appreciate the good wishes you send me, which I will not forget. However, in addition to the experience I've acquired in every type of business during my long life, I'm convinced that it's time for me to take care of "NUMBER ONE" first. Number one is you and me. We've already fulfilled our mission in society. We had a large and extensive family; we raised them, educated them, and gave them standing which was not against their will, based on what is demanded by religion and society. So we should derive some satisfaction from this, without vanity, but yes with pride to think that we have lived long enough to see fulfilled the obligation we entered into in our marriage more than fifty years ago. Thank God that He granted us such a long life so we could see our children's children and die in peace, blessing all of them. Amen.

Family Trees

Because the names of Mariano Guadalupe's and Francisca Benicia's children, sons-in-law, daughters-in-law, and grandchildren appear in much of their parents' correspondence, often years or decades apart, we provide this series of family trees as an aid to understanding the many relationships that constituted this extended family. We do not include family trees for Andrónico, who was unmarried, or for Uladislao, who did not marry before he moved to Mexico. Children whom Mariano Guadalupe fathered with women other than Francisca Benicia all appear frequently in the letters, so we include family trees for these six individuals as well.

※ Children of Mariano Guadalupe and
Francisca Benicia Carrillo de Vallejo

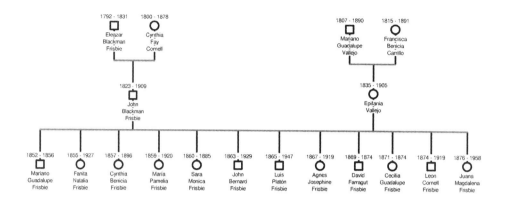

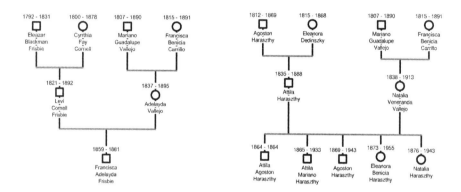

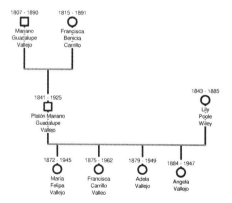

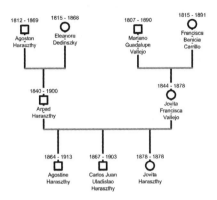

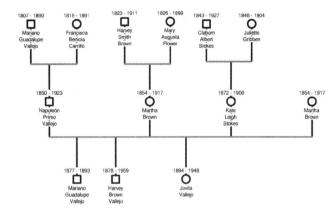

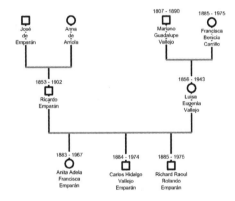

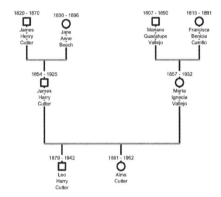

❋ Children Fathered by
Mariano Guadalupe Vallejo and Other Women

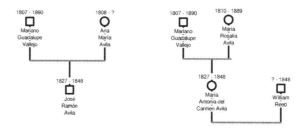

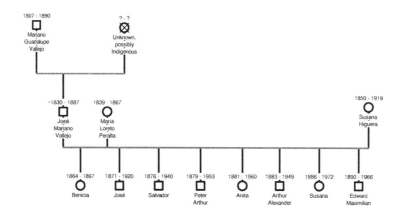

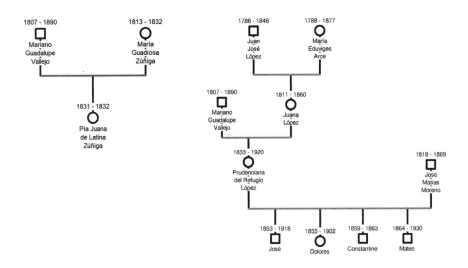

1807 - 1890
Mariano
Guadalupe
Vallejo

1813 - 1832
María
Guadiosa
Zúñiga

1831 - 1832
Pía Juana
de Latina
Zúñiga

1786 - 1846
Juan
José
López

1788 - 1877
María
Eduviges
Arce

1807 - 1890
Mariano
Guadalupe
Vallejo

1811 - 1860
Juana
López

1833 - 1920
Prudenciana
del Refugio
López

1818 - 1869
José
Matías
Moreno

1853 - 1918
José

1855 - 1902
Dolores

1859 - 1863
Constantine

1864 - 1930
Mateo

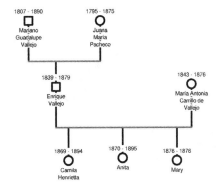

1807 - 1890
Mariano
Guadalupe
Vallejo

1795 - 1875
Juana
María
Pacheco

1839 - 1879
Enrique
Vallejo

1843 - 1876
María Antonia
Carrillo de
Vallejo

1869 - 1894
Camila
Henrietta

1870 - 1895
Anita

1876 - 1876
Mary

Biographical Sketches

Joseph Sadoc Alemany (1814–1888) was born in Catalonia, Spain. He entered the Dominican Order and served as a missionary in parts of the United States. He was appointed bishop of Monterey in 1850 and archbishop of San Francisco in 1853. He served in the latter position until he resigned in 1884 and returned to Spain. (McGloin, *California's First Archbishop*)

Juan Bautista Alvarado (1809–1882) was born in Monterey to José Francisco Alvarado and María Josefa Vallejo. His father died shortly after his birth, and his mother then married José Raymundo Estrada, brother of José Mariano Estrada. Alvarado served as secretary of the Diputación from 1828 to 1834 and was a member of that body for the next three years. He led the revolution against Nicolás Gutiérrez in 1836 and served as governor until 1842. He was also a leader in the movement against Micheltorena in 1844–45. (Bancroft, *History of California*, 2:693–94; Alvarado, *Vignettes*, vii–xiv)

José Amesti was a native of the Basque region of Spain. He came to Alta California in 1822 and became a merchant based in Monterey. He married Prudenciana Vallejo, Mariano Guadalupe's older sister, in 1823. He served in public office, including as alcalde in 1844. He was granted Rancho Corralitos in Santa Cruz in that same year. In 1846, Frémont's men seized his horses, saddles, and blankets on the rancho. He died around 1856. (Bancroft, *History of California*, 2:696; 5:358–59; Northrop, *Spanish-Mexican Families*, 1:351)

Margarita Angulo de Navarrete, a native of Baja California, was the daughter of Asunción Montaño and Juan de Dios Angulo, an important political figure in the mid-nineteenth century Baja California peninsula. In 1857 she married Pedro Magaña Navarrete, who served for a time as governor of Baja California in the 1860s. After he was overthrown they moved to San Francisco, although she was able to continue visiting Baja California during the early 1870s. She died in 1887. (Martínez, *Guía Familiar*, 462; Martínez, *Historia de Baja California*, 400, 410–11; Valadés, *Historia de la Baja California*, 147–67)

FAXON D. ATHERTON (1815–1877) was a native of Massachusetts. After developing a hauling business at Boston Harbor, in 1833 he moved to Valparaíso, Chile, a key port in the developing California–New England trade. After three years in California (1836–39) he settled in Valparaíso and married into a prominent Chilean family. He moved to California again in 1860 and lived on the San Francisco peninsula for his remaining years. (Atherton, *California Diary*, xiii–xxxii)

HUBERT HOWE BANCROFT (1832–1918) was a native of Ohio who came to San Francisco as a bookseller in 1852. He became a book collector and publisher and ultimately produced thirty-nine volumes on the history of the American West, including the seven-volume *History of California*. The seventy-eight oral histories and the thousands of pages of primary documents that Californios provided his staff are indispensable sources for the history of pre-U.S. California. (Caughey, *Hubert Howe Bancroft*; Clark, *Venture in History*)

JOHN BIDWELL (1819–1900) was born in New York. He was one of the leaders of the first North American overland party to California, in 1841. He worked for John Sutter for a few years and was tangentially involved in the Bear Flag movement. After the Mexico-U.S. war, he served with Mariano Guadalupe Vallejo in the first session of the California State Senate. He also served as a representative from California in the U.S. Congress in the mid-1860s. (Gillis and Magliari, *John Bidwell*)

WILLIAM W. BOGGS was the son of Lilburn Boggs, governor of Missouri in 1836–40. He spent the winter of 1846 at the Vallejo rancho in Petaluma and was alcalde of the Northern District in 1847–49. (Bancroft, *California*, 2; 722–23; Hyde, *Empires, Nations, and Families*, 352–53; Palmer, *History of Napa and Lake Counties*, 384 (Napa County section))

BENJAMIN S. BROOKS (1820–1884) was a native of Connecticut who came to gold rush San Francisco and quickly established himself as a leading lawyer. He represented Vallejo for several years. (California State Census 1852, San Francisco, 424; Langley, *San Francisco Directory 1871*, 122; *Daily Alta California*, May 3, 1884)

HENRY S. BURTON (1819–1869) was born in New York and graduated from West Point in 1839. He served in the Second Seminole War in the early 1840s. As an officer of the New York Volunteers, he served in Baja California during the Mexico-U.S. war. After the peace treaty was signed, he escorted a group of Baja Californians who had supported the American troops to Alta California and married one of them, María Amparo Ruiz, at Monterey in 1849. He later served in the American Civil War. (Bancroft, *History of California*, 2:737)

JOAQUÍN CARRILLO (1820–1899) was a younger brother of Francisca Benicia Vallejo. After the death of his father, he, his mother, and younger brothers moved to the Santa Rosa area. He married Guadalupe Cáceres in 1842. In 1846, Francisca managed to hide him from the Bear Flaggers. After they lost their ranch lands to squatters and legal proceedings, he and Guadalupe opened a hotel in Sebastopol. Two years after her death in 1874 he married Mary Springer of Bodega. (McGinty, "Carrillos of San Diego," 281–85)

JULIO CARRILLO (1824–1899) was a younger brother of Francisca Benicia Vallejo. He was arrested by the Bear Flaggers in 1846. After the American conquest of California, he lived in the Santa Rosa region. (Northrop, *Spanish-Mexican Families*, 2:46–48; McGinty, "Carrillos of San Diego," 294–300)

RAMÓN CARRILLO (1821–1864) was a younger brother of Francisca Benicia Vallejo. He moved to the Sonoma region with his mother in the late 1830s. In 1846 he was involved with the Californio resistance to the Bear Flaggers and was accused of complicity in the killings of Thomas Cowie and George Fowler. After fighting against the Americans in southern Alta California, he remained there after the war. In 1864 he was murdered at Cucamonga, most likely by Americans who blamed him for the killings of the two Americans. (McGinty, "Carrillos of San Diego," 285–93)

RAMONA CARRILLO (1812–1886) was an older sister of Francisca Benicia Vallejo. In 1827 she married a member of Governor José Echeandía's staff, Romualdo Pacheco, who was killed in 1831. In 1836 she married Scottish trader John Wilson, and they lived in various locations in central Alta California until his death in 1860. Drought in the first half of the 1860s severely damaged her rancho lands, and she spent much of the remaining years of her life in San Francisco. (McGinty, "Carrillos of San Diego," 128–32)

ENRIQUE CERRUTI (1836–1876) was a native of Turin, Italy. As a youth he journeyed to Latin America, where he said he became involved in various political and military activities in Bolivia. He came to California in 1873 and was hired by historian Hubert Howe Bancroft to interview various Californios, beginning with Vallejo. When his extensive speculation in mining stocks failed, he committed suicide. (Beebe and Senkewicz, *Testimonios*, xxiii–xxiv)

JOHN B. R. COOPER, a native of the Alderney Islands in the English Channel, arrived in Massachusetts as a young boy. He first came to California in 1823 as master of the Boston vessel *Rover*. Settling in California as a merchant in 1826, he married Encarnación Vallejo the next year and became active in public affairs.

He received several land grants during the Mexican period. He divided his time between living in Monterey and making trading voyages in the Pacific. He died in 1872. (Woolfenden and Elkinton, *Cooper*; Bancroft, *History of California*, 2:100–101)

CAROLINA DÍAS was born around 1832 in Mexico. By 1860 she was living in San Francisco and found employment as a piano teacher and Spanish tutor there. Her piano instruction activities probably brought her into contact with the Vallejo family. (1860 U.S. Census, San Francisco District 4, 203; Langley, *San Francisco Directory 1861*, 119, 406)

CARMELITA DOMÍNGUEZ was born around 1839 in Mexico. At some point during the 1860s her husband became a soldier in the forces of Mexican president Benito Juárez and fought against the French intervention. Carmelita and her young son Ricardo came to the United States and she began to work for Francisca Smith, a dressmaker in San Francisco. By the end of the 1860s, Carmelita had become acquainted with the Vallejo family and became a valued housekeeping worker at Lachryma Montis. (1870 U.S. Census, San Francisco Ward 8, 137; Langley, *San Francisco Directory 1875*, 246)

JOSÉ MARÍA ECHEANDÍA, a lieutenant colonel of engineers, was engaged in surveying the boundaries of the newly created Federal District in Mexico when he was appointed political and military governor of Baja and Alta California in 1825. Because he disliked the chilly and foggy climate of northern California he made his headquarters in San Diego. Little is known about him outside of his service in Alta California. He returned to Mexico in 1833 and was reported to be practicing his profession as an engineer in the 1850s. He died sometime before 1871. (Bancroft, *History of California*, 3:243–45; Hutchinson, *Frontier Settlement*, 124–25)

ESTANISLAO was the Spanish name given to Cucunuchi, a twenty-eight-year-old Laquisamne man when he was baptized in 1821 at Mission San José. He became an Indigenous alcalde there, an indication that he enjoyed the favor of the local clergy. Along with some companions, he refused to return to the mission after visiting his ranchería after the 1828 harvest. His forces defeated those of veteran fighter José Sánchez in 1829 and then forced the withdrawal of a combined Monterey–San Francisco expedition led by Mariano Guadalupe Vallejo. Cucunuchi/Estanislao was pardoned thereafter and continued to live at Mission San José until his death in 1838. (Holterman, "Revolt of Estanislao"; Osio, *History of Alta California*, 89–94; Bojorques, "Recuerdos sobre la historia de California," 21, C-D 46, TBL; San José Baptism 4471)

VÍCTOR FAURÉ was born in France around 1815 and became a physician. Mariano Guadalupe Vallejo hired him to manage his vineyards and wine cellars in Sonoma. He died in 1875. (Emparán, *Vallejos of California*, 103, 117)

HENRY DELANO FITCH (1799–1849) was a native of Massachusetts who came to San Diego in 1826 as master of a ship owned by Mexico-based trader Enrique Virmond. In 1829 he eloped with Josefa Carrillo and they were married in Chile. On their return, Fitch was briefly arrested but eventually released. He became a significant merchant in San Diego. In 1841, through the agency of his brother-in-law, Mariano Guadalupe Vallejo, he received a land grant slightly north of Sonoma. (Beebe and Senkewicz, *Testimonios*, 71–74)

JOHN CHARLES FRÉMONT (1813–1890) was born in Georgia. He was a lieutenant in the U.S. Army Corps and made journeys to Oregon in 1842 and California in 1843 and 1844. He appeared at Sutter's Fort in the winter of 1845 and then, claiming to be short on supplies, at Monterey in January 1846. He was active in the U.S. conquest of California and accepted the surrender of Andrés Pico at Cahuenga. He served California in the U.S. Senate and was the first Republican candidate for president in 1856. After serving in the American Civil War, he spent the rest of his life as a territorial governor and promoter of various western development projects. (Denton, *Passion and Principle*, 102–56)

JOHN FRISBIE (1823–1909) was a native of New York. He received some legal training as a young man. When the Mexico-U.S. war broke out, he joined the New York Volunteers. While stationed in Sonoma he met Mariano Guadalupe Vallejo's daughter Epifania, whom he married in 1851. Frisbie managed many of Vallejo's financial matters, not always well. After Frisbie filed for bankruptcy in 1876, he determined to start anew in Mexico. Remaining there the rest of his life, he attained a degree of success and eventually was able to purchase a ranch. (Frisbie, "Reminiscences," M-M 351, TBL)

LEVI FRISBIE (1821–1892) a brother of John Frisbie, was born in New York. He graduated from Albany Medical College in 1841 and practiced medicine in New York for the rest of the decade. He came to California in the early 1850s and married Mariano Guadalupe Vallejo's daughter Adela in 1858. He continued to practice medicine in Solano County until his death. (Munro-Fraser, *History of Solano County*, 351–52).

ARCHIBALD GILLESPIE (1812–1873) was born in Pennsylvania. In 1846 he was a lieutenant in the U.S. Marines. He arrived in Monterey in April of that year with a message to Thomas O. Larkin appointing him a confidential agent assigned to persuade the Californios to join the United States. He also delivered secret messages to John Frémont, which appear to have encouraged Frémont to become more belligerent. Gillespie served in the military during the U.S. conquest of California. His arbitrary behavior while in charge of the Los Angeles garrison sparked a Californio revolt. He was wounded in the military skirmish at San Pascual during the Mexico-U.S. war. He spent most of the rest of his life in California. (Marti, *Messenger of Destiny*; Harlow, *California Conquered*, 78)

PIETRO AND GOTARDO GIOVANARI, brothers, leased land from Vallejo and were involved in the wine business with Arpad Haraszthy. (McGinty, *Toast to Eclipse*, 36–38)

JOHN GRIGSBY (1806–1876) a Missouri farmer, came to California in 1845 with William Ide. He was an active member of the Bear Flag movement and eventually settled in Napa. He left California in the 1870s to return to Missouri, where he died. (Bancroft, *History of California*, 3:767; Warner, *Men of the California Bear Flag Revolt*, 174–88)

PABLO DE LA GUERRA (1819–1874) was a son of José de la Guerra y Noriega and María Antonia Carrillo. He attended his brother-in-law William Hartnell's school at Rancho Alisal and worked at the customs house in Monterey from 1838 until the American invasion. He later served in the 1849 Constitutional Convention and as a member of the California State Senate. (Bancroft, *History of California*, 3:769; Pubols, *Father of All*)

AGOSTON HARASZTHY (1812–1869) was born in Hungary and came to the United States in 1840. After some time in the Midwest he moved to California, in 1849. He founded Buena Vista winery in Sonoma, but financial difficulties forced him to relinquish ownership in 1866. He moved to Nicaragua, where he accidentally drowned. (McGinty, *Strong Wine*)

ARPAD HARASZTHY (1840–1900) was born in Hungary, shortly before his family moved to America. He studied winemaking in France and worked with his father as cellar master at Buena Vista winery in Sonoma. In 1863 he married Jovita Vallejo. He later worked as a vintner of champagne and wine in San Francisco. (McGinty, *Toast to Eclipse*)

ATTILA HARASZTHY (1835–1886) was born in Hungary. He worked at Buena Vista winery in Sonoma and married Natalia Vallejo in 1863. He remained in Sonoma as an important winemaker and struggled with outbreaks of phylloxera at the vineyard. (McGinty, *Toast to Eclipse*, 17–32, 155–56)

TERESA DE LA GUERRA HARTNELL (1809–1885) was a daughter of José de la Guerra y Noriega and María Antonia Carrillo. In 1825 she married William Edward Petty Hartnell, a British merchant. They moved to Monterey, where he eventually opened a school at their Rancho Alisal. After his death in 1854, she married Manuel Maturano. (Beebe and Senkewicz, *Testimonios*, 49–54)

ANDREW HOEPPNER was a German musician who had worked for the Russians at Sitka. Mariano Guadalupe Vallejo drew up a contract with Hoeppner stipulating that he would provide piano lessons to the entire Vallejo family for five years in exchange for a large concession of land from Vallejo's Agua Caliente tract. (Beebe and Senkewicz, *Mariano Guadalupe Vallejo*, 205–6)

THOMAS OLIVER LARKIN (1802–1858) was born in Massachusetts and came to Alta California in 1832. He lived in Monterey as a trader. He supported Alvarado in 1836 and was appointed U.S. consul eight years later. In 1845, President Polk and Secretary of State Buchanan made him a confidential agent in an unsuccessful attempt to bring Alta California peacefully into the United States. He died in San Francisco. (Hague and Langum, *Thomas O. Larkin*)

JACOB PRIMER LEESE (1809–1892) was born in Ohio. He traded along the Santa Fe Trail in the early 1830s and moved to Alta California in 1834. He lived in Yerba Buena (San Francisco) from 1836 to 1841, then moved to Sonoma. He married Rosalía Vallejo, the sister of Mariano Guadalupe Vallejo. In 1846 he was captured by the Bear Flaggers. He was vice-president of the Society of California Pioneers in 1855. In 1864 he was granted almost two-thirds of Baja California as part of a colonization enterprise. After this project failed, he abandoned his family, left California in 1865, and did not return until his old age. (Bancroft, *History of California*, 4: 710–11; Martínez, *Historia de Baja California*, 406–12)

THOMAS MADDEN was an important real estate merchant in San Francisco who handled several transactions for Vallejo. (Langley, *San Francisco Directory 1861*, 222; *Daily Alta California*, July 29, 1871; Langley, *San Francisco Directory 1880*, 573)

IGNACIO MARTÍNEZ was born in Mexico City in 1774 and came to Alta California around 1800. He served at Santa Bárbara and San Diego before being sent to San Francisco as a lieutenant in 1817. He succeeded Luis Antonio Argüello as presidio commander there in 1822 and acted in that capacity until 1827. From 1828 to 1831 he had various stints as acting commander and commander. After retiring from the military in 1831 he held various public offices, such as alcalde of San Francisco, member of the Diputación, and regidor at San José. He owned a large ranch, Pinole, in Contra Costa, across the bay from San Francisco. He died before 1852. (Bancroft, *History of California*, 4:733)

JOHN S. MISSROON, a lieutenant on the U.S.S. *Portsmouth* in 1846, was sent by John Montgomery to Sonoma and New Helvetia to check on the condition of the prisoners being held by the Bear Flaggers. He invested in a San Francisco lot while in the area. (Bancroft, *History of California*, 4:742)

JOHN BERRIEN MONTGOMERY (1794–1873) was commander of the U.S.S. *Portsmouth*, which was stationed at San Francisco during the Bear Flag revolt. Later in life he commanded the Charlestown, Massachusetts, and Washington, D.C., naval yards. (Rogers, *Montgomery and the Portsmouth*)

JOSÉ MATÍAS MORENO, a native of Baja California, came to Alta California in 1844 and served as secretary to Governor Pío Pico in 1846. He married Prudenciana López, whose father was Mariano Guadalupe Vallejo. After the Mexico-U.S. war, he lived in San Diego for a time and later settled on his ranch in northern Baja California. He served as head of the Northern District of Baja California and died in 1869. (Bancroft, *History of California*, 4:745)

ANTONIO MARÍA OSIO (1800–1878) was born in Baja California. He came to Alta California in 1825, worked in the customs service in Monterey in the late 1820s, and served on the Diputación in the early 1830s. He supported the southerners against Alvarado in the mid-1830s and eventually moved back to northern Alta California, where he returned to the customs service in Monterey. After the Mexico-U.S. war, he composed a history of Alta California. Eventually he returned to Baja California, where he died. (Osio, *History of Alta California*)

ROMUALDO PACHECO was born in Guanajuato, New Spain. He accompanied Echeandía to California when the latter was appointed governor in 1825. From 1827 to 1828 he served as aide-de-camp and acting commander at Monterey and then, from 1828 to 1829, he was acting commander at Santa Bárbara. He was killed while fighting in support of Governor Victoria at the Battle of Cahuenga in 1831. His son, also named Romualdo, became governor of California in 1875. (Bancroft, *History of California*, 4:764; Genini and Hitchman, *Romualdo Pacheco*, 3–13)

CHARLES PICKETT, a lawyer, arrived at Sutter's Fort in 1846 after a three-year stay in Oregon. Pressed into service as a guard, he impressed Vallejo with his sympathy and kindness to the prisoners held by the Bear Flaggers, and they remained close from that time on. (Powell, *Philosopher Pickett*)

ANDRÉS PICO (1810–1878), the son of José María Pico of Sinaloa and María Eustaquia Gutiérrez of Sonora, was born in San Diego. In the late 1830s he was active in the southern opposition to Alvarado and was arrested and sent to Sonoma. From 1839 to 1842 he served as alférez at San Diego. He undertook a mission to Mexico for Governor Micheltorena in 1844. On his return he continued to serve in the military, mainly in the Los Angeles area. He commanded the Californios in their victory over the North Americans at San Pasqual and later negotiated the Treaty of Cahuenga with John Frémont. He was elected to the California state assembly in 1851 and served in the state senate from 1860 to 1861. (Bancroft, *History of California*, 4:776–77)

Pío Pico (1801–1894), older brother of Andrés Pico, was born at Mission San Gabriel. He served in the Diputación in 1828, and as a member of the assembly he was one of the leaders of the opposition to Governor Victoria in 1831. He served as one of the acting governors in 1832. As the administrator of Mission San Luis Rey in 1834–40 he was a leader in the 1836–37 opposition to Alvarado. After Micheltorena's expulsion, he became the political leader and in that capacity frequently quarreled with José Castro, the military leader. He fled to Mexico in 1845 but returned to southern California in 1848 and lived in Los Angeles until his death. (Salomon, *Pío Pico*)

Víctor Prudón was born in France around 1809 and went to Mexico in 1827. He arrived in California as a teacher with the Híjar-Padrés colonization group in 1834 and married Teodosia Bojorques. He served as president of the Los Angeles vigilantes in 1836 and as Governor Alvarado's secretary from 1837 to 1838. He worked in the same capacity for Mariano Guadalupe Vallejo in 1841 and was Vallejo's emissary to Mexico in 1842. Bear Flag soldiers arrested him with Vallejo in 1846. His whereabouts after 1853 are not recorded. (Bancroft, *History of California*, 4:784–85; Rhoades, "Foreigners," 70–71)

William Reed was an Englishman who came to California in 1837. He served two years as a pilot aboard the vessel *California* and then settled near Mission San Miguel. He and Petronilo Ríos were granted the secularized mission in 1846. Reed married María Antonia Vallejo. He and his family were killed at the mission in December 1848. (Bancroft, *History of California*, 5:690)

Joseph Warren Revere (1812–1880) was born in Boston and joined the U.S. Navy in 1828. He participated in deployments in the Pacific and the Caribbean. A lieutenant on the *Cyane* in 1846, he was reassigned to the *Portsmouth*. The man who raised the U.S. flag at Sonoma, he described his time in California in *A Tour of Duty in California* (1849). He later served in the American Civil War. (Revere, *Naval Duty*, foreword; Bancroft, *History of California*, 5:692)

José (Pepe) de la Rosa came to California in 1834 with the Híjar-Padrés colony. Like many of the colonists, he settled in the Sonoma area. A printer by trade, he worked as a handyman for Mariano Guadalupe Vallejo, mending clothes and tinware. He served as Sonoma alcalde in 1845. In 1846, Vallejo sent him to Yerba Buena to alert John B. Montgomery, captain of the *Portsmouth*, about the Bear Flag incident and to seek the captain's intervention to free Vallejo. Montgomery refused to become involved. An accomplished musician, Pepe de la Rosa also spent time in the East Bay region, where he taught Mexican songs to Adelaida Cordero Kamp, who eventually recorded some of them for Charles Lummis. (Koegel, "Mexican-American Music," 66–72; Bancroft, *History of California*, 5:704)

FRANCISCO MARÍA RUIZ was born in Loreto, Baja California, about 1754. He enlisted in the military around 1780 and was sent as a sergeant to Santa Bárbara in 1794. Promoted to alférez in 1801 and then to lieutenant in 1805, he became commander of the San Diego presidio in 1806. He retired from that post as a captain in 1827. He was granted Rancho Peñasquitos over the objections of the missionaries in 1823. He died in San Diego in 1839. (Bancroft, *History of California*, 2:540–41)

MARÍA AMPARO RUIZ (1831–1895), born in Baja California, was the daughter of Jesús Maitorena and Isabel Ruiz, the daughter of former Baja California governor José Manuel Ruiz. She came to Alta California with the American forces in 1848 and married one of their officers, Henry S. Burton, the next year. She left California in 1859 when her husband was assigned elsewhere and returned after his death in 1869. She published two novels, *Who Would Have Thought It* and *The Squatter and the Don*. (Sánchez and Pita, *Conflicts of Interest*)

ROBERT SEMPLE (1806–1854), a native of Kentucky, came overland to California in 1845. He worked as a carpenter at Sutter's Fort and became a leader of the Bear Flag revolt. After the war, he became copublisher of the *Californian*, the first newspaper published in California. He speculated in land around the San Francisco Bay area and was president of the Constitutional Convention in Monterey in 1849. He moved to Colusa County and died after a fall from a horse. (Warner, *Men of the California Bear Flag Revolt*, 107–23; Bancroft, *History of California*, 5:715)

FRANCISCO SOLANO was the Spanish name given to a ten-year-old Suisun boy whose Indigenous name was recorded as Sina when he was baptized at Mission San Francisco de Asís in 1801. Mariano Guadalupe Vallejo later indicated that his full Indigenous name was Sem-Yeto. He moved to Mission San Francisco Solano in 1824 and quickly became a major figure at the mission and in the surrounding Suisun communities. When Vallejo founded Sonoma in 1835, Solano became his ally and together they fought against the Patwin Suisunes' traditional enemies to the north. He died in the early 1850s. (Beebe and Senkewicz, *Mariano Guadalupe Vallejo*, chap. 3)

ROBERT FIELD STOCKTON (1795–1866) was born in New Jersey and joined the U.S. Navy as a young man. After serving in the War of 1812, he arrived in Monterey in command of the U.S.S. *Congress* in July 1846 and soon thereafter was appointed as commander to succeed John Sloat. He resigned in 1847 and returned east. He was a New Jersey senator from 1851 to 1853. (Bancroft, *History of California*, 5:735)

JOHN AUGUSTUS SUTTER (1803–1880) was born in Germany. After failing in business in Switzerland, he traveled in northern Mexico, Alaska, and Hawai'i before settling in Alta California. Seeking to check Mariano Guadalupe Vallejo's influence, Governor Alvarado gave Sutter a huge land grant in the Sacramento

Valley. Using Indigenous laborers practically as serfs, he turned his New Helvetia into an almost feudal estate. In 1845 he assisted Governor Micheltorena against the Californio rebels and later supported the North American invasion of California. He was a member of the California Constitutional Convention in 1849, the year after gold was discovered on his property. By the mid-1850s squatters had taken most of his land, but he managed to survive on a pension from the California legislature. When the pension terminated, he moved to Lititz, Pennsylvania, where he died. (Hurtado, *John Sutter*)

Encarnación Vallejo (1809–1902) was a younger sister of Mariano Guadalupe Vallejo. In 1827 she married John Cooper, a ship captain from Massachusetts who had recently settled in Alta California. She bore seven children. Her husband became a trader in Monterey with regular sea voyages to Mexico, Hawai'i, and China. (Woolfenden and Elkinton, *Cooper*; Bancroft, *History of California*, 2:765–66)

Ignacio Vicente Ferrer Vallejo (1748–1831), founder of the Vallejo dynasty in Alta California, was born in Jalisco, Mexico. He entered the army at an early age and arrived in San Diego in 1774. He worked at Missions San Luis Obispo and San Carlos in the 1780s. After reenlisting in 1787, he was promoted to corporal in 1789 and to sergeant in 1805. He died in Monterey. His wife, María Antonia Lugo, bore thirteen children. (Bancroft, *History of California*, 5:756)

José de Jesús Vallejo (1798–1882), the older brother of Mariano Guadalupe Vallejo, was born in San José. He was an active participant in the defense of Monterey against Hipólito Bouchard. Later he held various military and civilian offices in Alta California, including service as administrator of Mission San José after 1836. After the North American conquest, he remained at Mission San José, serving for a time as postmaster there. (Bancroft, *History of California*, 5:757)

Juan Antonio Vallejo (1816–1857) was the youngest brother of Mariano Guadalupe Vallejo. He served in several minor political positions in the 1840s. Before his mother passed away in 1855, she named him executor of the family estate. However, his sudden death meant that his brother Mariano Guadalupe had to assume the executorship, which continued until 1864. (Bancroft, *History of California*, 7:757; Emparán, *Vallejos of California*, 100–103)

Rosalía Vallejo (1811–1889) was a younger sister of Mariano Guadalupe Vallejo. In 1837 she married Jacob P. Leese, a native of Ohio who had established himself as a merchant at Yerba Buena. They moved to the Sonoma region in 1841 and Rosalía ultimately bore six children. They moved to Monterey in 1850 and Leese abandoned his family in 1865. (Beebe and Senkewicz, *Testimonios*, 16–24)

SALVADOR VALLEJO (1814–1876), a younger brother of Mariano Guadalupe Vallejo, was born in Monterey. In 1836, Mariano appointed him captain of the militia at Sonoma, and he engaged in many campaigns against the Indigenous peoples in the area. He was married to María de la Luz Carrillo. He served as justice of the peace and as administrator of Mission San Francisco Solano. He was held prisoner by the Bear Flaggers in 1846. During the American Civil War he served in Arizona on the Union side. Later he lived at his rancho in Napa and with brother Mariano in Sonoma. (Bancroft, *History of California*, 5:759; McKittrick, "Salvador Vallejo"; Sánchez, Pita, and Reyes, *Nineteenth-Century Californio Testimonios*, 92)

PLÁCIDO VEGA (1830–1878) became governor of the Mexican state of Sinaloa in 1859. A supporter of Benito Juárez, he came to San Francisco in the mid-1860s. He raised money from Mexican Americans, including Mariano Guadalupe Vallejo, to support the fight against Emperor Maximilian. After his return to Mexico, Vega was accused of misappropriation of funds and became alienated from his former allies. (Miller, "Californians against the Emperor")

JOHN L. VER MEHR was a native of Belgium. He was ordained an Episcopalian priest and came to San Francisco during the gold rush. There he founded Grace Church, which eventually became Grace Cathedral. He moved to Sonoma and started a school there. After four of his children died from a diphtheria epidemic, he returned to San Francisco, where he started another school. After that burned in 1860, he spent his remaining years ministering in the North Bay region. He died in 1886. (Ver Mehr, *Checkered Life*)

RAMÓN DE ZALDO was born in Spain and became a merchant on the East Coast in the 1840s. He moved to California in the early 1850s and became an attorney specializing in the land claims and other issues central to the concerns of Californio landowners. He died in 1878. (Shuck, *History of the Bench and Bar*, 545; Harris, Bogardus, and Labatt, *San Francisco City Directory 1856*, 41, 114)

Bibliography

ARCHIVES
Archive of the Archdiocese of San Francisco
Mariano Guadalupe Vallejo to Archbishop Joseph Alemany, May 10, 1878

The Bancroft Library, University of California, Berkeley
The Archive of California. C-A 1-62
Bancroft Family Papers, 71/18c
Bancroft, Hubert Howe, "Personal observations during a tour through the line of missions of upper California." C-E 113
Hubert Howe Bancroft Records of the Library and Publishing Companies, 1864–1910. B-C 7
Juan Bojorques, "Recuerdos sobre la historia de California." C-D 46
Jacob N. Bowman, "Indices to California Land Cases." 1941 and 1964. C-R 16
Julio Carrillo, "Statement." C-E 67
Documents Pertaining to the Adjudication of Private Land Claims in California. Land Case Files
John B. Frisbie. "Reminiscences." M-M 351
Thomas Savage. "Report on Archives." C-E 191
Manuel Torres, "Peripecias de la vida Californiana, 1843–1850." C-D 15
The Mariano Guadalupe Vallejo Papers. C-B 1-36
The Vallejo Family Papers, approximately 1824–1938. C-B 441
The Vallejo Family Papers, approximately 1835–1938. C-B 441 FILM
The Vallejo Family Papers: Additions, 1846–1950. 76/79c
Mariano Guadalupe Vallejo. "Recuerdos históricos y personales tocantes a la Alta California, 1769–1849." C-D 17-21

Benicia Historical Museum
Rev. Charles Morris Blake to Mariano Guadalupe Vallejo, October 12, 1854. 1985.015.0009

California Digital Newspaper Collection, University of California, Riverside
Californian
Daily Alta California
Napa County Reporter
Petaluma Weekly Argus
Sacramento Daily Union
Sacramento Record Union
San Diego Union
Sonoma Democrat
Tuolumne Independent

California Historical Society, San Francisco
Comunicaciones del General M. G. Vallejo. Vault 979.4 v. 24
Melville Schweitzer Collection of California Miscellany. MS Vault 55
Sloat Collection. MS Vault 57, 146
Mariano Guadalupe Vallejo Miscellany. MS 2204
M. G. Vallejo's Release from Fort Sutter. PAM 4131

California State Historic Parks, Sonoma
Madie Brown Emparán Research Collection
Vallejo Family Papers. 243.1

The Huntington Library, San Marino
Helen and Robert W. Long Collection of Moreno Documents. HLG 1-1132
Monterey Collection. MR 1-407
Mariano Guadalupe Vallejo papers. VA 1-257
Mariano Guadalupe Vallejo to Thompson and West, September 20, 1879. TW121

Santa Bárbara Mission Archive-Library
California Mission Documents
De la Guerra Papers
De la Guerra Papers—Vallejo
Zephyrin Engelhardt Papers

Santa Clara University Archives and Special Collections
College Prospectus for the Year 1860–1861

The Society of California Pioneers, San Francisco
Letters of M. G. Vallejo. C059027
Vallejo Scrapbook. C058528

Sonoma Valley Historical Society
Bascom, Wayne Arthur, "The Robin Family of Sonoma"
Wilkins, Sandra, "1852 Sonoma Census–The Robin Family"

PUBLISHED PRIMARY SOURCES
Alvarado, Juan Bautista. *Vignettes of Early California: Childhood Reminiscences of Juan Bautista Alvarado*. Translated by John H.R. Polk with an introduction and notes by W. Michael Mathes. San Francisco: Book Club of California, 1982.

Atherton, Faxon. *The California Diary of Faxon Dean Atherton, 1836–1839*. Edited by Doyce Blackman Nunis. San Francisco: California Historical Society, 1964.

Beebe, Rose Marie, and Robert M. Senkewicz, eds. *Lands of Promise and Despair: Chronicles of Early California, 1535–1846*. Norman: University of Oklahoma Press, 2015.

———. *Testimonios: Early California through the Eyes of Women, 1815–1848*. Norman: University of Oklahoma Press, 2015.

Bolton, Herbert Eugene, ed. *Anza's California Expeditions*. 5 vols. Berkeley: University of California Press, 1930.

Browne, J. Ross, ed. *Report of the Debates in the Convention of California, on the Formation of the State Constitution, in September and October, 1849*. Washington, D.C.: J.T. Towers, 1850.

Cerruti, Henry. *Ramblings in California: The Adventures of Henry Cerruti*. Edited by Margaret Mollins and Virginia E. Thickens. Berkeley: Friends of The Bancroft Library, 1954.

Dana, Richard Henry. *Two Years before the Mast and Other Voyages*. Edited by Thomas Philbrick. New York: Library of America, 2005.

Dublin, Thomas, ed. *Immigrant Voices: New Lives in America, 1773–1986*. Urbana: University of Illinois Press, 2014.

Font, Pedro. *With Anza to California, 1775–1776: The Journal of Pedro Font, O.F.M.* Edited by Alan K. Brown. Norman: Arthur H. Clark, 2011.

Gibson, James R., ed. *California through Russian Eyes, 1806–1848*. Norman: University of Oklahoma Press, 2014.

Green, Thomas J. *Journal of the Texian Expedition against Mier; Subsequent Imprisonment of the Author; His Sufferings, and Final Escape from the Castle of Perote*. New York: Harper and Bros., 1845.

Haraszthy, Agoston. *Father of California Wine, Agoston Haraszthy: Including Grape Culture, Wines and Wine-Making*. Edited by Theodore Schoenman. Santa Barbara: Capra Press, 1979.

Harris, Bogardus and Labatt. *San Francisco City Directory for the Year Commencing October 1856*. San Francisco: Whitton, Towne, 1856.

Hoffman, Ogden. *Reports of Land Cases Determined in the United States District Court for the Northern District of California: June Term, 1853 to June Term, 1858, Inclusive*. San Francisco: Numa Herbert, 1862.

Journal of the Senate of the State of California at Their First Session. San José: J. Winchester, State Printer, 1850.

Langley, Henry G. *The San Francisco Directory for the Year Commencing September 1861*. San Francisco: Commercial Steam Presses, S.D. Valentine and Sons, 1861.

———. *The San Francisco Directory for the Year Commencing April 1871*. San Francisco: Francis and Valentine Commercial Steam Presses, 1871.

———. *The San Francisco Directory for the Year Commencing March 1875*. San Francisco: Henry G. Langley, 1875.

———. *The San Francisco Directory for the Year Commencing March 1877*. San Francisco: Henry G. Langley, 1877.

———. *The San Francisco Directory for the Year Commencing April 1880*. San Francisco: Henry G. Langley, 1880.

———. *The San Francisco Directory for the Year Commencing April, 1882*. San Francisco: Francis, Valentine, 1882.

———. *The San Francisco Directory for the Year Commencing May 1887*. San Francisco: Francis, Valentine, 1887.

Larkin, Thomas Oliver. *The Larkin Papers: Personal, Business, and Official Correspondence of Thomas Oliver Larkin, Merchant and United States Consul in California*. Edited by George P. Hammond. 11 vols. Berkeley: Published for The Bancroft Library by the University of California Press, 1951.

McKenney, L. M., *Business Directory of San Francisco and Principal Towns of California and Nevada*. San Francisco: L. M. McKenney, 1877.

Oak, Henry Lebbeus. *A Visit to the Missions of Southern California in February and March 1874*. Edited by Ruth Frey Axe, Edwin H. Carpenter, and Norman Neuerburg. Los Angeles: Southwest Museum, 1981.

Osio, Antonio María. *The History of Alta California: A Memoir of Mexican California*. Edited and translated by Rose Marie Beebe and Robert M. Senkewicz. Madison: University of Wisconsin Press, 1996.

Revere, Joseph W. *Naval Duty in California, with Map and Plates from Original Designs*. Edited by Joseph A Sullivan. Oakland: Biobooks, 1947.

Robinson, Alfred. *Life in California during a Residence of Several Years in That Territory*. New York: Wiley and Putnam, 1846.

Solano and Napa Counties Directory for 1871–72. Sacramento: H. S. Crocker, 1871.

Soulé, Frank. *The Annals of San Francisco*. New York: Appleton, 1855.

Vallejo, Mariano Guadalupe. *Recuerdos: Historical and Personal Remembrances Relating to Alta California, 1769–1849*. 2 vols. Edited and translated by Rose Marie Beebe and Robert M. Senkewicz. Norman: University of Oklahoma Press, 2023.

Ver Mehr, J. L. *Checkered Life: In the Old and New World*. San Francisco: A. L. Bancroft, 1877.

Wise, Henry Augustus. *Los Gringos*. New York: Baker and Scribner, 1850.

Woodward, Arthur. *The Republic of Lower California, 1853–1854: In the Words of Its State Papers, Eyewitnesses, and Contemporary Reporters*. Los Angeles: Dawson's Book Shop, 1966.

SECONDARY SOURCES

Bancroft, Hubert Howe. *History of California*. 7 vols. San Francisco: The History Co., 1884–90.

———. *History of the North Mexican States and Texas*. 2 vols. San Francisco: The History Co., 1884–89.

———. *The Native Races of the Pacific States of North America*. 5 vols. New York: D. Appleton, 1875.

Bancroft, Kim. *Writing Themselves into History: Emily and Matilda Bancroft in Journals and Letters*. Berkeley: Heyday and The Bancroft Library, 2022.

Beebe, Rose Marie, and Robert M. Senkewicz. *Mariano Guadalupe Vallejo: Life in Spanish, Mexican, and American California.* Norman: University of Oklahoma Press, 2023.

Beyreis, David C. "Dangerous Alliances in the New Mexico Borderlands: Charles Bent and the Limits of Family Networks." *Journal of the Early Republic* 39, no. 1 (Spring 2019): 57–80.

Bonner, Robert E. *The Soldier's Pen: Firsthand Impressions of the Civil War.* New York: Hill and Wang, 2006.

Brown, Madie D. "Gen. M. G. Vallejo and H. H. Bancroft." *California Historical Society Quarterly* 29, no. 2 (1950): 149–59.

Brown-Coronel, Margie. "Beyond the Rancho: Four Generations of del Valle Women in Southern California, 1830–1940." Ph.D. dissertation, University of California, Irvine, 2011.

———. "Intimacy and Family in the California Borderlands: The Letters of Josefa del Valle Forster, 1876–1896." *Pacific Historical Review* 89, no. 1 (February 1, 2020): 74–96.

Browne, J. Ross, and Alexander S. Taylor. *Resources of the Pacific Slope.* New York: D. Appleton, 1869.

Buelna, Eustaquio. *Breves apuntes para la historia de la guerra de intervención en Sinaloa.* Mazatlán, México: Imprenta y Estereotipia de Retes, 1884.

Camarillo, Albert. *Chicanos in a Changing Society: From Mexican Pueblos to American Barrios in Santa Barbara and Southern California, 1848–1930.* Dallas: Southern Methodist University Press, 2005.

Carr, Edward Hallett. *What Is History?* New York: Vintage Books, 1961.

Casas, María Raquel. *Married to a Daughter of the Land: Spanish-Mexican Women and Interethnic Marriage in California, 1820–80.* Reno: University of Nevada Press, 2007.

Caughey, John Walton. *Hubert Howe Bancroft: Historian of the West.* Berkeley: University of California Press, 1946.

Chalfant, W. A. *The Story of Inyo.* Bishop: Chalfant Press, 1933.

Chávez-García, Miroslava. *Migrant Longing: Letter Writing across the U.S.-Mexico Borderlands.* Chapel Hill: University of North Carolina Press, 2018.

———. *Negotiating Conquest: Gender and Power in California, 1770s to 1880s.* Tucson: University of Arizona Press, 2004.

Chávez-García, Miroslava, and Verónica Castillo-Muñoz. "Gender and Intimacy across the U.S.-Mexico Borderlands." *Pacific Historical Review* 89, no. 1 (2020): 4–15.

Clark, Harry. "Their Pride, Their Manners, and Their Voices: Sources of the Traditional Portrait of the Early Californians." *California Historical Quarterly* 53, no. 1 (1974): 71–82.

———. *A Venture in History: The Production, Publication, and Sale of the Works of Hubert Howe Bancroft.* Berkeley: University of California Press, 1973.

Clarke, James Mitchell. "Antonio Meléndrez: Nemesis of William Walker in Baja California." *California Historical Society Quarterly* 12, no. 4 (1933): 318–22.

Crosby, Harry W. *Antigua California: Mission and Colony on the Peninsular Frontier, 1697–1768.* Albuquerque: University of New Mexico Press, 1994.

Denton, Sally. *Passion and Principle: John and Jessie Frémont, the Couple Whose Power, Politics, and Love Shaped Nineteenth-Century America.* New York: Bloomsbury, 2007.

Dillon, Richard H. *Great Expectations: The Story of Benicia, California.* Fresno: Benicia Heritage Book, 1980.

Earle, Rebecca. "Letters and Love in Colonial Spanish America." *The Americas* 62, no. 1 (2005): 17–46.

Elliott, Bruce S., David A. Gerber, and Suzanne M. Sinke, eds. *Letters across Borders: The Epistolary Practices of International Migrants*. New York: Palgrave Macmillan, 2006.

Emparán, Madie Brown. *The Vallejos of California*. San Francisco: The Gleeson Library Associates, University of San Francisco, 1968.

Farmer, Jared. *On Zion's Mount: Mormons, Indians, and the American Landscape*. Cambridge: Harvard University Press, 2008.

Field, Kendra, and Daniel Lynch. "'Master of Ceremonies': The World of Peter Biggs in Civil War–Era Los Angeles." *Western Historical Quarterly* 47, no. 4 (2016): 379–405.

Fuhlhage, Michael. "Brave Old Spaniards and Indolent Mexicans: J. Ross Browne, Harper's New Monthly Magazine, and the Social Construction of Off-Whiteness in the 1860s." *American Journalism* 31, no. 1 (2014): 100–26.

Geiger, Maynard J. *Franciscan Missionaries in Hispanic California, 1769–1848: A Biographical Dictionary*. San Marino: Huntington Library, 1969.

Genini, Ronald, and Richard Hitchman. *Romualdo Pacheco: A Californio in Two Eras*. San Francisco: Book Club of California, 1985.

Gerber, David A. "Acts of Deceiving and Withholding in Immigrant Letters: Personal Identity and Self-Presentation in Personal Correspondence." *Journal of Social History* 39, no. 2 (2005): 315–30.

Gillis, Michael J., and Michael F. Magliari. *John Bidwell and California: The Life and Writings of a Pioneer, 1841–1900*. Spokane: Arthur. H. Clark, 2004.

Greenberg, Amy S. *Manifest Manhood and the Antebellum American Empire*. Cambridge: Cambridge University Press, 2005.

Gregory, Tom. *History of Sonoma County, California*. Los Angeles: Historic Record Co., 1911.

Guinn, J. M. *History of the State of California and Biographical Record to Oakland and Environs*. 2 vols. Los Angeles: Historic Record Co., 1907.

Gullard, Pamela, and Nancy Lund. *Under the Oaks: Two Hundred Years in Atherton*. San Francisco: Scottwall Associates, 2009.

Hager, Christopher. *I Remain Yours: Common Lives in Civil War Letters*. Cambridge: Harvard University Press, 2017.

Hague, Harlan, and David J. Langum. *Thomas O. Larkin: A Life of Patriotism and Profit in Old California*. Norman: University of Oklahoma Press, 1990.

Harding, George Laban. *Don Agustín V. Zamorano: Statesman, Soldier, Craftsman, and California's First Printer*. Spokane: Arthur H. Clark, 2003.

Hargis, Donald E. "Native Californians in the Constitutional Convention of 1849." *Historical Society of Southern California Quarterly* 36, no. 1 (1954): 3–13.

Harlow, Neal. *California Conquered: War and Peace on the Pacific, 1846–1850*. Berkeley: University of California Press, 1982.

Hart, John M. *Empire and Revolution: The Americans in Mexico since the Civil War*. Berkeley: University of California Press, 2002.

Hittell, Theodore. *History of California*. 4 vols. San Francisco: Pacific Press Publishing House, 1885.

Holterman, Jack. "The Revolt of Estanislao." *Indian Historian* 3, no. 1 (January 1970): 43–54.

Hurtado, Albert L. *John Sutter: A Life on the North American Frontier*. Norman: University of Oklahoma Press, 2006.

Hutchinson, C. Alan. *Frontier Settlement in Mexican California; the Híjar-Padrés Colony and Its Origins, 1769–1835*. New Haven: Yale University Press, 1969.

———. "An Official List of the Members of the Híjar-Padrés Colony for Mexican California, 1834." *Pacific Historical Review* 42, no. 3 (1973): 407–18.

Hyde, Anne Farrar. *Empires, Nations, and Families: A History of the North American West, 1800–1860*. Lincoln: University of Nebraska Press, 2011.

Kern, Ruy E. *The Vallejos of Mission San José*. Fremont: Mission Peak Heritage Foundation, 1983.

Koegel, John. "Mexican-American Music in Nineteenth-Century Southern California: The Lummus Wax Collection at the Southwest Museum, Los Angeles." Ph. D. dissertation, Claremont Graduate School, 1994.

Kryder-Reid, Elizabeth. *California Mission Landscapes: Race, Memory, and the Politics of Heritage*. Minneapolis: University of Minnesota Press, 2016.

Langum, David J. "Californios and the Image of Indolence." *Western Historical Quarterly* 9, no. 2 (1978): 181–96.

Lerma Garay, Antonio. *El general traicionado: Vida y obra de Plácido Vega Daza*. Culiacán Rosales, Sinaloa: Creativos7editorial, 2010.

Lugo, Don José del Carmen. "Life of a Rancher." *Historical Society of Southern California Quarterly* 32, no. 3 (1950): 185–236.

Lystra, Karen. *Searching the Heart: Women, Men, and Romantic Love in Nineteenth-Century America*. New York: Oxford University Press, 1989.

Marti, Werner H. *Messenger of Destiny: The California Adventures, 1846–1847, of Archibald H. Gillespie, U.S. Marine Corps*. San Francisco: J. Howell Books, 1960.

Martínez, Pablo L. *Guía Familiar de Baja California, 1700–1900: Vital Statistics of Lower California*. México, D.F., México: Editorial Baja California, 1965.

———. *Historia de Baja California*. México: Libros Mexicanos, 1956.

Martínez Martínez, Germán. "Inventing the Nation: The Pronunciamiento and the Construction of Mexican National Identity, 1821–1876." In *Forceful Negotiations: The Origins of the Pronunciamiento in Nineteenth-Century Mexico*, edited by Will Fowler, 226–45. Lincoln: University of Nebraska Press, 2010.

McGinty, Brian. "The Carrillos of San Diego: A Historic Spanish Family of California." *Historical Society of Southern California Quarterly* 39, part 1 (March 1957): 3–13; part 2 (June 1957): 127–48; part 3 (September 1957): 281–301; part 4 (December 1957): 371–91.

———. *Strong Wine: The Life and Legend of Agoston Haraszthy*. Stanford: Stanford University Press, 1998.

———. *A Toast to Eclipse: Arpad Haraszthy and the Sparkling Wine of Old San Francisco*. Norman: University of Oklahoma Press, 2012.

McGloin, John Bernard. *California's First Archbishop: The Life of Joseph Sadoc Alemany, 1814–1888*. New York: Herder and Herder, 1966.

McKittrick, Myrtle M. "Salvador Vallejo." *California Historical Society Quarterly* 29, no. 4 (1950): 309–31.

———. *Vallejo, Son of California*. Portland: Binfords and Mort, 1944.

Miles, Tiya. "The Long Arm of the South?" *Western Historical Quarterly* 43, no. 3 (September 2012): 274–81.

Miller, Robert Ryal. "Arms across the Border: United States Aid to Juárez during the French Intervention in Mexico." *Transactions of the American Philosophical Society* 63, no. 6 (1973): 1–68.

———. "Californians against the Emperor." *California Historical Society Quarterly* 37, no. 3 (1958): 193–214.

————. *Juan Bautista Alvarado: Governor of California, 1836–1842*. Norman: University of Oklahoma Press, 1998.

————. "Plácido Vega: A Mexican Secret Agent in the United States, 1864–1866." *The Americas* 19, no. 2 (1962): 137–48.

Monroy, Douglas. *Thrown among Strangers: The Making of Mexican Culture in Frontier California*. Berkeley: University of California Press, 1990.

Munro-Fraser, J. P. *History of Solano County*. San Francisco: Wood, Alley, and Co., 1879.

————. *History of Sonoma County*. San Francisco: Alley, Bowen, 1880.

Mutnick, Dorothy Gittinger. *Some Alta California Pioneers and Descendants*. 5 vols. Lafayette: Past Time Publications, 1982.

Nakayama A., Antonio. *Realidad y mentira de Plácido Vega*. Culiacán, México: Centro de Estudios Históricos del Noroeste, 1993.

Northrop, Marie E. *Spanish-Mexican Families of Early California, 1769–1850*. 3 vols. Burbank: Southern California Genealogical Society, 1984–2004.

Ohles, Wallace V. *The Lands of Mission San Miguel*. Fresno: Word Dancer Press, 1997.

Ortega Noriega, Sergio. *Breve historia de Sinaloa*. México: Colegio de México, Fideicomiso Historia de las Américas: Fondo de Cultura Económica, 1999.

Padilla, Genaro M. *My History, Not Yours: The Formation of Mexican American Autobiography*. Madison: University of Wisconsin Press, 1993.

Palmer, Lyman L. *History of Napa and Lake Counties, California*: San Francisco: Slocum, Bowen and Co., 1881.

Peeke, Carroll. "The Forgotten Man." *Historical Magazine of the Protestant Episcopal Church* 35, no. 2 (1966): 173–81.

Pérez, Erika. *Colonial Intimacies: Interethnic Kinship, Sexuality, and Marriage in Southern California, 1769–1885*. Norman: University of Oklahoma Press, 2018.

————. "The Dalton-Zamoranos: Intimacy, Intermarriage, and Conquest in the U.S.-Mexico Borderlands." *Pacific Historical Review* 89, no. 1 (2020): 44–73.

————. "'Saludos from Your Comadre': Compadrazgo as a Community Institution in Alta California, 1769–1860s." *California History* 88, no. 4 (2011): 47–62.

Pitt, Leonard. *The Decline of the Californios: A Social History of the Spanish-Speaking Californians, 1846–1890*. Berkeley: University of California Press, 1966.

Pomerleau, Claude. "French Missionaries and Latin American Catholicism in the Nineteenth Century." *The Americas* 37, no. 3 (1981): 351–67.

Powell, Lawrence Clark. *Philosopher Pickett: The Life and Writings of Charles Edward Pickett, Esq., of Virginia*. Berkeley: University of California Press, 1942.

Pubols, Louise. *The Father of All: The de la Guerra Family, Power, and Patriarchy in Mexican California*. Berkeley: University of California Press; San Marino: Huntington Library, 2009.

Rhoades, Elizabeth. "Foreigners in Southern California during the Mexican Period." M.A. thesis, University of California, Berkeley, 1924.

Rhoda, Richard, and Tony Burton. *Geo-Mexico: The Geography and Dynamics of Modern Mexico*. Vancouver Island, B.C.: Sombrero Books, 2010.

Rogers, Fred Blackburn. *Montgomery and the Portsmouth*. San Francisco: J. Howell, 1958.

Rosengarten, Frederic. *Freebooters Must Die! The Life and Death of William Walker, the Most Notorious Filibuster of the Nineteenth Century*. Wayne, Penn.: Haverford House, 1976.

Rosenwein, Barbara H. "Worrying about Emotions in History." *American Historical Review* 107, no. 3 (2002): 821–45.

Rothman, Ellen K. *Hands and Hearts: A History of Courtship in America.* Cambridge: Harvard University Press, 1984.

Salomon, Carlos Manuel. *Pío Pico: The Last Governor of Mexican California.* Norman: University of Oklahoma Press, 2010.

Sánchez, Rosaura. *Telling Identities: The Californio Testimonios.* Minneapolis: University of Minnesota Press, 1995.

Sánchez, Rosaura, and Beatrice Pita. *Conflicts of Interest: The Letters of María Amparo Ruiz de Burton.* Houston: Arte Público Press, 2001.

Sánchez, Rosaura, Beatrice Pita, and Bárbara Reyes, eds. *Nineteenth-Century Californio Testimonios.* Crítica Monograph Series 68. La Jolla: UCSD Ethnic Studies, Third World Studies, 1994.

Sandos, James A. "Because He Is a Liar and a Thief": Conquering the Residents of 'Old' California, 1850–1880." *California History* 79, no. 2 (2000): 86–112.

Schell, William. *Integral Outsiders: The American Colony in Mexico City, 1876–1911.* Wilmington: SR Books, 2001.

Shawcross, Edward. *The Last Emperor of Mexico: The Dramatic Story of the Habsburg Archduke Who Created a Kingdom in the New World.* New York: Basic Books, 2021.

Shuck, Oscar T. *History of the Bench and Bar of California.* Los Angeles: Commercial Printing House, 1901.

Smilie, Robert S. *The Sonoma Mission, San Francisco Solano de Sonoma: The Founding, Ruin and Restoration of California's 21st Mission.* Fresno: Valley Publishers, 1975.

Sollors, Werner. *Beyond Ethnicity: Consent and Descent in American Culture.* New York: Oxford University Press, 1986.

Suárez, Camille. "A Legal Confiscation: The 1851 Land Act and the Transformation of Californios into Colonized Colonizers." *Journal of the Civil War Era* 13, no. 1 (2023): 29–55.

Taylor, Alexander S. "Historical Summary of Lower California, from Its Discovery in 1532 to 1867." In J. Ross Browne and Alexander S. Taylor, eds., *Resources of the Pacific Slope.* New York: D. Appleton and Co., 1869.

Taylor, Lawrence D. "The Mining Boom in Baja California from 1850 to 1890 and the Emergence of Tijuana as a Border Community." *Journal of the Southwest* 43, no. 4 (2001): 463–92.

Tuomey, Honoria. *History of Sonoma County, California.* 2 vols. Chicago: S. J. Clarke, 1926.

Valadés, Adrián. *Historia de la Baja California, 1850–1880.* México: Universidad Nacional Autónoma de México, 1974.

Vásquez, Jessica M. *Mexican Americans across Generations: Immigrant Families, Racial Realities.* New York: New York University Press, 2011.

Warner, Barbara R. *The Men of the California Bear Flag Revolt and Their Heritage.* Spokane: Arthur H. Clark for the Sonoma Valley Historical Society, 1996.

Weber, David J., and David J. Langum. "Here Rests Juan Espinosa: Toward a Clearer Look at the Image of the 'Indolent' Californios." *Western Historical Quarterly* 10, no. 1 (1979): 61–69.

Woolfenden, John, and Amelie Elkinton. *Cooper: Juan Bautista Rogers Cooper, Sea Captain, Adventurer, Ranchero, and Early California Pioneer, 1791–1872.* Pacific Grove: Boxwood Press, 1983.

Index

References in *italics* refer to illustrative matter.